Translational Spaces

This book explores the concept of space, or rather spaces, in relation to translation, to construct a conceptual framework for research to better understand and solve translation problems. A number of interrelated spatial perspectives on translation supported by empirical evidence are presented to help better understand the complexities between China and the West in cultural exchanges and to offer a way of explaining what happens to translation and why it takes on a particular form. In the checkered history of Chinese-Western cultural exchange, effective communication has remained a great challenge exacerbated by the ultimate inescapability of linguistic and cultural incommensurability. It is therefore necessary to develop conceptual tools that can help shed light on the interactive association between performativity and space in translation. Despite the unfailing desire to connect with the world, transnational resistance is still underway in China. Further attempts are required to promote a convergence of Chinese and Western translation theories in general and to confront problems arising from translation practice in particular. This work will be of interest to students and scholars in translation studies around the world, as well as those working in cultural studies and cross-cultural communication studies.

Yifeng Sun is Chair Professor of Translation Studies in the Department of English and Senior Research Fellow in the Institute of Advanced Studies in Humanities and Social Sciences at the University of Macau. He is also an Honorary Professor at the University of Queensland and serves as Editor-in-Chief of *Babel: International Journal of Translation*.

Routledge Advances in Translation and Interpreting Studies

For more information about this series, please visit www.routledge.com/ Routledge-Advances-in-Translation-and-Interpreting-Studies/book-series/RTS

Translational Spaces
Towards a Chinese-Western Convergence

Yifeng Sun

Routledge
Taylor & Francis Group

LONDON AND NEW YORK

First published 2021
by Routledge
2 Park Square, Milton Park, Abingdon, Oxon OX14 4RN

and by Routledge
52 Vanderbilt Avenue, New York, NY 10017

Routledge is an imprint of the Taylor & Francis Group, an informa business

© 2021 Yifeng Sun

British Library Cataloguing-in-Publication Data
A catalogue record for this book is available from the British Library

Library of Congress Cataloging-in-Publication Data
Names: Sun, Yifeng, 1957– author.
Title: Translational spaces : towards a Chinese-Western convergence /
    Yifeng Sun.
Description: Abingdon, Oxon ; New York, NY : Routledge, 2021.
Subjects: LCSH: Translating and interpreting—Social aspects—China. |
    Translating and interpreting—Cross-cultural studies. | Language
    and culture—China. | Intercultural communication—China. | Space—
    Social aspects—China. | East and West. | China—Relations—Western
    countries. | Western countries—Relations—China.
Classification: LCC P306.8.C6 S85 2021 (print) | LCC P306.8.C6 (ebook) |
    DDC 495.18/04009—dc23
LC record available at https://lccn.loc.gov/2020038730
LC ebook record available at https://lccn.loc.gov/2020038731

ISBN: 978-0-367-65478-8 (hbk)
ISBN: 978-1-003-12962-2 (ebk)

Typeset in Galliard
by Apex CoVantage, LLC

Contents

Acknowledgments

A portion of Chapter 2 has been adapted from "The Shifting Distance of Translation" in *Translation and Cross-Cultural Communication Studies in the Asia Pacific*, published by Brill/Rodopi. Chapter 3 is a greatly expanded version of "Cosmopolitan Translation Cross-Cultural Paradigms," published in *Telos*. Thanks are due to Springer for permission to reuse parts of "World Literature in and through Translation" in *Neohelicon*. I wish to thank John Benjamins for allowing me to incorporate in Chapter 6 some material from an article that appeared in *Babel*. Some material in Chapter 8 is taken from "Deconstruction and Translation Research" in *Derrida Today*, published by Edinburgh University Press. Thanks are also due to Routledge for permission to reproduce a portion of "Translatability" in *Handbook of Chinese Translation* (pp. 101–114), edited by C. Shei and Z. Gao, 2017, and to reuse some material from "Translation and Back Translation: Transcultural Reinventions in Some Chinese American Literary Works" and "Empowering Translation" both in *Asia Pacific Translation and Intercultural Studies*, 2014 and 2018.

I am grateful to Katie Peace, Commissioning Editor for Routledge Research Books in Education, Linguistics and Psychology, for her interest in and support of this book. I would also like to thank Professor José Lambert for discussing and sharing ideas with me concerning the concept of translational spaces.

Introduction

China has a long history of translation of more than three thousand years. Because of the rich and compelling experience of translation, there has been no dearth of studies on translation. The translation of Buddhist scriptures occasioned some most insightful observations on and reflections of the operation and nature of translation. It is fascinating to identify the historical space of Chinese translation practice by integrating transnational and comparative perspectives into a broader understanding of how translation has functioned across different spatial and temporal dimensions in Chinese-Western intercultural relationships. Chinese and Western translation traditions and practices are traceable to different cultural spaces. One major objective of this book is to present an overview of the concept of translational spaces in a Chinese cultural context. By specifying a geographical setting, a critical spatial perspective is established to develop the argument that the nature and magnitude of translation can be better understood by examining the spatial implications for designing appropriate strategies. Translation is encapsulated by a continual process of recontextualization, and subsequent reconceptualization must be built on this awareness in order to enable translation to function for the target reader.

Notwithstanding the prevalence and long history of translation practice in China, the preponderant concern of some Chinese translation scholars is to find a way to develop the so-called Chinese Translation Studies, with its own theoretical system and methodology to justify the claim that a translation theory with Chinese characteristics should be constructed. An equally obsessive emphasis is given to a national academic space that may well function as a negative shaping force in resistance to cultural otherness. Different linguistic and cultural spaces can be congruent or overlap despite contested geopolitics and potential conflicts between different spatial representations. Chinese-Western interaction has proved to be a testing ground for an integrated approach to the multifaceted concept of spaces and is fraught with ideological and cultural complexities and conflicts associated with efforts to bridge cross-cultural gaps and perceptions. Bearing this in mind, it is important to construct new dialogic spaces in which boundaries between different cultural domains and practices are crossed, and as a result it becomes possible that new enlightenment is brought to both translation theory and practice in a drive towards a Chinese-Western convergence.

The concept of space or spaces can be better developed and more systematically theorized in shedding light on translation theory and practice alike. To start with, the in-between space or third space always exists between two languages in translation for the purpose of negotiation and re-negotiation. Accordingly, a cultural-political perspective is brought to bear on translation involving interventions and hybridization. The conceptual framework of spaces has and still is undergoing significant changes to meet the needs of redefining translation and perceiving it in an ever-changing light or perspective.

Translation Studies has been preoccupied with the endlessly fascinating and frustrating process of translation. It is time to rise above it by addressing the concept of translational spaces. On this account, it is essential to look at how translation can be empowered and given more choices in formulating strategies that are played out by exploring a series of related spaces. Such spaces are dynamic rather than static, and more dimensions and potentialities can be found to do fuller justice to the plurality and multiplicity of meaning, which are identified with the persistent inadequacy associated with translation, especially literary or philosophical translation that comprises multiple representations and their perceptions.

Source and target texts inhabit and belong to different spaces, be they linguistic, cultural, geopolitical, ideological, historical, or any combination of them, all of which represent often invisible or imperceptible forces that influence the outcome of translation. Situated at the interface of translation, these forces are correlated with a wide variety of factors amenable for the production and reception of translation. Quintessentially, translation is both aggressive and vulnerable. Its violent nature is expressed by George Steiner when referring to the decipherment of meaning (Steiner 1998: 315). Boundary crossings are unavoidable, which is frequently accompanied by spatial violation. The vulnerability of translation is related to its derivative nature and hence torn "between adequacy and acceptability" (Toury 2012: 84). Translation is always subject to certain constraints, and translators must be mindful of conflicting expectations from the target reading community.

Simply put, translation is the result of reproduction in another temporal space. The glaring linguistic and cultural distance between Chinese and English is widely recognized to constitute a formidable impediment to effective communication. Moreover, translation is seen as characteristic of being governed by different types and variables of distance: linguistic, cultural, political, and aesthetic. A temporal distance that exists between source and target texts is an unavoidable consideration when translation is initiated. A famous Chinese scholar, Qian Zhongshu, has pointed out: "There is bound to be some distance between one language and another" (Qian 1981: 19). This may seem patently obvious yet is central to any discussion regarding English-Chinese translation: the two languages are so vastly different that a general comparison between them reveals multitudinous linguistic gaps and cultural lacunae. Linguistic and cultural distance offers grounds for acculturation and can justify some degree of domestication in reconnecting any missing links between the two linguistic and cultural systems. It is thus important to develop a holistic understanding of the dimensional space of distance germane to translation in terms of temporality both at the cognitive and practical levels. It is clear that distance and displacement within a multi-temporal space are deeply intertwined, and spatial distance together with temporal distance is bound to change constantly, the adjustment of which is essential to the performativity of translation.

In today's globalized world, cosmopolitan spaces and participatory practice are inextricably linked. There is also an increasing need to improve adjustment to reduce alienation generated by dislocation. As a result, bridge-crossing movements and cross-cultural encounters become more commonplace and normative and far less exclusive. Cosmopolitan translation and adaptation are only possible when sufficient intercultural mediation and conflict resolution are developed and applied to translation practice. Different conceptions of cultural realities contribute significantly to the creation of cosmopolitan spaces to encourage moving beyond a provincial mindset. It can be observed that Translation Studies has borrowed extensively "theoretical paradigms and research methodologies from other disciplines, thus generating hybrid formations of transdisciplinarity" (Sun 2012: 32). The resultant interdisciplinarity that features translation research is of a cosmopolitan consciousness and spirit. In an increasingly globalized world, academic research in China has long extricated itself from its past state of isolation and stagnation. Furthermore, China has seen an unprecedented boom in Translation Studies thanks to its increasing intercultural interaction with the outside world, which is in no small measure brought about by massive translation practice, and Chinese translation scholars manifest an eagerness to learn from the West and also to play an increasingly active role in promoting the development of the discipline. An ever-growing number of Chinese scholars are eager to engage in academic exchange and dialogue with international counterparts through lectures and conferences. The flow of ideas and the exchange of scholarly information have prompted a critical rethinking of stereotypical assumptions about translation in China. A cosmopolitan ethos has been cumulatively established and subsequently practiced.

However, in contrast to the emergence of cosmopolitanism, over the years, some Chinese translation scholars have held overly antagonistic views about the erosion of Western domination in translation research. Their overarching concern is to establish and develop Translation Studies in China with its own theoretical system and methodology so as to be able to create so-called Chinese characteristics. The impassioned quest for identity is fundamentally about cultural politics, but it is also meant to effectively analyze and provide more definitive answers to translation problems related to continuous cultural and political change in a country longing to focus on its overall cultural promotion in a cosmopolitan space. But on no account is this a cosmopolitan approach.

In retrospect, there seems to be one historical opportunity for China to establish Translation Studies in a modern sense. Back in the 1950s, it became obvious that Translation Studies in China needed theoretical breakthroughs. Dong Qiusi, in an article entitled "论翻译理论的建设" ("On the Construction of Our Translation Theories") in *Translation Newsletter*, proposes to establish Translation Studies as a discipline, claiming that "China has a long history of translation and, despite the lack of systematic theorization, has acquired an abundance of scattered and unconsolidated experiences and ideas" Dong (2004: 225). Dong projects a sanguine prognosis largely based on this perception of China's long history of translation. With the wisdom that hindsight affords, Tan Zaixi ruefully notes: "In the 1950s China was behind no other country with regard to the construction of Translation Studies. Had Dong Qiusi's idea caught everyone's attention, our translation research might have been ahead of the West all along" (Tan 1995: 15). Regrettably, this optimism is retrospectively ungrounded partly because China was soon afterward plunged into great social and political upheaval, and its embryonic intercultural connectivity would be severed. However, the underlying assumption at the time was that it was possible to formulate a theoretical system capable of systematically exploring and elucidating the nature of translation.

For historical and political reasons, China is a late player in Translation Studies in its modern sense. After all, no one had access to the seminal paper by James Holmes entitled "The Name and Nature of Translation Studies" in 1972. Yet since the country resumed contact with the outside world in the late 1970s, the discipline has been gaining recognition and even popularity. Many graduate programs in Translation Studies and translation and interpreting training have cropped up in recent years. Meanwhile, however, aside from this exuberance, Western translation theories have met with voices of suspicion, doubt, and denigration. All this seemed to have immediately created a distinctly colonial experience, raising the central question of the possibility of cultural violence that poses a threat to the target culture. It has become a source of acute anxiety about cultural identity and the profound implications of extensive uncritical borrowings. It is plain that the issue of suitability and relevance has to be examined. It was not uncommon in the 1980s and 1990s that translation theories developed in the West and other parts of the world that were indiscriminately subsumed under the category of the West were considered not relevant to or suitable for translation practice in China; the underlying assumption was that the usefulness of theory was closely linked with whether it could be applied to the actual translation practice. But the disconcerting fact was that many of those holding antagonistic views about Western translation theories were contented with scant knowledge of them. The cultural and political prejudice in conjunction with Chinese chauvinism that formed the basis of this enmity contrasts sharply with the creative academic dialogue on which scholarly critiques of Western thinking on translation were based sometime later.

In any event, there is always a way to translate, but at what cost? What is at stake is the reputation of the profession. Translation is impaired by limited translatability or untranslatability. To be sure, translatability cannot be taken for granted, and the specter of untranslatability still hangs over the translator. Attention is drawn to the limits or impossibility of translation. It is never enough to simply translate meaning. Formal features of the original need to be reflected to an acceptable degree in translation, which can only be achieved by performing a spatial search for and development of what can be best described as the most appropriate solution. Chinese translation practice serves as an exemplar and demonstration of the usefulness of translational spaces in expanding the limits of translatability. Conceptual and metaphorical spaces between untranslatability and translatability, or between bad translation and good translation, can be constructed to open possibilities and perspectives so as to extend the limits of translatability. Arguably, if something is interpretable, it is translatable. An interpretative space gives rise to the necessary space(s) for translation. Spatial translatability may be understood to refer to the possibility of representing in the target text what is meant to be conveyed in the source text. In essence, this aligns translatability with transferability, which, however, defies easy assumptions. While the transfer of meaning is not impossible, although it is admittedly fraught with pitfalls and problems, the transfer of form, among other things, is a matter of serious concern. To transfer both meaning and form bears directly upon the very limits of translatability. The lack of formal correspondence between source and target texts is evinced by limited translatability. Since formal substitution is hard to come by, overall or essential similarity needs to be demonstrated in the target text.

Meaning is based and dependent on other signs, which should be sharable, but at the same time, it is also based and dependent on references and allusions, which are not necessarily sharable, hence the greater need to explore and maximize whatever is sharable or universal. Enablement and improvisation as reflected in an interplay of relationships that permeate all forms of cross-cultural communication are integrated into dynamic and manipulative spaces, which are necessitated and constructed through intertextual references involving cross-spatial boundaries. The multiplicity of translated variants results from and also signifies spatial possibilities. In experiencing both decontextualizing and recontextualizing, translation is subject to transformation leading to a dynamic reconfiguration in which the target language reshapes the source language and creates spaces of difference as well as homogeneity. Chinese-Western convergence has been hard to come by, but there is an increasing awareness of and demand for the need to increase academic dialogue and exchange to better tackle translation problems in this cross-cultural context.

From a cross-cultural perspective, to foreignize translation is highly desirable but may risk unintelligibility and a low degree of readability. Foreignization is a cultural-political issue, and as a translation strategy, it is subject to constraints of many kinds. Temporal and cultural gaps tend to create difficulties in interpretation and representation, and cultural pluralism can easily lead to multiple and discrete interpretations. Spaces for acculturation and transculturation are made available to overcome barriers to intercultural communication and interaction. To foster cross-cultural understanding and collaboration, a spatial perspective is needed to dissipate conflicts of political and aesthetic incommensurability. This is particularly so in Chinese-English translation, which is influenced by a host of overt and covert variables. Translation takes place in a multi-dimensional ideological space, and some degree of ideological pluralism allows for cultural diversity marked by tolerance of difference and foreign otherness. Chinese-Western differences are more reliably interpreted and shaped in cross-cultural spaces. It is a matter of practical importance for translators to enter intentional spaces. In view

of the difficulty or even impossibility to ascribe authorial intention, both participatory and dialogical spaces are crucial to encompassing unintended possibilities. Contextual spaces are positioned and repositioned through translation, and
both the author and the reader are responsible for context or its construction.
The translator plays the double role of reader and author in the sense of transferring or (re)constructing the contextual situation for a different text and audience. While the translator can interpret with many aims, the act of interpretation
is culturally and ideologically governed, and the ensuing complicated remapping is such that translation is always somewhat adrift across multi-dimensional
spaces.

The cases of Chinese American literature are exemplars of the spatial trajectories of cultural translation and "back" translation in relation to Chinese American
literature. This translation practice brings two different cultural traditions and
domains into one spatial counterpoint consisting of the availability of cultural
and cross-cultural resources. Chinese American literature is analogous to, and
in crucial aspects, an extension of cultural translation. The retelling of Chinese
stories brings about indirect translation and direct rewriting based on transnational experiments. Chinese stories are retold in a different language to a different audience and re-retold to the "same" audience who are supposed to be
culturally familiar with these stories. The spatial transfer of Chinese culture from
and back to its origin is refreshing and reviving, which involves spatial perception and manipulation. The travel of culture through this special form of translation constitutes a basis for this transformation process during which acculturation
and assimilation unfold in developing and enriching the creative potential of the
writer/translator. Cross-cultural transformation is the natural tendency of this
form of writing, where the invisibility of a source text does not mean its non-
existence. The linguistic and cultural traces of the "original" are visible, and it is
not difficult to see the extent of borrowing from the Chinese source. A profusion
of cultural references and connotations, as part of spatial performance, are used
to produce the writing of these Chinese American authors.

With regard to a spatial mode of thinking, deconstructive space is of great significance and has drawn considerable critical attention from Chinese translation scholars.
But what is controversial is that it may make translation impossible, considering that
it explicitly acknowledges the impossibility of translation, as shown clearly in the early
resistance to deconstruction by many translation scholars, including some in China.
As viewed by some translation scholars in other parts of the world, deconstruction
provoked fierce resistance in China. Traditionalists were understandably perturbed
by the fear that deconstruction would lead to nihilism (Feldman 2000: 51). Deconstruction signifies an appreciable shift from linear models of space to more dynamic
spatial models and engages a ceaseless movement, making it possible to expand the
space to discover traces and alterity. In a deconstructive space, translation represents
a re-synthesis of signs involving the complex interplay of signifiers and signifieds.
Derrida rejects the static spaces associated with traditional criticism, and according to
deconstruction language is forever incomplete, hence the need to explore spaces for
more possibilities. A series of spaces is where solutions to specific translation problems

can be made available and considered. The emphasis on the primary importance of context that is regulated and also regulates meaning makes translation possible despite endless deferral or play of meaning, which also makes it possible for what is repressed to be made visible. The interactive reader-cum-translator is intricately related to the concept of subjectivity and intersubjectivity, which helps to dissolve the traditional boundary between self and other as well as other in the self, generating the ability to transform what comes from other texts. Chinese translation scholars have been singularly fascinated by the concepts of subjectivity and intersubjectivity, which is reflected in a large number of articles focusing on this discussion. In a related vein, indeterminacy forces creation, thus posing a great challenge to translation. The impact of deconstruction on the traditional Chinese concept of fidelity in translation is very profound and even polemical, resulting in some heated and sometimes irascible debates.

In addition to untranslatability or limited translatability, translation needs to grapple with lack of vigor and vitality. A translated text, which is not genetically identical with or even similar to the original, tends to compare unfavorably with it. The derivative nature of translation is often stressed, and thus it is regarded as secondary. In addition, so many constraining factors amount to a hindrance to translation, which is forced into a position of inferiority. These factors, which can be weak at times and strong at others, need to be mediated and moderated to address the disempowered position of translation. In any case, translation must get around what seems untranslatable or compensate for whatever causes loss. Torn between accuracy and adequacy, it is always difficult for translation to meet and balance the conflicting demands that are imposed on the translator, whose endeavor is compromised by their weakened position due to constraints, expectations, and demands. To explore spatial possibilities in the event of suffering from constraints seems to be the best antidote to the frustration over lack of resources in dealing with difficult translation problems. In sum, translation is beset with conflicts, tensions, and contradictions, and is variously and ultimately compromised by ideology and poetics, patronage and power relations, gender and reception, functionality, and inadequacy.

Moreover, translation is justly regarded as an act of negotiation, but how and with what are rarely investigated. Appropriation may be the result of compromise, and it is often necessary although not always necessarily coveted. Both semantic and syntactic constraints are placed upon the operation of translation, which is in the chronic state of being comparatively powerless. It seems that if translation is deeply committed to something, it can also be at the same time deeply compromised by something else. However, this either/or dilemma can be avoided if there is a way to make more resources available to account for spatial dimensions and also to enable and empower translation. The temporal and spatial nature of writing and rewriting should be fully recognized and examined, and it can be well illustrated by the English-Chinese or Chinese-English translation practice. As is shown by numerous examples, unless they are lackadaisical in their efforts to tackle constraints, translators are never powerless to intervene or manipulate. How translation can be energized in mediating and negotiating particular ways of translating is what really matters.

The immanent plurality and multiplicity of the original are susceptible to infelicitous compromise in translation, whose performativity may thus be questioned. The fundamental question of what happens to translation requires, by virtue of its essential function and design, an imaginative grasp of what is or can be involved in making translation not only possible but also efficacious. What happens to translation entails a negotiated system of meaning. To be able to mediate and negotiate successfully, spaces are of critical importance in avoiding dysfunction or less optimal solutions to translation problems. Numerous interrelated predicaments define the limits of translatability and are predisposed to debilitate translation. How to overcome many of the perilous predicaments is a continual struggle. Because of the inherent incomparability and incommensurability between the two systems involved in translation, the modes of signification are or can be different, yielding the possibility or even inevitability of manipulation. Once the fusion of content and form in the original is broken in translation, transformation invariably ensues. The widely held assumption that the target reader only passively consumes the translated product due to their lack of knowledge of the original has proved to be questionable and outmoded in the current age of globalization. The scope of the implied freedom for the translator is of course limited. Translation needs to be sufficiently empowered to transcend the limits and constraints of what may well amount to untranslatability or lame translation. It is therefore vital to engage with complexity in searching for preferable alternatives by probing the spaces of possibilities to cultivate Western-Chinese convergence.

For over a century, translation research in China was dominated by what was identified as three major difficulties in translation by Yan Fu in the note to his translation of *Evolution and Ethics* by T. H. Huxley: namely faithfulness, lucidity, and elegance (Yan 1981: 1). The real challenge is to overcome the three at the same time. The combination of these difficulties has since been construed as a tripartite criterion or standard. Fan Shouyi, among many others, calls them "the three-character criteria" (Fan 1999: 33). Notwithstanding its practical usefulness and fruitfulness, this acclaimed dictum has been seen by many as responsible for the longstanding impasse of translation research in China as an institutionalized framework. There have been endless debates and expositions of the tripartite criterion to revive its relevance and bring it up to date. Nevertheless, it is sometimes argued that adherence to the tripartite dictum or obsession with its various expositions will only hamper rather than help Translation Studies in China. In truth, the tripartite dictum has been polemical since its inception: many attempts have been made to define or redefine it but generally without much success. It has been pointed out that the tripartite dictum has derived from Alexander Fraser Tytler's *Essay on the Principles of Translation* (1907), while others have taken pains to demonstrate the substantial differences between the two. Curiously, while Tytler's principles of translation are almost forgotten in China and the West, Yan Fu's dictum still receives critical attention with some Western translation scholars showing a great interest in it as well. All this is encouraging and suggests the possibility to establish and promote productive China-Western scholarly dialogue. However, such cross-spatial comparisons and interactions are still comparatively rare. More spaces are needed to foster and strengthen cross-cultural research.

References

Dong, Qiusi (trans. by Tan Zaixi) (2004) "On Building Our Translation Theories," in Leo Tak-hung Chan (ed.) *Twentieth-Century Chinese Translation Theory: Modes, Issues and Debates*, Amsterdam and Philadelphia: John Benjamins Publishing, 225–229.

Fan, Shouyi (1999) "Highlights of Translation Studies in China since the Mid-Nineteenth Century," *Meta* 44(1): 27–43.

Feldman, Stephen M. (2000) "Made for Each Other: The Interdependence of Deconstruction and Philosophical Hermeneutics," *Philosophy and Social Criticism* 26(1): 51–70.

Qian, Zhongshu (1981) "林纾的翻译" (Lin Shu's Translation), in Qian Zhongshu et al. (eds.) 《林纾的翻译》(*Lin Shu's Translation*), Beijing: Commercial Press, 18–52.

Steiner, George (1998) *After Babel: Aspects of Language and Translation*, Oxford and New York: Oxford University Press.

Sun, Yifeng (2012) "The Shifting Identity of Translation Studies in China," *Intercultural Communication Studies* 25(2): 32–52.

Tan, Zaixi (1995) "中西现代翻译学概评" (A General Survey of Chinese and Western Translation Theories), 《外国语》(*Journal of Foreign Languages*) 16(3): 12–16.

Toury, Gideon (2012) *Descriptive Translation Studies–and beyond*, Amsterdam and Philadelphia: John Benjamins Publishing.

Yan, Fu (1981) "译例言" (Translator's Note), in T. H. Huxley (trans. by Yan Fu), 《天演论》(*Evolution and Ethics*), Beijing: Commercial Press, 1–3.

1 Translation and spaces

Introduction

This chapter intends to explore the concept of space, or rather spaces concerning Translation Studies, a conceptual framework for research to better understand and solve translation problems. Translation takes place in a space between two languages but also emanates from and operates within different spaces. Further, translation entails movement from one site to another, in whose process the creation/production of spaces allows for multiple representations. In order to make translation work better, it is necessary to adopt a broad definition of the concept of spaces. Here the concept of space(s) is understood not only as the bridging of a gap or distance between two languages and cultures but, more importantly, as a tangible strategy to understand and disentangle exactly what happens to translation. It is sometimes necessary to shift focus from process to space in exploring ways to negotiate and enhance the availability of linguistic and stylistic resources by addressing varying degrees of polarity between accuracy and acceptability. The perennial challenge to reconcile the conflicting demands of both needs requires a series of spaces to handle the substantial amount of intricate negotiation and mediation that are required. Translation leads to an assemblage that mediates the recognition of incommensurability, multiplicity and, ultimately, the inherent irreducibility of meaning. Given the semantically uncertain and aesthetically precarious position of translation, translators need to traverse varied spaces while working with multiple cultural codes and conventions. Only through a heightened awareness of the polymorphic interfaces between linked national, social, cultural, historical, and aesthetic spaces can it become possible to produce a translation version that is reasonably balanced and coherent.

Space and spaces

As a fertile conceptual tool, a miscellany of spatial metaphors has been closely associated with Western translation theory (Guldin 2016: 48). However, they all seem to refer to linear transference rather than multi-dimensional representation. There is thus a need to present a reconceptualization of translational spaces to illuminate the underlying multifaceted causes behind translation problems. Translation is first and foremost concerned with the space of distance between the source and target texts, and between the linguistic and cultural systems thus represented, as well as the author and the translator. Moreover, it entails translocation from one geographical or cultural space to another, depending on and complicated by a multitude of interrelated factors. It can be observed that the spatialization of translation remains under-theorized and unsystematically treated. Its theoretical importance and practical significance warrant further investigation and wider recognition. More specifically, it is the spatialization of linguistic resources and cultural knowledge that can shed light on understanding the nature of translation.

Notably, translation is encapsulated by a continual process of recontextualization, and subsequent reconceptualization must be built on this awareness with a focus on enabling translation to function at least proximately if not exactly maximally. Since different cultural and knowledge systems are intertwined in intersecting with one another, if more spaces are made available, mediation and negotiation in translation can be significantly enhanced to become more effective. Since translation is subject to constraints arising from demands for both accuracy and readability, its success depends on whether such constraints can be overcome. With the growing demand for cross-cultural communication, it is increasingly felt that translatability cannot be taken for granted, and translation is an unremitting struggle against various degrees of untranslatability. Indeed, as an impossible necessity, translation establishes the nexus between the possible and the impossible. Apart from its functional role in empowering translation practice, a spatial concept about translation has the potential to gain more explanatory power, and a working understanding of space should thus be obtained. Growing diversity and global interconnectedness require and create more conceptual and operational spaces with unprecedented and profound implications. Transnational spaces bring into play transnational and transcultural challenges and experiences encompassing difference as well as commonality. There is not an overarching theory for capturing all the aspects of space. Kant famously contends that "space is essentially one" and that "the manifold in it, and therefore the general concept of spaces, depends solely on [the introduction of] limitations" into one general space (quoted by Hatfield 1990: 90). There are, however, claimed/created spaces involving the practices of inclusion and exclusion, and admittedly they are concurrent and interacting, as well as overlapping and branching. Translation covers more than one-dimensionality that contains corresponding spatial relations and correlations. William J. Spurlin argues that "translation also includes the spaces where various cultural systems, in addition to language, intersect, converge, and transform" (Spurlin 2017: 173). Further, the dynamics of inclusion and exclusion are linked to merging and division. For Homi Bhabha, the "third space," as an in-between space, is an overarching singular concept. However, it must be pointed out that it cannot be an all-embracing one. The third space provides a different site away from both source and target texts, and in this site different forces operate into hybridization. Moreover, the "third space" is said to be an indication of a contact zone (Pratt 1992: 6), which eventually results in hybridity, or as Bhabha later would prefer, a continuous process of hybridization. Yet before and during hybridization, translation must necessarily operate at different levels and as a result in dissimilar spaces. For example, as Ovidio Carbonell puts it, cultural translation involves an exotic space (Carbonell 1996: 79). The third space emerges out of two cultures in translation, each of them inhabiting in its own cultural space. The concept of spaces should be viewed conceptually or metaphorically to better elucidate what happens in translation, which engenders the dynamic reconfiguration of connectivity by invoking a series of discrete but related spaces intertwined with linguistic conceptualizations, cultural representations, and signifying processes in connection with beliefs and values. This also problematizes the singular of space predicated on the assumption that there is only one single space involved in translation, which would overlook the fact that it is in reality the aggregation of spaces.

Walter Benjamin compares the relationship between the original and the translation to a tangent and a circle (Benjamin 2000: 22). Translation must "touch" the original as Benjamin explicitly states in this simile. These touches occur "at the infinitely small point of the sense of the original, thereupon pursuing its course according to the laws of fidelity and in the freedom of linguistic flux" (Benjamin 2000: 22). The act of touching lies at the heart of "fidelity" to disallow unwarranted deviation, yet significantly, "freedom" is also found to be prerequisite to translation. The point mentioned by Benjamin is small and can be related to the image of fragments, which suggests a sense of destruction. However, there is only one possibility that source and target languages can intersect at a certain point, namely the translation and the source text being completely equivalent. This can rarely be the case, of course, since the two may well have moved on separate trajectories. Nevertheless, it is still possible to prompt translation to keep in touch with the original, and no less importantly, to increase the frequency of the tangent touching the circle. Moreover, although the points of contact can be sparsely distributed, it is possible to capture them, even though only fleetingly and to a small extent. The elusiveness or non-fixedness of the original, in tandem with latent variables interminably activated and emerging, shows that as "a relational process," translation consists essentially of movement in an effort to capture the meaning of the original, which is, on the other hand, not exactly possible due to the non-fixed nature of the original (Waggoner 2012: 197).

By implication, it is through a series of spaces traversed by the movement of translation that the relations of distance and proximity are restructured and transformed. Inevitably, translation induces spatial displacement, interactively engaging with the multitudinous spaces in relation to culture, ideology, politics, and aesthetics. It is thus necessary to theorize space(s) in relation to translation as is demonstrated in a series of questions posed by Robert-Foley:

> What lies in between languages in translation? Is that space (if it is a space at all) empty or full, visible or invisible, loud or quiet? Is it a lost space full of unknown truths waiting to be uncovered, or a new space waiting to be created?
>
> (Robert-Foley 2016: 905)

This may imply a degree of vagueness and uncertainty, but points to possibilities associated with translational space. The centrality of the concept of space to translation is exemplified by the palpable need to develop it as a multi-dimensional concept to make out different ways in which translation enters into dialogue with different linguistic and cultural realities.

The special relevance of spaces to translation can be seen as a useful determinant in perceiving perspectives and subsequent spatial representations. Translation brings into place different perspectives, some of them imperceptible, and these perspectives naturally bear directly on the strategies and approaches subsequently adopted. Therefore, cross-cultural perspectives can be limited one way or another, thus causing an impediment to the opportunity to choose or create appropriate spaces. Sometimes perspectives can be held to be spaces for achieving their corresponding purposes. These spaces are both physical and virtual in nature, with conceptual or metaphorical dimensions. For this reason, their boundaries are not always clear or definite, and it may well be impossible to distinguish or separate these spaces, which can also cut across diverse types of boundaries. Moreover, what is important is that these spaces should be properly coordinated to bring out their operational and functional potentials. If properly chosen and interconnected with the resources available, a network of experimental, explorative, and diagnostic operational spaces can be constructed and applied. Spaces can overlap and are rarely isolated. The concept is necessarily a collective one because when one space ends and another space begins, this may continue until a feasible and optimal solution is obtained. Through the development of operational spaces, the systematic disempowerment of translation can be avoided or ameliorated. Different translators may tackle and solve problems in a plurality of different sets of spaces. As a result, their approaches are correspondingly different, and therefore a different degree of empowerment or disempowerment can be observed.

Meanwhile, it is also important to establish a spatial understanding of the operation of translation in dealing with untranslatability. In this regard, thick translation has emerged as a pragmatic solution by providing intervening paratextual spaces to accommodate the necessary amount of linguistic and/or cultural information, typically in the form of description and explication, in attending to references and allusions contained in the original, thus making translation less restrictive and thus more perceptible. Given the objectively irreducible distance between source and target texts in both linguistic and cultural terms, to resort to "thickness" points to the apparent lack of an inherent space to accommodate the requisite amount of information for adequate communication, be it linguistic or cultural, which makes necessary cultural and linguistic explication. It can be construed as a creditable, albeit sometimes perhaps misguided, attempt to carve out a significantly larger space to remove constraints. Furthermore, the switching between different spaces heralds an irreducible desire to capture more facets of the original without inevitably resorting to thick translation or annotated translation, which after all hampers readability and is detrimental to the literary value inherent in the original.

To put it another way, translation problems can be appropriately placed in a most suitable space to be better tackled. Different types of meaning, be they denotative, connotative, figurative, or other types, require different approaches in translation. And such approaches are best designed and employed in and from different spaces. Clearly, a different space (or more spaces) is needed to cross a seemingly uncrossable space embodied in references and allusions. It is worth noting that space is inextricably linked to possibilities. To be able to function properly, translation necessarily vacillates between proximity and distance, and in so doing, a series of spaces are mapped out and explored and perhaps traversed as well in order to work out the best obtainable solutions.

The so-called transfer of meaning takes place at the risk of losing depth and dimensionality. To start with, it is advisable to spatially understand ontological dimensions that are aligned with one another in spatial relations, considering the fact that unfolding of meaning over time through rereading and rewriting engenders time-space transfiguration in response to external contextual dimensions in an unmediated form. A multi-dimensional conceptualization of complex spatial interactions is informed by the potential for infinite possibilities. The "contact zone" involved in translation is defined by Mary Louise Pratt as "the space and time where subjects previously separated by geography and history are co-present" (Pratt 1992: 7). It should not come as a complete surprise to recognize the necessity to refocus attention on what makes translation possible and workable in terms of both accuracy and acceptability.

The concept of interconnected spaces includes such salient attributes as diversity, sensibility, flexibility, and so on and is used as a lens for rethinking how translation is done and presented to illustrate the concept as a remedial strategy that can be useful in dealing with dysfunctional or disempowered translation. The production and reproduction of spaces increase the capacity for resilience and resourcefulness. It can also be said that a spatial form is not only an organic whole of entity form and a void form in the real space but also a subjective judgment of the existence of factors in an ideological space. The interdependence between these spaces holistically reflects a range of potentially ostensibly competing but also complementary strategies and practices. It is thus very necessary to develop a spatial perspective on translation to gain a better understanding of how translation can be done more resourcefully.

Friedrich Schleiermacher's much-quoted spatial metaphor about translation entails a mutually exclusive movement: the translator either brings the original to the target reader or takes them to it (Schleiermacher 2012: 43). These spatial movement strategies were motivated by cultural politics, and it should be placed securely in a historical space: Schleiermacher only encouraged one movement: to take the target reader to the original, which is supposed to be stationary and unchanged. Although the third way of translating is precluded, translation methods are more than two, which suggests multiple movements, practices, and spaces can be involved. More importantly, it is often the combination of these methods and manifestations that define and shape the experience of translation. What this clearly shows is that the concept of space is dynamic rather than static and heterogeneous rather than homogeneous. It is also susceptible to changing and changed circumstances and contexts in which spatial configurations are constantly generated. On this account, translational spaces are malleable, continually expanded or reinvented to meet the need or challenge arising from a given situation, which explains their unabated relevance to translation.

Distance and space

If we say a translation unfailingly entails an act of reading, an obvious question needs to be asked: How does the translator read the source text in the first place? The way in which he/she reads it determines the way in which it is translated, at least to some extent. Almost equally, however, the way in which meaning is conveyed what has been read informs the end-result of translation. There can well be a distance between the translator/reader and the translator/writer. However, by and large, a bad reader can barely be a good translator, although there is no guarantee that a good reader will make a good translator. Moreover, the attitude of the translator is also a relevant factor. For instance, an emotionally engaged reader is more likely to generate an emotionally engaging translation. Translation is essentially an impossible but necessary practice as stated by Derrida. But necessity does not necessarily solve the problem of impossibility. What makes translation possible warrants further investigation. As pointed out by de Man, "The relationship of the translator to be original is the relationship between language and language" (De Man 2000: 81). Such a relationship is demonstrably fraught with hazards. But we now realize more acutely than ever that it is also the relationship between culture and performance. The nature of the relationship is influenced by many factors, such as historical and cultural variants, of the production and reception of translation.

Guo Moruo, a famous Chinese poet and scholar, once recalled his experience of translating *Faust*, a tragic play growing out of Goethe's 60 years of life experience. The play is divided into two parts. Guo spent nearly 30 years translating it. He was in his twenties when starting the translation project. As the first part was the product of Goethe's youth, the translation went smoothly thanks to the emotional proximity between Goethe and Guo, and the ideological distance between them was not unbridgeable. The source text was proverbially reminiscent of the May Fourth Movement in China. However, when it came to the translation of the second part – Goethe composed it when he was an elderly man – the job became much more laborious and painstaking. As Guo recalls, the writer's "thoughts and feelings" seemed to persistently elude him at that time (Guo 1984: 22). Subsequently, he lost interest in the play and even began to doubt its literary value as a world-famous work. Almost three decades elapsed before the translator accumulated sufficient life experience through some tumultuous times. Only then did he find the play powerfully resonating with his own understanding of life. The two spatial systems and perspectives associated with the author and the translator began to converge with the shortening of the earlier emotional distance separating them. The stalled translation project was then resumed and finished within a short period of time (Guo 1984: 22). The main impediment of the antecedent emotional distance or lack of commitment ceased to exist.

In a similar vein, while translating *Uncle Tom's Cabin*, Lin Shu was weeping unrestrainedly, overwhelmed by primal empathy and humanity when emotional distance decreased concomitantly. As a result, his translation was richly evocative and heart-warming. According to Qian Zhongshu, "He established a close relationship with what he was translating, and a commanding overpowering emotion halted his dashed pen so that he could manage to wipe his tears" (Qian 1981: 35–36). In telling contrast to the earlier emotional commitment, however, his later translations reveal a detachment or unwillingness to get involved. Qian points out that "He no longer appreciated and was not even interested in the texts for him to translate. He was only interested in payment" (Qian 1981: 36). Lin's two sharply divergent attitudes towards translation underline the importance of an appropriate level of emotional involvement on the part of the translator in shortening the distance between source and target texts. In the course of moving information from one location to another, at least two spaces of separate belonging and potential exclusion can be observed. While it is necessary to acknowledge the irreducible distance separating a text and its translation, closing the gaps between the source and target languages is very important and prompts the translator to acquire and develop a spatial understanding of distance.

Additionally, in terms of translation, "the distance between the two cultures is an obstacle to information transfer" (Santamaria 2010: 517). Cultural distance is susceptible to causing defamiliarization and can be identified as the main and paramount cause of untranslatability. While cultural spaces may overlap, they operate as an arena for clashes or conflicts. Pratt's notion of "contact zones" has been widely adapted for translation. It refers primarily to cross-cultural encounter and to the contact zone in which there are

> social spaces where disparate cultures meet, clash, and grapple with each other, often in highly asymmetrical relations of domination and subordination – such as colonialism and slavery, or their aftermaths as they are lived out across the globe today.
>
> (Pratt 1992: 4)

In the process of translation, the transfer of information is fraught with perils, which is partly caused by different distances, not only representing differences but also reinforcing them. Moreover, cultural distance is invariably compounded by historical distance, and the spaces thus generated as a result underscores the necessity to establish discrete connections by historicizing and contextualizing interpretations of the cultural material to be conveyed in translation.

It is therefore meaningful to examine how translation forms the nexus between cultural referents whose congruity or incongruity is likely to be and often is experienced differently by the target reader. Spaces are necessary for these referents to make sense in a different cultural context and in response to linguistic and cultural displacement. The fixed referential space in the original becomes a shifted referential space in the target text. The spatial relations between the two texts can be understood as artificial connectivity that is employed through translocations.

The spatial nature of writing and rewriting is obvious, and the latter requires space to materialize, deductively implying a temporal or spatial distance between source and target texts as exemplified in etymological tracing, which affirms the inevitability of rewriting and concomitant appropriation. Rewriting means belated participation in the writing process and contributes to the meaning to be consumed by the target reader and is responsible for giving it a final shape. As a result, a pluralistic approach to translation is constructed in keeping with the nature and extent of rewriting with the aim of finding solutions to translation problems. When different ways of translating the same source text are made available for comparison, it is only too clear that different spatial dimensions are represented, where cultural referents, for instance, may well be treated differently. References and allusions in the source text are spatial in nature, denoting referential spaces where the translator is challenged to explore various ways to articulately communicate what is intended to be expressed by the author without losing much of the rhetoricity and specificity in the original.

In terms of distance, "hard translation," which is an extreme form of literalism, posited and espoused by Lu Xun, arguably the most influential modern Chinese writer, in a series of acrimonious debates over how translation should be performed in the late 1920s and early 1930s provides an illuminating perspective on linguistic and cultural borrowing. Hard translation would leave little space for rewriting. There is no denying that it can serve a specific purpose, but due to its seemingly insouciant disregard to readability or even intelligibility to some extent, "hard translation" came under feverish attack by Liang Shiqiu, who was labeled as a "liberal-conservative critic" (Wang 2013: 324). An interesting case is presented, in which how "hard translation" purports to minimize the distance between the source and target texts is unveiled, thereby potentially reducing separation and deviation, as well as the chance and space for rewriting. The resultant shortest possible distance signifies minimum space in an operational sense and minimizes the chance of distortion. In order to address the acute problem of inadequate vocabulary and syntactic representations concerning the Chinese language, "hard translation" demands hard efforts to be made by the target reader, not only to expand themselves but also, more importantly, to enrich the Chinese language. The true significance of Lu Xun's hard translation can only be understood in the larger context of cultural strategy that occupies a correspondingly larger space.

During the late Qing and early Republic periods of China, most translations were via Japanese, and such spatial movements are of critical importance. The dominance of Japanese was created and sustained by the influx of Chinese students into Japan. Indirect translation via Japanese was prevalent, the reason for which is twofold: first, most translators only knew Japanese. Second, they trusted that what had been selected to be translated into Japanese was worthy of being translated into Chinese (Chi 2018: 18–19). Most of the translated texts were originally written in English or other European languages. Before 1949, when the People's Republic of China was founded, most Russian texts were indirectly translated via English and Japanese. This practice of indirect translation via an intermediary third language signals a spatial trajectory, outlining the contours of the effort to access the original in a viable, albeit compromised mode. Unarguably, it is a makeshift means of satisfying the urgent demands of society in great need of knowledge and understanding of the advanced countries in the world. In short, indirect translation represents a short-cut substitute for direction translation despite following a seemingly circuitous route to what can be provided to the target reader. The spatial implications of indirect translation are such that China benefited greatly from these translations in a timely manner.

Contextual spaces

A distance also exists between content and context. Any act of reading and interpretation must be subject to contextualization. The spatial and contextual relationships of words must be re-established within a different language and culture. It is an accepted fact that translators must be able to make sense of the source text before starting to translate. For this reason, stimulating contextual awareness is essential for producing reliable translation. In the context of translation, it is a cultural situation in which meaning is originally constructed and subsequently displaced. Accordingly, the success of translation depends in large measure on an understanding of the spatial situation surrounding how information is processed and converted to the target language. Translation occurs in a given spatial situation, calling forth a context that provides an interpretative scaffolding, and what that entails is a matter of historical and contextual interpretation. Widdowson observes that "contextual interpretation, which yields referential meaning, and textual interpretation which yields representational meaning" (Widdowson 1992: 55). The distance between textual interpretation and contextual interpretation can be significant. Meanwhile, surface meaning acquired through textual interpretation can belie the real meaning, thus suggesting an inherent pitfall in translation. Contextual interpretation, as argued by Widdowson, is "essentially . . . *convergent*" (Widdowson 1992: 55). Consequently, spatial configuration and heterogeneity are formed to free the otherwise imprisoned literary referents and allegories. After all, the transfer of the original space of reading, especially allegorized reading, is often close to impossibility.

Moreover, it can be observed that translation usually moves from an immediate context to an extended, hence broader context in which both linguistic and cultural interpretation is guided and governed. For the purpose of translation and reception, a unified comprehension space is required to accommodate interpretation on the part of the translator and intelligibility on the part of the target reader. Clive Barnett states:

> There is a taken-for-granted consensus that ideas, discourses and representations need to be placed in historical, economic or social contexts if they are to be properly interpreted, explained and criticized.
>
> (Barnett 1999: 281)

In all likelihood, more directly relevant to translation is the conceptualization of linguistic and cultural contexts and influences. To further compound the situation, there are also, among others, political and ideological contexts to be considered. What is less obvious is that all these can be interrelated and competing contexts. Depending on the contexts or the one that seems to be more relevant than others, the translator may decide what to prioritize and what to relinquish. Translation is intrinsically related to place and space, and a host of problems are imputed to the distance between discrete systems characterized by spatial heterogeneity. It means that oftentimes meaning cannot be literally interpreted, or otherwise it could cause serious communication problems.

The instability of meaning is disallowed to become unmanageable through Derrida's repeated emphasis on the determining role of context, which is of particular significance to translation. The re-inscription depends primarily on what is interpreted in taking into account the context or related contexts, which creates the necessary enabling conditions for meaning that is culturally coded in the original to be re-encoded in the target language, during which process cross-culturally communicative competence can be promoted. In this sense, cross-cultural spaces in which cross-cultural information is processed and reproduced are decisive in relativizing contextual parameters to determine meaning as a result of contextual control by the translator.

Closely related to the aforementioned spaces are intertextual spaces, which are of abiding relevance to adequate cross-cultural translation. In terms of adequacy, the intertextual references and possibilities constitute an irreducible part of translation, and it is therefore important to require and maintain the function of intertextual space:

> A text is perceived in another intertextual space which turns out to be the field of more or less casual connections with other texts where the text acquires new meanings and often loses its inherent meaning.
>
> (Torop 2003: 275)

The networks of connections are often notably absent in the target language and very difficult to reproduce in translation in a different intertextual space. Translation can be seen as an especially intensive form of intertextual connections (Torop 2003: 275). In general, the allusive erudition displayed in the source text is a nightmare for the translator in less than successful attempts to sort out the intertextual weaving and reconstruction in the target language.

However, such attempts can lead to a somewhat reductionist approach, as exemplified by explicitness to increase accessibility and shareability. Because translation is only possible through interpretation, a contact zone in translation charts a semantic space where a general tendency is exhibited towards explicitness in the translated text:

> In its most basic meaning in the field of linguistics, the term explicitness refers to the overt encoding of information. In other words, the part of a

message that is encoded linguistically is explicit, while the information which can be understood from the message without being directly referred to by linguistic material is implicit.

(Baumgarten et al. 2008: 177)

The truth is that since translation is integral to the act of decoding, varying levels of explicitness are observable, and this can be construed as an ingrained inclination to achieve a minimum level of communication. It is the change of context that necessitates a higher level of explicitness. Translocation induced by translation is conducive to establishing a somewhat different contextual framework to introduce foreignness to the target language. And this foreignness tends to be blamed for indeterminacy and lack of intelligibility. It cannot be denied that in translation the shift from implicitness to explicitness reduces the interpretative space, and the aesthetic challenge of decoding is weakened accordingly. Consequently, the pleasure of reading diminishes.

There is no doubt that contextual information is essential for interpretation, which, for the reason stated earlier, can lead to explicitness, consciously intended or otherwise. It should also be pointed out that denotational explicitness compromises connotational significance and restricts the formal features of the original. Intertextual interpretation in a cross-cultural sense is profoundly enabling in that it empowers translation to function adequately under a multifactorial condition. Meanwhile, sufficient contextual information and intertextual knowledge can help to reduce the need for explicitness. This requires translators to translate contextually and hermeneutically. A more contextualized understanding of the translated text is certainly a desirable condition for decoding, not to mention the fact that meaning can be regulated and shaped. Translation is the perpetual undoing and redoing of what has been done. Effective interpretation is based on sound cultural knowledge and is subsequently capable of enlarging the sense-making capacity of translation. Various and complex mappings of the spaces in which the translator first tries to make sense of things and then make sense of the ways in which sense is made of the original. The translator then works out ways in which to present what they have made sense of in translation. The referential and intertextual processes of interpretation play an important role in creating and shaping the aesthetic reading experience of translation. These processes entail the related spaces for cues and clues to the intended meaning, which can be implicit rather than explicit, and suggestive rather than unequivocal. In other words, if the original implicitness can be retained to a certain extent and not at the expense of intelligibility, translation can be significantly empowered. For this reason, if sufficient contextual clues are made available for the target reader to follow, the construction of an interpretative framework will help them to decode meaning successfully.

Translation represents a legitimized and expected form of rewriting in a given context that functions to regulate the whole reproduction process, and it is within a specific context that this rewriting brings source and target texts together. Derrida's concept of iterability suggests that signs are repeated and repeatable with difference. This difference introduces a spatial dimension of its own into translation. Nevertheless, translation is not an unbridled or willful act, but the result of interpretation aided by intertextuality through context that gives rise to rewriting. However, dislocation of the target reader's usual frame of reference results in a disorienting reading experience. The space of otherness signifies other spaces, which, if anything, further heightens contextual complexities. Various competing contextual spaces signify that translation, or at least good translation, is not about searching for an exact one-to-one match between words in source and target texts but about moving words from one system of meaning to another and meaning is intended to be rendered more processable and thus more translatable. Translation is cross-cultural communication within a cross-cultural context since the message that is conveyed in translation is culturally encrypted. Furthermore, cultural meaning itself is interpreted and prioritized according to the needs of the target system in respect of cultural contextual interactions made possible through cultural spaces in which cultural constraints can be overcome.

Function and approach

In contrast to contextual control, the functionalist approach to translation reverses the central focus. With an emphasis on reception, the possibility of a different function, as opposed to that embedded in the original, creates a space to gain freedom of a different kind by removing constraints on the translation practice that is associated with staying close to the original. If priority is given to specific communicative purposes, the desired reception is largely predetermined. As a result, a considerable distance between source and target texts is allowed to exist. To re-prioritize is not uncommon, especially in media translation. This can be easily justified since there are often a variety of source materials, none of which seem to be more authoritative, but some of which are certainly more relevant. Transediting, signifying more flexible forms of writing or rewriting or re-rewriting, has become the norm and has gone beyond the traditional realm of translation, giving rise to "a complex, integrated combination of information gathering, translating, selecting, reinterpreting, contextualizing and editing" (Van Doorslaer 2010: 181). Also, shifts of focal points induced and set in motion by varying agendas and agents lead to different arrangements or organizations of source material, coupled with additions and deletions while reframing the source text to improve acceptability. Indeed, new connections are made in the process of re-articulation and restoring coherence. Furthermore, competing forces of more elaboration and contraction generate more re-prioritization, causing further spatial reconfiguration and re-territorialization.

The broader definition of translation in this sense is to make sure that its reception is favorable. From the point of view of the functionalist approach, the most important outcome is that translation works for a particular purpose by performing its intended function. In order to overcome the restrictions of the source text together with its culture, once again, it is necessary to produce translation spaces. However, it is not necessarily a strategy to avoid any contact with strangeness or foreign otherness because the potential lack of correspondence with the original would be an unmistakable hallmark of bad translation as posited by Benjamin. The function of the original may well be changed in view of the significantly different purpose of translation compared with that of the original. Regardless of its "sins," this approach assertively recontextualizes the text for translation, thereby establishing a different contextual space. As a result, the translated text is made to function in a certain way and becomes a product of overt transformation.

The multiple functions of space are steeped in different cultural conditions and subject to variables that can destabilize translation. More often than not, source and target languages do not share a contextual space, and they also tend to function differently in different contextual spaces. This being the case, translation needs to identify or come up with a shared space for communication between the translated text and the target reader. In this sense, the task of translation is defined and performed according to the underlying purpose. In this situation, the task of the translator is to meet the needs of his/her patron. In order to meet such needs, the translator needs to be given unhindered freedom. The liberating nature of freedom is most salient in that spaces can be formed for the purpose of exploring related possibilities. Over the years, the underlying nature of the relationship between source and target texts, particularly with regard to equivalence, has undergone some subtle yet fundamental changes. Functions related to denotative, connotative, pragmatic, and formal equivalence represent different spaces respectively. At any rate, target-orientedness has liberated translation from the old imprisonment of faithfulness to the original in every detail. However, a higher degree of independence from the original seems to indicate a lower degree of accountability of the translated text, which may appear to be a potential source of controversy.

As a practically valid and workable approach, functional translation was once hailed to be a truly enlightening and liberating in reconceptualizing translation. However, both "the theoretical foundations and applicability of functionalist approaches" have been under heavy criticism, as acknowledged by Christine Nord (Nord 2011: 32). In recapturing one of the "basic principles of functional translation," Nord writes:

> A translation that achieves the intended purpose may be called "functional," which means that a text (in this case, a translation) "works" for its receivers in a particular communicative situation, i.e., in the way the sender wants it to work. If the purpose is information, the text should offer this in a form comprehensible to the audience; if the purpose is to amuse, then the text should actually amuse its readers. The text producer (and the translator as text producer, too) has, therefore, to evaluate the audience's capacities of comprehension and cooperation, and anticipate the possible effects that certain forms of expression may have on the readership.
>
> (Nord 2011: 34)

First of all, the "intended purpose" is unclear and left unexplained. Whose intended purpose? Presumably, it is the author's intended purpose, but it is by no means clear what this purpose really is. There seems to be an unwarranted assumption for functionalist scholars that this purpose can be inferred or established unproblematically. Moreover, the purpose or purposes involved can be much more complex than just providing information or amusement, despite the distinct possibility to identify the primary function of a given text.

The situational relevance of functional translation seems to be conditional, and as Nord contends: "Functionality is not an inherent quality of a text. It is a quality attributed to the text by the receiver, in the moment of reception" (Nord 2011: 34). It seems to mean that whatever the intended purpose, it is the reception that truly matters since it defines or validates what is supposed to be the intended purpose, or rather, the actual function. Simply put, purpose and function are not necessarily the same thing and should not be used interchangeably: they may derive from different spaces and are susceptible to manipulation by means of misrepresentation. Nord has offered a definition for "functional":

> A translation that achieves the intended purpose may be called "functional,"
> which means that a text (in this case, a translation) "works" for its receivers
> in a particular communicative situation, i.e., in the way the sender wants it
> to work.
>
> (Nord 2011: 34)

This "functional" translation can serve the purpose of preventing translation from drifting away from the original. It can offer an ethical containment of what would otherwise be excessive manipulation by setting "an ethical limitation on" infinite possibilities related to equivalence (Nord 2011: 33). The sender is presumably the translator in this particular context. Since there is only one sender here, who is ultimately responsible for "the way" in which a translation works, his/her intention controls the actual function of the translated text. But this could be problematic. The underlying assumption that the two intentions of author and translator are the same is open to question. Likewise, the client or commissioner who may have a different purpose may prevail and play a decisive role in shaping the final product.

Nevertheless, despite the patron's overriding intentions among other intentions, the basic communicative intentions can be inferred by the translator with the help of the context involved in a given situation. While some degree of functional deviation is inevitable, source and target texts are expected to function analogously, which is the basic principle of dynamic equivalence so that accountability and receptivity discussed by Nord are interrelated and conjoined. While a productive space between the spheres of production and consumption is necessary, in the case that matching communicative intention with the supposed function proves to be insurmountable, the transfer of situations to another space may be considered as a panacea. Once the function of the text to be translated is identified or established, the translator can use an imaginary space into which the situation related to the original is reconstructed. Subsequently, a range of linguistic and cultural resources intrinsic to the target system becomes available for whatever is needed for the situation to function in a similar or comparable way. Admittedly, a certain degree of formal deviation may well result from this strategy. To be sure, not every detail in the original can be matched in the target text, but a similar overall function can be comparably performed in the target system. This conceptualization of situation in relation to translation is useful in holistically representing what is meant to be achieved in the original by way of circumventing the seemingly unmanageable and should be fecund for generating solutions to difficult translation problems.

This relocation of situation engenders an opportunity for complete rewriting and is semantically contextualized to make possible lexical perception and access. It falls within the scope of transwriting or transcreating yet with more spatial configurations that allow for the possibility of reconstructing the meaning embedded in the original situation in the source text. It can be argued that this strategy will provide and enable the dynamic functionality of the otherwise untranslatable parts of the source text. By circumventing serious translation problems, the otherwise unprivileged position of the translator has become a privileged one in which it is possible to create new parts of the translated text. The newness, in this case, does not necessarily form hybridity in the absence of a third space, which is not exactly involved here. The newly created parts are meant to capture something of the same quality and flavor of the original. A different space of representation is found to function in a parallel way in the target language, establishing connections in a hierarchy of relevance and adequacy in translation practice.

Expanded or condensed spaces

As noted earlier and as a last resort to bypass spatial constraints, thick translation is called for to address the distance between self and other, particularly with regard to cultural referents and concepts. Thick translation as a paratextual extension reveals, at least to some extent, a central concern about irreducibility, primarily serving to fill the gaps and lacunae in translation in which multiple reference points may not be recognized as they are located outside the familiar cultural space of the target reader. The thickness can be seen as an expansion of the space infrastructure of the original to bring into existence extra spaces needed to accommodate cross-cultural information purported for the benefit of the target reader, given the fact that the dense intertextual and interspatial resonances cannot be reproduced within the parameters of the original space. For sure, as asserted by Yuste Frías, thick translation is different from the translation of paratexts, which is included in paratranslation (quoted by Nord 2012: 404). Its main function is to contextualize the translated text "with its annotations and its accompanying glosses" (Appiah 2000: 427). It is necessary to transcend the circumscribed limits of the space allocated to the translation. The kernel of this expansion is that what is foreign may turn out too strange to be intelligible without some detailed annotated texts. Moreover, to allow the translated text to retain its foreignness is in conformity with translational ethics. As maintained by Lacayo, "An ethics of irreducibility in translation would call for a foreign text to maintain its autonomous right to remain foreign" (Lacayo 2014: 224). The concern about irreducibility leads to the formation of more spaces for translation to function adequately. For this reason, the asymmetrical forms of source and target texts can cause the target reader to be semantically frustrated and culturally disoriented and must, therefore, be converted into functional capability. An elongated space is needed to prevent cultural information from being curtailed. As cultural outsiders, the target reader needs extra space for more explanatory annotations to be provided. By means of the footnotes, endnotes, or sidenotes, thick translation, through these extra spaces, provides the target reader with the necessary historical and cultural knowledge for the sake of effective cross-cultural communication.

The emergence of the paratextual space extends the scope of textual representation. Aside from paratextual annotations and glosses as part of thick translation, there are also textual annotations interwoven in the translated text. On a smaller scale and in a more common form, explanatory translation is used to expand the original spatial dimension by inserting the requisite amount of information to control signification and enhance performativity. Such added information increases the elasticity of the space that is used in parenthetical constructions. Strictly speaking, translation of this kind does not entail an extra space. In the event that references and allusions turn out to be unfamiliar and uncharted for the target reader whose cross-cultural knowledge is inadequate, the translator is compelled to intervene in order to assign meaning to what is semantically elusive. When the unfamiliar is perceived to put too great a semantic strain on the target reader, a sense-making solution must be found in the paratextual productions situated outside the main text. In expanding space in the text, tropes and metaphors also have a chance to be retained rather than rephrased or substituted so that an expanded version of translation is produced. This seems to be a compromised way to allow and encourage the target reader to experience the foreign, albeit somewhat obliquely. It is the combination of sense-making and cross-cultural encounter that gives rise to this mode of expanded translation, which is different from annotated translation. Still, this historically and culturally contextualized translation, though stretched with a moderate amount of extra information, evades creating burdensome reading, and is less intrusive or distracting than thick translation or annotated translation. When there is something susceptible to multiple readings, paraphrasing is required.

Dao'an (312–385), a Chinese Buddhist monk, was responsible for overseeing the translation of Buddhist scriptures into Chinese. Despite some ambivalence and caution, he was predisposed to condense the translation space by excluding what was thought to be the unnecessary elements from his translation when confronting

> the dilemma which ever faced Buddhist translators: whether to make a free, polished and shortened version adapted to the taste of the Chinese public, or a faithful, literal, repetitious and therefore unreadable translation.
>
> (Zürcher 2007: 203)

An adaptive translation strategy is preferred here out of necessity. There are of course different reasons for a preference for shortened translation. On the surface, the source text is partially or selectively translated, but in reality, the eliminated parts are not consequential. To condense translation with discretion is to enhance readability without causing too much damage to the basic information being conveyed.

Similarly, Arthur Waley's English translation of *Monkey: Folk Novel of China*, "has entertained a broad readership since its first publication in 1943" (Levy 1984: 507). One could certainly argue that the condensation of space highlights the entertaining quality of the novel. The translation is an abridged one. According to Hu Shi, who wrote an introduction to the translated text, Waley translated only 30 chapters out of 100, and he further pointed out:

> Freed from all kinds of allegorical interpretations by Buddhist, Taoist, and Confucianist commentators, *Monkey* is simply a book of good humor, profound nonsense, good-natured satire and delightful entertainment.
>
> (Hu 2007: 4–5)

The novel contains numerous allusions and references, which would be most likely to overburden the target reader, who was not familiar with traditional Chinese cultural thought and religious practice. Thus, expunged and appropriated, the condensed space of rewriting makes it possible for the target reader to enjoy a compact reading of a Chinese classic. The spatial compactness makes "delightful entertainment" possible, and by drastically reducing allusions and references, readability is secured.

Translation entails rewording and signifies the manipulation of signifiers. In audiovisual translation, there is scarcely any space for paratextual information and constraints are more stringent and may well result in instances of unintelligibility or confusion. The limited space available can also increase the risk of doing insufficient justice to the original. However, a high degree of spatial elasticity in light of non-verbal signs in the form of multimodality lessens the pressure for semantic transmission, in view of which various forms of contractions are permissible, allowing or tolerating inadequacy. Pérez-González observes that

> [t]ranslators should therefore give careful consideration to the manifold connections between verbal and non-verbal resources in the source text: overlooking them may be detrimental to the target reader's holistic perception of the overall semiotic ensemble.
>
> (Pérez-González 2014: 120)

Audiovisual translation affords spaces for the interplay between verbal and non-verbal signs. Meaning is contingent on and open to the possibility of the combination and interaction of verbal and non-verbal aspects of what is holistically presented to and experienced by the target audience. Significantly, it is these connections that generate the overall results of communication. The functional equivalence is achieved through the connections that are successfully made.

In respect of audiovisual translation, Jorge Díaz-Cintas and Aline Remael have referred to "all the spatial and temporal limitations imposed by the medium itself" (Díaz-Cintas 2014: 9). In this light, functional equivalence is probably the most relevant and imperative to our understanding of what constitutes the core of audiovisual translation, for which the contracted spaces are of primary consideration for the translator. These non-verbal signs include "visual, gestural, aural and linguistic signifiers" (Hale and Upton 2000: 2). The power of these non-verbal signs can be demonstrated almost as a universal language, which can be directly transferred and processed without any conscious efforts to "translate." Intersemiotic translation is a holistic exercise defined by Jakobson as "an interpretation of verbal signs by means of signs of nonverbal sign systems" (Jakobson 1959: 233). It can be seen as a set of non-verbal signs that provide assistance to verbal signs. And the verbal and paraverbal (phonetic and kinetic) features of utterances are underscored and heightened by spatial dynamics as well.

Intersemiotic translation involves different verbal and non-verbal signifiers and covers more spatial situations and levels. Different semiotic systems co-exist and interact with one another, yielding a hybridized "text." Hybridized on different levels, image and sound as non-linguistic signs ultimately contribute to the final effect on the target reader. All the multilayered spaces involved in this process, if properly integrated and combined, facilitate an interactive capability to produce multiple representations from and within these different spaces. All this entails, in essence, an adaptive translation as manifest in multimodal texts, requiring and stimulating participatory engagement. Verbal signs are alternately foregrounded and recede as governed by the actual needs of the particular situation. Intersemiotic textuality is dynamically expanded and enhanced by the role of multimodality, inherently triggering more corresponding spaces for omissions, condensation, and adaptation, all of which comprehensively address the concern about irreducibility. Moreover, due to the specific interpretative contexts in specific situations, spatiotemporal referentiality is established as self-referentiality in many cases to make reasonably clear sense to the target audience.

Conclusion

Translation brings together various different kinds of spaces, representing an articulation of global and local spaces in which culturally situated references and normative constraints are entangled to interact with one another. A variety of disparate spaces are connected by the need for translation across linguistic and cultural divides, where interaction and participation feature prominently. Thanks to such spaces of participation and production, the power of resourcefulness and liberation thus generated is brought into sharp focus. The acknowledgment of the irreducible distance separating a text and its translation prompts probing into the variety of perspectives, attitudes, beliefs, and values embedded in translation. Historical belatedness of both distance and space provides the possibility to bring in something different. When initiated from a distance, be it temporal, geographical, discursive, epistemological, or empathic, translation is situated in a series of corresponding spaces. The pronounced change of distance reshapes the operation of translation. How the two culturally different texts are related to each other projects the trajectory of translation and its adaptation to the target cultural system. Translation hinges on distance and the various distances thus involved are constitutive of spatial configurations, which contributes to the understanding of the multifaceted nature of transmission concerning cross-cultural dialogue and adaptation. With a larger range of possibilities becoming available, the practice of translation is expressly empowered. Movement in or through spaces is a primary perceptual fact, bringing together otherwise disparate perspectives and divergent perceptions.

Translation necessitates searching and mapping out multi-dimensional spaces, and instead of being confined to the surface meaning, more dynamic and interconnected approaches arise from a complex spatial awareness and perception in relation to translation. Anxiety about the presumed confinement of space can be decidedly weakened through an engagement with various translation problems related to irreducibility. In terms of compensation, if something is lost in one space, it may be possible to obtain compensation in another. The circulation of newly, and for this reason perhaps differently, produced meaning is made possible via more productive spaces where a multiplicity of approaches can be formed and developed. The spatialization of translation improves the chance to examine possible ways to empower translation by making it more resourceful and less constrained. Further, by taking into account variability, complexity, and reciprocity, different spatial realities, when metaphorically extended, can facilitate discursive engagements with all relevant factors in translation.

References

Appiah, A. K. (2000) "Thick Translation," in Lawrence Venuti (ed.) *The Translation Studies Reader*, London and New York: Routledge, 417–429.

Barnett, Clive (1999) "Deconstructing Context: Exposing Derrida," *Transactions of the Institute of British Geographers* 24(3): 277–293.

Baumgarten, Nicole et al. (2008) "Explicitness in Translation and Interpreting: A Critical Review and Some Empirical Evidence (of an Elusive Concept)," *Across Languages and Cultures* 9(3): 177–203.

Benjamin, Walter (2000) "The Task of the Translator," in Lawrence Venuti (ed.) *The Translation Studies Reader*, London and New York: Routledge, 15–25.

Carbonell, Ovidio (1996) "The Exotic Space of Cultural Translation," in R. Alvarez and M. C. A. Vidal (eds.) *Translation, Power, Subversion*, Clevedon: Multilingual Matters, 79–98.

Chi, Limin (2018) *Modern Selfhood in Translation: A Study of Progressive Translation Practices in China (1890s–1920s)*, Singapore: Springer.

De Man, Paul (2000) "Conclusions: Walter Benjamin's 'The Task of the Translator'," in Paul de Man (ed.), *The Resistance to Theory*, Minneapolis: University of Minnesota Press, 73–105.

Díaz-Cintas, Jorge, and Aline Remael (2014) *Audiovisual Translation, Subtitling*, London and New York: Routledge.

Guldin, Rainer (2016) *Translation as Metaphor*, London and New York: Routledge.

Guo, Moruo (1984) "谈文学翻译工作" (On Literary Translation), in Translators Association of China *Translation Newsletter* Editorial Office (ed.) 《翻譯研究論

文集(1949–1983)》(*Translation Research Papers [1949–1983]*), Beijing: Foreign Language Teaching and Research Press, 21–24.

Hale, Terry, and Carole-Ann Upton (2000) "Introduction," in Carole-Ann Upton (ed.) *Moving Target: Theatre Translation and Cultural Relocation*, Manchester: St. Jerome, 1–13.

Hatfield, Gary (1990) *The Natural and the Normative: Theories of Spatial Perception from Kant to Helmholtz*, Cambridge and London: MIT Press.

Hu, Shi (2007) "Introduction," in Cheng'en Wu (ed.) *Monkey: Folk Novel of China*, New York: Grove Press, 4–5.

Jakobson, Roman (1959) "On Linguistic Aspects of Translation," in Reuben Arthur Brower (ed.) *On Translation*, Cambridge, MA: Harvard University Press, 232–239.

Lacayo, Aarón (2014) "A Queer and Embodied Translation: Ethics of Difference and Erotics of Distance," *Comparative Literature Studies* 51(2): 215–230.

Levy, Dore J. (1984) "A Quest of Multiple Senses: Anthony C. Yu's *The Journey to the West*," *The Hudson Review* 37(3): 507–515.

Nord, Christiane (2011) "Manipulation and Loyalty in Functional Translation," *Current Writing: Text and Reception in Southern Africa* 14(2): 32–44.

Nord, Christiane (2012) "Paratranslation: A New Paradigm or a Re-Invented Wheel?" *Perspectives: Studies in Translatology* 20(4): 399–409.

Pérez-González, Luis (2014) "Multimodality in Translation and Interpreting Studies: Theoretical and Methodological Perspectives," in Sandra Berman and Catherine Porter (eds.) *A Companion to Translation Studies*, Oxford: John Wiley, 119–129.

Pratt, Mary Louise (1992) *Imperial Eyes: Travel Writing and Transculturation*, London and New York: Routledge.

Qian, Zhongshu (1981) "林纾的翻译" (Lin Shu's Translation), in Qian Zhongshu et al. (eds.) 《林纾的翻译》(*Lin Shu's Translation*), Beijing: Commercial Press, 18–52.

Robert-Foley, Lily (2016) "Writing with Translational Constraints: On the 'Spacy Emptiness' between Languages," *MLN* 131(4): 905–918.

Santamaria, Laura (2010) "The Translation of Cultural Referents: From Reference to Mental Representation," *Meta: Translators' Journal* 55(3): 516–528.

Schleiermacher, Friedrich (trans. by Susan Bernofsky) (2012) "On the Different Methods of Translating," in Lawrence Venuti (ed.) *The Translation Studies Reader*, London and New York: Routledge, 43–63.

Spurlin, William J. (2017) "Queering Translation Rethinking Gender and Sexual Politics in the Spaces between Languages and Cultures," in B. J. Epstein and Robert Gillett (eds.) *Queer in Translation*, London and New York: Routledge, 172–183.

Torop, Peeter (2003) "Intersemiosis and Intersemiotic Translation," in Susan Petrilli (ed.) *Translation, Translation*, Amsterdam and New York: Rodopi, 271–296.

Van Doorslaer, Luc (2010) "Journalism and Translation," in Yves Gambier and Luc van Doorslaer (eds.) *Handbook of Translation Studies*, Amsterdam and Philadelphia: John Benjamins Publishing, 180–184.

Waggoner, Matt (2012) "Is There Justice in Translation?" in Scott S. Elliott and Roland Boer (eds.) *Ideology, Culture, and Translation*, Atlanta: Society of Biblical Literature, 187–200.

Wang, Pu (2013) "The Promethean Translator and Cannibalistic Pains: Lu Xun's 'Hard Translation' as a Political Allegory," *Translation Studies* 6(3): 324–338.

Widdowson, H. G. (1992) *Practical Stylistics: An Approach to Poetry*, Oxford: Oxford University.

Zürcher, Erik (2007) *The Buddhist Conquest of China: The Spread and Adaptation of Buddhism in Early Medieval China*, Leiden: Brill.

2   Distance and temporality

Introduction

The present epoch of globalization redefines the concept of distance in the course of negotiating spaces between nations and cultures. However, in a smaller world, cross-cultural exchanges are more contested and challenged by details and particulars, which, though seemingly insignificant, concerns the reception of the translated text. In adapting to the changed conditions and circumstances, translation vacillates between proximity and distance, with the latter taking precedence and emerging as the most dynamic, multivalent force at work. The pursuit of proximity entails coping with or adjusting to distance. Thus, translation is characteristic of different types and variables of distance: linguistic, cultural, political, and aesthetic. That there exists a temporal distance between the source and target texts is undoubtedly a concern. Aside from it, linguistic and cultural distance necessitates acculturation and sometimes justifies domestication. This chapter aims to offer a holistic way of understanding distance regarding translation, at both cognitive and practical levels. Distance and displacement are deeply intertwined, and moreover, distance between the author and the source text reader and distance between the author and the target reader are very different in nature. Since distance is also characterized by dislocation, it generates alienation, and despite the overt desirability to minimize the distance between the source and target texts as a gesture to address disparities between two languages and cultural values, in an overtly experimental mode of translation, distance is bound to change constantly and can function to enhance the efficacy of cross-cultural communication. Close textual engagement or affirmative disengagement is seen to be strategic because an increased distance creates the necessary space for control and manipulation. The translator plays a pivotal role in the articulation and re-articulation of distance, particularly in literary translation.

Objective distance

Translation leads to dislocation and is closely related to distance involving differences in beliefs, attitudes, and preferences that exist in different translation traditions and practices. The sheer ubiquity of distance of various sorts embedded in translation cannot be overlooked. It can be said that the distance that separates source and target languages is sometimes synonymous with difference, which is at the core of translation. Moreover, difference deriving from dislocation creates distance between languages and mindsets of different audiences reading the source and target texts respectively. The resultant distancing effect is manifest in the sense that alienation rooted in foreign otherness distances the target reader from the source text. In commenting on Lin Shu's translation practice, Qian Zhongshu refers to different types of distance to be traversed by translation concerning the travel of texts across spatial and temporal boundaries:

> There is bound to be some distance between one language and another. Distance also occurs between the understanding of the translator together with his/her writing style and the content of the original and its form. This is followed by yet another type of distance, i.e., the distance between the understanding of the translator and his/her ability to express what is embedded in the original.
>
> (Qian 1981: 19)

There is, of course, no symmetrical equivalence of signification between two languages, thus representing the most potent source of anxiety and tension. An important part of the task of the translator is to understand the nature of such distance and to know how to make use of adjusting distance of different kinds accordingly.

More generally, an existential distance between the source and target languages, which may be called objective distance, makes translation susceptible to untranslatability, largely due to incommensurability or partial commensurability between the two languages. (Un)translatability is essentially due to the nature of the distance that "separates the cultural background of source text and target audience in terms of time and place" (Snell-Hornby 1995: 41). The cross-cultural awareness and recognition of the distance are prerequisite for establishing an appropriate translation strategy because such a distance has potentially profound implications for a broad understanding of the way in which a translation is produced and received. This distance, no matter how indeterminable, is bound to require a somewhat different cultural, not to mention historical, perspective on a given textual situation. Therefore, it is necessary to perform a basic assessment of the objective distance prior to translation. As Giovanni Pontiero states:

> If the initial analysis of the distance is appropriate and the translator has fixed the necessary temporal and spatial parameters correctly, i.e., appropriately to his ability and the task in hand, then later detailed decisions a rational to fall back on and are not taken piecemeal. In other words, the cultural unity of the translation as a work of literature depends crucially on the basic decisions on distance in time and space that separate it from the source content.
>
> (Pontiero 1997: 28)

Time and space are key factors contributing to the distance that is subjected to and governed by a host of parameters to be formulated in solving translation problems. The processes of decision making also depend on other types of distance involved in a given situation, which means that any decision making about solutions to translation problems has some kind of bearing on distance.

Distance implies change, and as such, even an existential distance is not a fixed one. Above all, it is worth pointing out that translation is driven and controlled by a sense of direction. As mentioned by Schleiermacher, translation operates in two opposite directions: the target reader is either sent abroad (to the author) or brought home. Either way, distance is involved: how far away from home is a translation considered to be exciting and safe at the same time? Similarly, George Steiner observes that "Any model of communication is at the same time a model of translation, of a vertical or horizontal transfer of significance" (Steiner 1998: 47). This brings to the fore the issue of perspective, which in turn decides on distance. Any shift in perspective not only allows new elements to come to the fore but also changes the distance of observation and, when necessary, acts of intervention. Since the source and target audiences seldom share the same perspective, they observe the same thing from different distances as well.

In a cross-cultural context, distance may be caused by, or be the cause of, bias or prejudice. Post-colonial and feminist translators, for instance, are prone to rewrite the original in an overtly radical way in response to, or in anticipation of, the need for transformation, often for a good reason. Referring to the alienating effect caused by distance, Steiner points out:

> By far the greater proportion of art and historical record has been left by men. The process of "sexual translation" or of the breakdown of linguistic exchange is seen, almost invariably, from a male focus.
>
> (Steiner 1998: 46)

The result is only too apparent: such translation practice is likely to distance the female target reader. Not surprisingly, a feminist interpretation of the source represents a perspective that is radically different. Sometimes, a politically motivated rewriting constitutes an action that moves in exactly the opposite direction to the source text, thereby completely subverting what is originally intended.

Thus, the translator is typically faced with two diametrically different approaches to translation, both of which can be effective and successful, as stated by Wilhelm von Humboldt in his correspondence to A. W. Schlegel:

> All translation seems to be simply an attempt to solve an impossible task. Every translator is doomed to be done in by one of two stumbling blocks: he will either stay too close to the original, at the cost of the taste and the language of his nation, or he will adhere too closely to characteristics peculiar to his nation, at the cost of the original.
>
> (quoted by Pontiero 1997: 55)

Creating artificial proximity to either the source or target culture seems fit and convenient at times, but it can produce inhibiting or facilitating effects. However, this either/or dichotomous thinking precludes the possibility of translation standing an equal distance from both the source and target texts. Of course, it is the initial decision concerning the direction in which translation moves that determines the distance to be traversed and how.

Temporal distance

Evidently, temporal or historical distance falls into the category of objective distance. Much has been written about the temporal distance that separates the source text from the target reader. In this light, there is above all the question of archaic language, which understandably tends to be updated in translation for contemporary consumption. The result is a simultaneously intralingual and interlingual translation to bridge both the historical and linguistic distance. For this reason, the temporal distance may be subject to change, although it can be consciously preserved by the translator, and in some cases, it is even re-created. Nevertheless, whether the archaic language of the original should be reproduced has been the subject of much debate. For no such text exists that is perfectly acceptable to all readers, then and now, source and target. This difficulty is further compounded by the consideration that normally the source language is not archaic to the source text reader who first reads it. So can modernizing the text in translation be warranted? What about the historical distance that does exist to separate the text from the reader now, be they source or target readers? Yet if an archaic language is recreated only to be forced upon the target reader, there is a good chance that the translation in question will risk unintelligibility. This seemingly zero artificial distance (which I shall discuss further later in this chapter), despite imparting an air of historical authenticity, may not make translation functionally available to the target reader.

In translation, distance marked by a certain degree of textual difference between different translation versions is almost omnipresent. Different translation versions of the same source text over the years often reveal different distances, either preserved or created, separating the source text in various degrees from the target reader. In terms of chronology, moreover, any retranslation is further away from the original, but the temporal distance involved may not decrease. In brief, translation is at the crossroad of the past and present: whatever the case may be, translation is invariably associated with temporal distance between the historical contexts surrounding the production and reproduction of the source and target texts. The underlying dilemma is whether to bring the past to the present or to view the former with the appropriate historical distance and analysis. Recreating the historical atmosphere generates representational immediacy to enhance the reading experience; for if the distance is too great, it is difficult to elicit empathy and to establish relevance. And as a result, the target reader is kept at an emotional as well as temporal distance from the original text.

Updating or appropriating the original means to collapse distance. Mildred L. Larson argues: "Extreme archaization has no place in a translation because it renders an original false, if not meaningless to the modern reader" (Larson 2008: 54). It does seem to diminish the relevance of the source text to the target reader. But to present the illusion that no historical distance actually exists is largely ineffective and counterproductive and only casts doubt on historical authenticity. It is not difficult to see the need to re-construct temporal distance in translation in order to keep past and present distinct. A proximal temporal distance, while useful in enhancing readability, which is sometimes achieved at the expense of recognizing the historical setting of the time of the original, is potentially misleading and confusing. Similarly, a cultural borrowing is likely to produce a distancing effect on the relationship between a narrated event in the past in the original and the target reader of today. A related question is: Does the translator distance him/herself from the original author or prefer to be identified with the latter? It is true that if the translation keeps a temporal distance from the original, the irreducible needs of the target reader can be better addressed. But admittedly, this may lead to an ahistorical production of the source text.

Sometimes to historicize the translated text is usually an indispensable starting point. But this does not necessarily require archaization to produce a distancing effect that may be regarded as less than desirable for smooth reading. Commenting on Antoine Vitez's translation of *Hamlet*, Déprats observes:

> Vittoz's translation belongs to no particular period: it is no closer to Shakespeare's time than it is to our own. The main effect is to distance Hamlet from us and to mark it as an old, archaic text, connected to dramatic rhetoric that we no longer remember except as a literary keepsake. The stylistic processes that are used here are designed to suggest what a great distance separates us from Hamlet.
>
> (Déprats 2001: 80)

This temporal distance is deliberately and scrupulously maintained. The translated play is thus invested with a sense of history necessary for a proper understanding of the special circumstances in which the plot is designed and unfolded, thus conveying as many of the nuances of the complex character of Hamlet as possible into the target language. The corollary is a delicate equilibrium that at once historicizes Hamlet and makes the play accessible to the modern target reader.

The archaization or modernization of the text under translation results in creating or bridging the distance between the source and target texts. It is important to argue for the primacy of historical awareness in reading a historical play or novel. However, the distance between the signifier and the signified, susceptible to further increase if extreme archaization of the language of translation is favored, can cause problems for reading and understanding the translation. It is known that some translators make use of historical distance to critique contemporary events so that this objective distance tacitly functions as a means of self-protection to allow criticism to be made with impunity. Lin Shu's translation was done in terse archaic language. As a result, the foreign is further distanced from the target reader. But it is a safe distance. The use of classical Chinese – an archaic form of Chinese – was motivated by the desire to reduce the aesthetic distance of the target reader from the foreign. Classical Chinese was demonstrably at odds with the narrative form of the novel for, as observed by Hu Shi, prior to Lin's translation, classical Chinese had not been used for novel writing (Hu 1924: 21). However, this was more than merely antiquarian interest displayed by Lin Shu, and the supposed collapse of the aesthetic distance was an inducement for the target reader to read foreign texts. The entirely artificial recreation of temporal distance is tantamount to controlling and manipulating the aesthetic distance in question.

Guo Moruo's translation of *The Sorrows of Young Werther* by Johann Wolfgang von Goethe was hugely popular with young Chinese students, and the novel became the subject of enthusiastic and laudatory rhetoric. The publication of this translation in 1922 coincides with the May Fourth Movement when the Chinese youth found the novel resonating with their frustration and aspiration. There was a "Werther fever" at the time.[1] Yang Wuneng retranslated the novel, and it was published by Renmin wenxue chubanshe in the 1980s. According to Wu Yuetian, it was a blockbuster and sold 152,000 copies.[2] It was reported that despite Guo's exquisite style of translation, his language is somewhat antiquated, not complying with today's mode of expression.[3] Temporal distance has considerable bearing on reception, which explains the essential need for retranslation "when older versions get dated" (Paloposki and Koskinen 2010: 34). In the course of retranslating existing translations, spatial distances are traversed and shown to represent or reflect the patterns of dynamic distancing, which entails various perspectives and interactions.

Artificial distance

In contrast to objective distance, artificial distance, which can also be called translational distance, is deliberately created by the translator for the purpose of mediation and intervention. It should be conceptually clarified by, first and foremost, defining what constitutes this translational distance. The prefix "re-" is repeatedly and consistently associated with translation, as in "re-writing," "re-interpreting," "re-contextualizing," "re-possessing," "re-locating," "re-prioritizing," "re-working," "re-presenting," "re-configurating," "re-appropriating," "re-structuring," "re-mapping, "re-territorializing," and "re-translating." This artificially but also consequently effected distance is meant to, on the one hand, suggest an optimal translation strategy to ensure that the meaning of the original is correctly and properly decoded and reproduced, or adopt an approach that is driven by ideological or political interests, on the other. Additionally, the cultural and aesthetic dimension is amenable to spatial/temporal aggregation and manipulation of cultural meaning. The "re-" prefix suggests both temporality and spatiality. Translation gives rise to a temporal separation and, consequently, disruption of the original textual relationships. Such distancing is attributed to the inherent nature of translation.

As an artificial act, translation is inseparable from distance. As opposed to natural distance, artificial distance is placed between different linguistic and cultural settings. The language of translation is artificial utterance, and whatever that is reprioritized or reconfigured is artificially enacted. Similarly, translation is known to be manipulative and concerned with cultural reconstruction and the perceived purpose or function of a particular translation task. To be specific, when inherent foreignness is reduced, it is artificially administered. Even if perfect resemblance to the original is achieved, the inevitable question is: in what sense? The manipulation of translation is always artificial and involves continual shifts of perspectives, viewpoints, spatial attention, focal points, and framing effects in the process of recreating and reshaping the translated text. The manipulation of translation is an act that leads to the creation of artificial distance, which makes it possible for manipulation to take place. There is an obvious need to provide sufficient space to manipulate translation in order for it to function in the particular way intended by the translator. This manipulative space is the result of extending distances to allow for fertile possibilities.

Artificial distance is also an interpretive and operative distance necessitated by the functionality of translation. On the other hand, however, excessive translational distance from the original, as evidenced in unrestrained domestication, can barely do justice to the original and fails to deliver cross-cultural authenticity. The target reader is deprived of experiencing foreign otherness closely and intimately. There is no denying that any translation approach that generally works well is attributable to optimal translational distance, which eschews the two extremes of reducing or increasing distance unduly and is considered to be flexible in balancing both objective distance and artificial distance. Thus, artificial distance here primarily signifies necessary detachment from unnecessary entanglement with irresolvable linguistic and cultural specificities in the original. It is also a dynamic distance, and through cross-cultural interaction of the objective distance with the artificial distance comes the realization of vivacious end-results of translation.

Either blurring or sharpening is applied to certain images, as a way to design an optimally balanced method, to achieve the desired performance of translation. It is therefore important to find or create an optimal distance between specificity and abstraction, and to shun a confrontational approach, circular translation will necessarily increase the distance. And the reproduction of certain meaning is only possible through detours. Translation often implies some degree of adaptation, alteration, transformation, all contributing to the change of distance. In the case of two languages that are notably different from one another, no unmediated translation of the surface meaning is likely to function properly. If the distance is too short to allow sufficient space for adjustment, appropriation, and localization, it is no doubt necessary to open the space for mediation and intervention. In many cases, rhetorical artifices or devices, including metaphor, metonymy, synecdoche, and irony, cannot be translated literally – and can only be translated at a distance. The constant adjustment of distance plays an important role as an enabling lubricant to assuage the concern over awkward translation. More specifically, the satisfaction of the urgent demand for creating an artificial distance to stave off the problems of untranslatability rests on operational adjustments of stylistic form that adds to the aesthetic appeal to the target reader.

Moreover, the distance between source and target texts can be artificially adjusted as in indirect translation. As mentioned in the previous chapter, indirect translation via Japanese during the late Qing and early Republic periods of China was very common. Liang Qichao published Chinese translations via Japanese of "The Ghost of the Winter Palace" by Allen Upward, *Deux Ans de vacances* (*Two Years' Vacation*) by Jules Verne and *La Fin du monde* (*The Last Days of the World*) by Flammarion Camille. Zhou Zuoren translated into Chinese Arthur Conan Doyle's "The Man from Archangel" and Edgar Allan Poe's "The Gold-Bug," also from Japanese translations. The widespread use of indirect translation continued until the 1950s, when for ideological polarization, China wished to foster ties with other socialist countries. All the literary works from Czechoslovakia, Poland, Hungary, Bulgaria, Romania, and Albania that were made available in Chinese belonged to the practice of indirect translation (Wang 2008: 28). The limited availability of direct translations apparently resulted from the lack of translators who knew the source languages. The linguistic proximity and cultural affinity between Chinese and Japanese can be seen as an alternative or compromised way of accessing the original: the circuitous nature of this indirect translation represents a longer distance, which is, at the same time, somewhat paradoxically, also a shorter distance reality.

In addition, distance adjustment or orientation is part of the driving force for the formation of translation strategies. Schleiermacher's either/or methods concerning translation entails an approaching movement of the reader, who is moved to the author, and the latter is left in peace. This is foreignizing translation. Alternatively, the opposite movement is observed: the author is moved to the reader, who is left in peace. These two methods are not just "different," but they are antithetical and seem to be irreconcilable because it is clear that Schleiermacher prefers the first method or movement. Either movement represents an attempt to address the issue of distance, whose existence makes it necessary to initiate the movement. And the purpose of this movement is to shorten the existential distance between the author and the (target) reader, and for that matter, between source and target texts in a truculent way. At any rate, this distancing strategy is considered absolutely necessary to enable translation to function.

Contrary to common belief, to establish the minimum distance between source and target texts is not necessarily a safeguard against unfaithfulness because the minimum distance is not always an optimal distance. In the event of untranslatability, distance is intended to make space for the translator to resort to the linguistic and cultural resources available to them in the target language. In general, distance is determined by the consideration of how best translation problems can be tackled. In reality, distance denotes selection, inclusion, and exclusion. The question of distance needs to be analyzed in conjunction with other related factors that affect translation. In practical terms, the translator may wish to keep distance between themselves and what is advocated in the original. This is particularly so during a politically sensitive period in certain countries like China. Such practice is best exemplified by the translator, often in the prefaces to their translations, repeatedly reminding the target reader to maintain a critical stance to what they are about to read.

Distance, in a nutshell, is manifest in the complex, multivalent processes of cultural translation. Translation is often preceded by interpretation, which always produces a distancing effect. John W. Stanley maintains that "the translator is forced to do some interpreting, thereby distancing the translation from the original text and, hence, from the otherness embedded in the linguistic structures of the original language" (Stanley 1994: x). To capture optimally and accurately what is embedded in the original, distance is introduced and also adjusted from time to time in response to whatever challenges the source text may present. Again, the multivalent character of interpretation regarding the different semantic possibilities of a given word, phrase, or metaphor engenders distance shifts in translation.

Adjustment of distance

At first glance, foreignizing translation minimizes the distance between source and target texts, but there is the risk of alienating the target reader because the resultant historical and cultural distance that is increased can present obstacles to reading, although it is sometimes possible for a new way of reading to be suggested. There is no doubt that foreignization brings about intimacy – admittedly in a somewhat discomforting manner: the target reader is brought into direct contact with the original, more or less unmediated or unassisted as the case may be. But since this intimacy can be imposed, it may appear to be an unnerving and formidable reading experience on the part of the target reader.

Moreover, foreignization is unequivocally identified with unidiomatic rendering, and usually, devoid of sufficient mediation, engenders a sense of alienation, which almost unavoidably results in reduced readability or even accessibility. In reference to foreignized translation, the extant linguistic or/and cultural distance can be underestimated or even overlooked as if to induce the target reader to ignore or circumvent it. While maintaining the cultural distance between source and target languages, foreignization distances translation from the norms of the target language and culture. In practicality, the target reader is invariably uprooted from their linguistic and cultural context, thus triggering a sense of cultural alienation. Venuti champions foreignization in the specific context of Anglo-American translation practice, and asks the rhetorical question: "Can a translator maintain a critical distance from domestic norms without dooming a translation to be dismissed as unreadable?" (Venuti 1998: 84). This can indeed happen. Yet from a cross-cultural perspective, foreignization is a perfectly legitimate and even desirable translation strategy. While directness and immediacy can be empowering and emancipatory, it is advisable not to lose sight of the basic requirement of acceptability concerning any translated texts.

At the same time, it is worth mentioning that foreignization, which brings the target reader into close contact with the original can increase the alienating cultural distance between the two. This dialectic of intimacy and alienation, estrangement and reconciliation, strikes at the heart of how to make foreignization work as a translation strategy, which allows the difference between the past and the present to emerge in the reading process. Despite seemingly relentless efforts to create close proximity as shown in an intimacy with the source text that suggests closeness or the reduction of distance, sometimes the translator encourages the target reader to distance themselves from the source text for all sorts of reasons, one of which is that they are able to stand back to have a better view of a larger picture since too close viewing only obscures the vision. On the other hand, however, foreignization tends to curtail the role of mediation so that a somewhat undesigned, uncontrolled strangeness is produced. The paradox is that unmediated closeness as reified in strangeness creates a sense of distance in terms of understanding and responding to the translated text. And it is precisely distance that is culpable to some translation problems as in the case of metaphors being directly transferred to the translated text: on the surface, the same distance is maintained, yet metaphors in many cases are not exactly transferrable, and inevitably, they are either transformed or replaced.

Translation is concerned principally with the relative distance between source and target cultures and languages. Although proximity and match are not the same, they are often brought to bear on particular acts of translation. Proximity is the closest possible match between the source and target texts, representing the maximum overlap of the two semantic fields. In March 2011, the then Chinese Premier, Wen Jiabao appealed to real estate developers in China, saying: "你们的身上也应该流着道德的血液" ("in you should flow moral blood"). The outcome of translation is in closest proximity to the original. The directness and the immediacy of experience come effectively into play. However, if the English translation reads like: "blood of moral responsibility (decision, courage, life, principles, values)," proximity is practically vitiated, the result of which is the creation of some unnecessary distance, only to weaken the effect of articulation. However, in contrast to "moral blood" which coincides with its Chinese equivalent, "moral fiber," if directly translated into Chinese, would be problematic because there is no such thing as "道德纤维" in Chinese. The word "fiber" has to be substituted by something like "力量" (strength). So the direct distance between the two linguistic codes has to be changed: directness to be replaced by indirectness, hence the shift of distance resulting in the loss of the original proximity to the target language with the concrete image of "fiber" removed in translation. The cultural meaning of directness and indirectness is significantly related to the difference in distance. It is axiomatic that overcoming barriers to cross-cultural communication relies on the enabling power of adjusting the distance to ease the burden of estrangement.

Distance not only separates source and target texts but also alienates them, and while foreignization brings source and target texts closer, it alienates the target reader due to the noticeably increased linguistic and cultural distance between the translated text and the target reader who are naturally much more familiar with the norms of the target language. This, of course, does not disprove the value of foreignization: the target reader may enjoy a certain degree of estrangement to experience the foreign. And the directness that stems from the minimal distance between the source and target texts is a powerful demonstration of how the target language and culture can be enriched and expanded. The adjustment of distance indicates that foreignization is conditioned and constrained by the (un)willingness of the target reader, and tolerance of, or even eagerness for, the unfamiliar is a necessary precondition for foreignization. In addition, it should be noted that the distance between self and other varies considerably from case to case. It can be said that foreignization at once gives rise to proximity and distance. After all, it is possible for self to identify with other whereas the distancing effect of foreign otherness is felt by some who prefer to learn about other at a distance, with the help of adaptive translation. In a sense, the perceived upshot of foreignization provides a larger space for cultural contestations by turning the familiar linguistic form of the target language into something unfamiliar, which leads to negotiating the distance of perception and appreciation.

The adjustment of distance in translation is necessitated by various factors, including the constant change of conditions that pose challenges. Juan C. Sager states:

> Translators have to adapt their strategy to the choice of the author's persona in a work of literature. Through the persona the author creates the emotional (or aesthetic) distance he or she wishes to establish between the narrator and the story and therefore the degree of involvement or detachment at which the work should be read. In translation, this distance has to be redefined because the different cultural setting of the environment in which the translation is read inevitably increases the physical and emotional distance. The translator's definition of his or her persona, as the alter ego of the author, can be used to increase or bridge these distances.
>
> (Sager 1998: 83)

The existence of various distances in the original cannot normally be transferred directly to the target text. The subtlety of reading to be expected of the source reader and target reader respectively is very difficult to recapture. On the surface, emotional distance is different from aesthetic distance, though they often are inseparable. Moreover, due to cultural barriers and historical changes, an emotional distance exists between the source and target readers, who respond to the same parts of a text differently. And partly as a result of it, their aesthetic experiences of reading are different. Such distances need to be bridged. Additionally, to "redefine" this distance is to justify attempts to adjust it. To produce a successful translation, all kinds of distance adjustments need to be made from time to time. A certain dynamic distancing between aspects of translation is involved to create different distances in response to the functional demands of translation.

Meanwhile, it is worth reiterating that other types of distances can feature significantly in translation such as emotional distance and psychological distance. How to enable emotional expression to be conveyed in translation that can be perceived and shared by the target audience is a serious challenge. As an integral part of dynamic equivalence, there is good reason to expect emotionally laden reading experience to be reproduced in translation. Part of the task of the translator is to elicit an emotional response from the target reader. By creating an emotional connection (by means of minimizing emotional distance) with the target reader, a given translation, mainly referring to a literary translated text, can provide a more or less equally rich and fulfilling reading experience enjoyed by the source reader. Crucially though, "The translator should . . . get into the original and create emotional resonance with the author" (Tu and Li 2009: 13). Whether emotion can be shared cross-culturally can be an issue, and it is possible that "a debilitating sense of cultural exile and loss" is created, "usually accompanied, if not caused, by emotional distance" (Sun 2018: 135). Therefore, to capture sufficient emotional weight to be reflected in translation is no doubt important so that the target reader is emotionally involve.

Viewed in this way, cross-cultural alienation requires acculturation: to create some distance to make the two different cultural perspectives involved compatible or less incompatible, and consequently, the psychological distance between source and target readers can be bridged. Psychological distance is identified as one of the key differences between the two reading experiences, and the resultant lack of resonance gives rise to the need to control and manipulate such distance. The inevitably increased psychological distance for the target reader does not ensure that cross-cultural contextual information is accurately represented in translation, which can be evaluated differently depending on the psychological distance. The target reader's psychological distance, not properly aptly decreased, is predisposed to weaken their textual engagement and dialogic interaction. In a general sense, translation is meant to embrace difference as exemplified in foreign otherness, but perceptual or emotional difference arising from psychological distance can potentially impede effective cross-cultural communication. Decrease in psychological distance is necessary and considered to be desirable.

In literary translation, especially poetry translation, a certain degree of deviation is inevitable to avoid dysfunctional consequences of adhering closely to the original in terms of lexicon, syntax, and morphology. According to Zheng and Xu, when literary translation is done,

> the principle of "faithfulness" is forsaken. When it comes to poetry, a faithful translator is at the end of his/her resources. Therefore, knowing perfectly well that this is something we can't do, we have to relinquish this principle and deviate from being faithful. "Distance" thus emerges, and we end up giving up either translation or the original.
>
> (Zheng and Xu 2002: 47)

The frustrating impasse is, from their point of view, "顾此失彼" ("attending to one means neglecting the other"). The binary nature of this either/or statement, as in the last sentence of the afore-quoted argument, is clearly exhibited. Of course, it can be argued that deviation from the original is not necessarily tantamount to infidelity. The increased distance by virtue of deviation can generate an artificial space to attend to both the original and its translation.

It needs to be emphasized that the shortest possible distance is not the only determinant of faithful translation. Zheng and Xu have provided insight into the dynamic function of distance in maximizing the potentials embedded in translation:

> Literary translation requires "distance," and only by maintaining a certain distance from the original, can the translator overcome the "resistance to translation" posed by the original (or alternatively called untranslatability), and bring creativity into play. The traditional Chinese translation theory emphasizes "spiritual resemblance," which is recreation. It is a strategy specifically designed to overcome "untranslatability." Spiritual resemblance is concerned with "distance," recognizing the aesthetic significance of "distance" in the process of literary translation. "Distance" is the origin of the art of translation.
>
> (Zheng and Xu 2002: 48)

The search for spiritual resemblance is not meant to counter the impossibility of formal equivalence but also to achieve what really matters in translation. To this end, increasing distance is the only choice to bring translation to aesthetic parity with the original, to which considerable weight is given, especially in literary translation. It can be observed that adjustment of distance is the norm of translation.

Shifts of distance

When distance becomes adjustable, translation can be under the constant shifts of distance and also, possibly, alignment or perspective. For lack of distance, formal equivalence appears to be more unattainable. Nevertheless, in many instances, formal equivalence is still preferred (Tymoczko 2014: 63); this is probably about the closest proximity to the original, which gives a false impression of accuracy and reliability. While this may well be the case, there is the risk of incomprehension or rejection. An appropriate distance from the original allows for the necessary space for translation to function. As such, a distancing space between source and target texts is created, concerned with the position or perspective from which the translation is made and shows a distance shift in treating the original material.

Translation makes it possible to communicate to a different audience across a temporal, spatial, and cultural distance. So the original cultural intimacy which is shaped by familiarity with the source culture may not be retained in translation. However, intimacy, as epitomized by foreignization, can be a frightening prospect, for it constrains the translator presenting the general meaning of the original. To this end, distance is required to activate the complicated process of reconfiguration to capture the relatively indeterminate meaning of the original, without being trammeled by adhering closely to its syntax and other formal features. This entails making translation decisions, and any decision making is explicitly connected with establishing a frame for a holistic approach to semantic, lexical, grammatical, and stylistic aspects with regard to the pertinent parameters including norms, conventions, and properties. For instance, when wordplay turns out to be untranslatable, the preferred and common solution is to translate meaning at the cost of losing some formal features. If the playfulness of language is eschewed for fear of its possible untranslatability, the shift of focus has patent implications to the distance between the two languages. A translation unit framed in such a way enables the reader to see different things, and spatial proximity and distance are also affected as a result of the way it is framed.

Translation calls for a variety of changes of distance, subtle or not so subtle, and explores cultural difference through the systematic articulation of nuances and tensions by amplifying or weakening certain aspects of the original. Some specific modes of translational distance are of strategic use and convenience in terms of coming to grips with cultural alienation. Maria Tymoczko points out: "a literary translator chooses an emphasis or privileges an aspect of the text to be transposed in translation (e.g., linguistic fidelity, tone, form, cultural content, or some combination thereof)" (1999:34). This is typically symptomatic of Chinese translation practice in the late Qing period. In Lin Shu's translation of David Copperfield by Charles Dickens, it is obvious that the translator conceals some of the Western values and beliefs in the original and replaces them with traditional Chinese ones as in Miss Betsey's pronouncement: "From the moment of this girl's birth, child, I intend to be her friend." Lin renders it as "此女一生,吾即极力将护之." A back translation would be: "I will do my utmost to protect her *at her* birth" (my italics). What is foregrounded in translation is her role as a patron rather than a friend. The complete absence of "friend" in translation merely emphasizes the translator's refusal to accept or convey what is specifically characteristic of the Western value of egalitarianism. Apparently, the implied equality does not correspond to the Chinese cultural values perceived by the translator, who sees the age difference between the two characters of different generations as a hierarchical distance to be maintained on account of the prevailing attitude of the target culture at the time, who would find it inconceivable for an elderly lady to make friends with an unborn baby. Thus, a deliberately distancing effect is in order.

In this respect, concretization results primarily from focalization, with the sharpening of focus on singling out certain quintessentially representative parts for translation. Literary concretization culminates in enhancing the reading experience. It is aesthetic distance that plays a pivotal role here. Sometimes concretization is a means of cultural contextualization, or rather, re-contextualization, and can also be an enrichment through specific added details to foreground what is regarded as relevant and important by the translator. To give one example from *The Call of the Wild* by Jack London: "It was beautiful spring weather, but neither dogs nor humans were aware of it." It is rendered as "时值莺呖燕啭, 阳光明

媚, 但是不论狗或者人都没有觉察到这一点." When we move to a back translation, we know how focalization is privileged and enacted: "It was springtime with birds trilling and the sun shining, but neither dogs nor humans were aware of it." The modifier "beautiful" in the original is concretized as "birds trilling and the sun shining" in the translated text to convey the beautiful spring season visually. Whether this variation of the basic meaning as a form of visual performance is justifiable or not is an obviously different matter. Something subjective seems to creep into the translation, and the added details are not irrelevant, as they help increase the attractive liveliness of the translated text.

An intimate act of reading offers an intimate way of doing translation, and the target reader is given the chance to share the same intimacy enjoyed by the source reader. However, it turns out that such intimacy is not provided, for presence and absence are co-constitutive of translation practices to bypass the most difficult or problematic part of the translation process. The necessary appropriation of surface meaning leads to its erasure, considering that it may otherwise be untranslatable. Let us examine one example that fits into this category: "我友有一妻, 极贤惠, 日日举案齐眉, 家中颇有世外桃源之感." If the surface meaning is kept intact, it may well verge on the ridiculous: "My friend has a wife, who is extremely virtuous. She holds the serving tray all the way up to her eyebrows (to serve him). And his home is reminiscent of a garden of idyllic beauty." Obviously, a sense of humor is registered in the original, yet the playfulness can be risky in translation: any contextual shifts would make such translation problematic, for there is no way to delimit the perception of the potentially disturbing image of a wife who behaves like a servant. An alternative version is something like: "My friend has a loving wife who tries everything in her power to look after him, which makes their home like Xanadu" (my translation). By simplifying and zooming out the original image, it increases the distance that is safe enough to stave off any literal interpretation by the target reader. As for the lost humor, some compensatory measure can be taken: "His every whim is indulged." Or "His every whim is her command."

A similar example also shows the necessity to remove or change a specific image: "她是一贯爱翘尾巴的." In Chinese, the phrase "翘尾巴" literally means "stick up one's tail" to describe someone who is haughty or snooty, but it does not work in the target language. Several versions to avoid this problem are suggested as follows:

> She tends to get swollen-headed. She is too big for her britches.
> She is a bit caught up in her own self-importance.
> She has suffered chronically an inflated sense of self-importance She is always a self-important figure.
> She is always insufferably cocky.

The first two versions also use images, albeit different ones without mentioning "tail," because "tail" does not have the same function in the target language. In like manner, "tail" in Chinese often conjures up a negative image: 他那在上司面前摇尾讨好的样子让我恶心. Its English translation would be: "He is fawning and obsequious to his superiors, which just makes me feel sick." In Chinese, it literally means that he behaves like a tail-wagging dog. As briefly indicated earlier, there is little need to bring "tail" into close-up, and in translation, the originally framed part is taken out with telescopic detachment. However, because of different cultural perceptions of a tail-wagging dog, the removal of the image in the original precludes the possibility of inappropriate association on the part of the target reader.

Through a process of abstraction as opposed to concretization as a means of spatial manipulation, the strange and unfamiliar is contained and normalized to some extent. When aesthetic proximity cannot be introduced in translation, de-visualization becomes a preferred option on the grounds that an appropriate degree of cultural conformity is required to overcome barriers to cross-cultural communication. In many ways, to capture something quintessential about the original, be it semantic or formal or both, remains the most important task of the translator, who would find it useful to establish a frame for working out specific ways to tackle the details and particulars to be translated. Essentially, a contextual frame is needed to better focus on, interpret, and present those indispensable parts of the original. Of course, it is not always possible to create the same semantic or formal properties as the source text. Thus, when an identical or verbatim reproduction is out of the question, an abstract representation is more suitable for enacting the readjustment of focal points and gives more scope for flexibility and change of cultural and aesthetic distance. A translation may be distanced from the original visual language by using a different linguistic and cultural frame based on an understanding of the cultural and aesthetic distance involved by forming a feasible alternative for battling what may turn out to be serious translation problems.

After translation leads to recontextualization, shifts and susceptibilities are the natural outgrowth of translation manipulation. Temporal, linguistic, and cultural distances are susceptible to change and shift. As Catford points out, in translation there can be "departures from formal correspondence between source and target texts" (1965: 73). Consequently, a series of shifts in distance are performed as part of rewriting and reconfiguration. The shift away from "formal correspondence" makes way for spatial extension to allow the translator to reorganize the source material and re-present it in a coherent way to the target reader. This is primarily motivated by the consideration of temporal or historical specificity. Other competing factors are manifested in this active process of re-prioritizing a variety of demands. Shifts in distance can mirror the shifting perspectives on the role and function of translation and means to manipulate the source text at various levels, as is presented in the target text. It goes without saying, by way of shifting distances, untranslatability can be addressed holistically and in an integrated manner. This is critical for an understanding of the dynamic and transformative mechanisms of translation.

Conclusion

There is no doubt that distance is a key concept in relation to translation, which is concerned with the transmission of meaning across historical, linguistic, and cultural distance. To reflect upon the causes and implications of distance is to better understand how translation works in a cross-cultural sense. The adjustment of distance leads to blurring or sharpening of certain details in the original so as to impact the overall effect of translation. Distance refers fundamentally to perceived differences, similarities, registers, and so on. Relatedly, negotiations about distance adjustment determine how distance function in translation in general and foreground the impact of focalization and adaptation in particular. To shorten the objective distance between the source text and target reader by adjusting the translational distance prepares the way for understanding the nature of translation. The dissolution of the idiom in the original performs the function to overcome strangeness inherent in cultural distance.

Translation focuses on contingency or undecidability, which conditions and defines how translation decisions are made. Given that no complete translation is attainable, and its manifestations may be elusive and shifting, a translation is constantly prompted to vacillate between presence and absence, explicitness and implicitness, as well as the literal and the figurative. It is often difficult to approach translation from an objective perspective for translation is often produced by a displacement of perspective, thereby causing distance shifts between the two sets of linguistic and cultural values. Furthermore, interpretive undecidability risks destabilization of the translated text. Because the notion of "perspective" is associated with the visual effect of reading and translating, the shifting array of factors affecting distance suggests that translation is characterized by perpetual contingency, historicity, and arbitrariness. The endless change and adjustment of distance are therefore driven by the exigencies of primary needs for translation to work in a certain way.

Notes

1 https://book.douban.com/subject/1047138/discussion/19713708. Retrieved on 5 July 2020.
2 www.library.sh.cn/dzyd/spxc/list.asp?spid=1123. Retrieved on 5 July 2020.
3 https://zhidao.baidu.com/question/378093445.html. Retrieved on 5 July 2020.

References

Catford, J. C. (1965) *A Linguistic Theory of Translation: An Essay in Applied Linguistic*, London: Oxford University Press.
Déprats, Jean-Michel (2001) "Translation at the Intersections of History," in Michael D. Bristol, Kathleen McLuskie, and Christopher Holmes (eds.) *Shakespeare and Modern Theatre: The Performance of Modernity*, London and New York: Routledge, 75–92.
Hu, Shi (1924)《五十年来之中国文学》(*Fifty Years of Chinese Literature*), Shanghai: Shenbao guan.

Larson, Mildred L. (2008) *Translation: Theory and Practice, Tension and Interdependence*, Amsterdam and Philadelphia: John Benjamins Publishing.

Paloposki, Outi, and Kaisa Koskinen (2010) "Reprocessing Texts. The Fine Line between Retranslating and Revising," *Across Languages and Cultures* 11(1): 29–49.

Pontiero, Giovanni (1997) "Essays by Giovani Ponteiro," in Pilar Orero and Juan C. Sager (eds.) *The Translator's Dialogue*, Amsterdam and Philadelphia: John Benjamins Publishing, 1–83.

Qian, Zhongshu (1981) "林纾的翻译" (Lin Shu's Translation), in Qian Zhongshu et al. (eds.) 《林纾的翻译》 (*Lin Shu's Translation*), Beijing: Commercial Press, 18–52.

Sager, Juan C. (1998) "What Distinguishes Major Types of Translation?" *The Translator* 4(1): 69–89.

Snell-Hornby, Mary (1995) *Translation: An Integrated Approach*, Amsterdam and Philadelphia: John Benjamins Publishing.

Stanley, John W. (1994) "The Translator's Preface," in H. G. Gadamer (trans. By John W. Stanley), *Heidegger's Ways*, Albany: State University of New York Press, ix–xiv.

Steiner, George (1998) *After Babel: Aspects of Language and Translation*, New York: Oxford University Press.

Sun, Yifeng (2018) *Translating Foreign Otherness: Cross-Cultural Anxiety in Modern China*, London and New York: Routledge.

Tu, Guoyuan, and Li Jing (2009) "距离合法性视角下译者当译之本的知情选择与情感同构" (Legitimate Choice/TL Distance in Translation), 《中国翻译》 (*Chinese Translators Journal*) 29(4): 13–18.

Tymoczko, Maria (1999) "Post-Colonial Writing and Literary Translation," in Susan Bassnett and Hari Trivedi (eds.) *Post-Colonial Translation: Theory and Practice*, London and New York: Routledge, 19–40.

Tymoczko, Maria (2014) "How Distinct are Formal and Dynamic Equivalence?" in Theo Hermans (ed.) *The Manipulation of Literature*, London and New York: Routledge, 63–86.

Venuti, Lawrence (1998) *The Scandals of Translation: Towards an Ethics of Difference*, London and New York: Routledge.

Wang, Yougui (2008) "中国翻译传统研究：从转译到从原文译 (1949–1999)" (From Translating through Translations to Translating from the Original: China's Approach to Rendering Literary Works in "Minor" Languages [1949–1999]), 《中国翻译》 (*Chinese Translators Journal*) 28(1): 27–32.

Zheng, Hailing, and Xu Jing (2002) "文学翻译过程中的'距离'问题" (On "Distance" in Literary Translation), 《中国翻译》 (*Chinese Translators Journal*) 23(3): 27–32.

3 Cosmopolitan space and transnational resistance

Introduction

This chapter proposes to investigate the shifting cross-cultural paradigms in response to cosmopolitan thinking and consciousness, as well as the nature of cultural translation concerning cosmopolitanism. The perception of cosmopolitan translation, referring primarily to cultural translation situated fully within the cosmopolitan constellation, is closely linked to cognitive, social, and cultural change in a global and globalizing context. The rapid development of globalization raises questions about nationalism, cultural identity, and above all, translation itself. Psychological differences between different ethnic groups are centrally concerned with the production and reception of cultural meaning and its dependence upon cross-cultural awareness. Different conceptions of cultural realities contribute significantly to the creation of cosmopolitan spaces to encourage moving beyond a provincial mindset. Fear of and resistance to cultural homogeneity may well result in a strong sense of nationalism radically antipathetic to the practice of cultural translation as is manifest in the doubt of and resistance to "Other" spaces as exhibited by some Chinese translation scholars. However, increasing hybridization between different cultures through translation moves inevitably towards cosmopolitanism. This chapter provides a sobering look at academic nationalism and contends that if cultural translation is mainly about cross-cultural communication, cosmopolitan translation is more concerned with intercultural communication. Increasingly, cultural references, in a cross-cultural sense, are constitutive of cross-cultural intertextuality and are poised to develop into intercultural allusions. These are new challenges to reassess the changed and changing nature of cultural translation, which radically redefines the spatial network of local affinities and allegiances in the process of globalization and calls for an elaborate analysis of the emergent concept of cosmopolitan translation in the Chinese cultural context.

Cultural translation

The force of culture is increasingly recognized; its central relevance to translation can barely be denied or overlooked, especially in the broader cross-cultural context. Appropriately, the cultural translator can considerably enhance performance by reacting appropriately to changed circumstances within the cosmopolitan frame of translation and showing respect for other cultures while (re) negotiating to ensure the survival of cultural message in translation. Cosmopolitanism is fostered and underpinned by the practice of cultural translation in which culture itself represents a powerful and dynamic form of translation. Thus, in a traditional or conventional sense, cultural translation can be said to be a cosmopolitan cultural practice that moves beyond the translation paradigms. This is a preliminary attempt to investigate the possibility of introducing the concept of cosmopolitan translation in a nascent cosmopolitan space, constituting a further step beyond cultural translation to embrace a cosmopolitan conception of cultural diversity, hybridization, identities shift, and transcultural exchanges, which can be understood as the fundamental characteristics of cosmopolitan translation. Cosmopolitan translation is thus best seen in light of a general conception of translation concerning cultures that can be better accounted for in terms of envisaging a cross-cultural attitude of flexibility and tolerance.

Most directly related to cosmopolitanism is cultural translation, which entails interpretation and reproduction of cultural meaning, negotiation of cultural forms, and assessment of cultural performance and production. In other words, cultural translation is prerequisite of cosmopolitism, and fundamentally metaphorical in nature, it signals a first necessary step towards the construction of cosmopolitanism. Furthermore, cultural translation represents a multi-dimensional approach to understanding and analyzing the fundamental problems in cross-cultural communication. For instance, it is possible to produce a linguistically fluent but culturally empty translation. Indeed, if what is culturally loaded becomes culturally empty devoid of certain cultural values, it is a highly unsatisfactory result of translation. Cultural translation involves a more acute awareness of and serious interest in cultural difference deeply ingrained in cultural meaning. Therefore, the primary concern about cross-cultural communication is whether the cultural meaning with its nuances embedded in the source language is captured by the translator to be conveyed to the target language. In general, it is a matter of liberating translation from the conventional constraints of referring to direct transmission from a source text to a target one. But the operation of cultural translation is a great deal more complicated and encumbered with unsettling constraints. In this respect, cross-cultural adaptation is unavoidable. And this unavoidable operation opens up space for cross-cultural and intercultural negotiation for appropriate terms and approaches to potential translation problems.

As part of cultural translation, something is appropriated for a different situation and context to be made operationally appropriate for translation, and in this sense, cultural translation is different from foreignization. There are of course many cases of cultural misappropriation, but it can be argued that it is the designated outcome of translation that really matters in terms of the effectiveness of cross-cultural communication. In addition, what it is meant by appropriating or misappropriating a source text is not always easy to establish and can be open to interpretation. But the essential point of it is simply that the target reader is made to be culturally related to the source text, one way or another. Moreover, since the ultimate aim of translation is to foster cross-cultural communication, the phrase "cultural translation" has gained a certain currency in recent years. To start with, a culturally translated text is a contextually translated one; namely, it is translated with the relevant cultural context(s) being taken into consideration. In other words, what is originally culturally situated must be cross-culturally re-situated in translation to give prominence to the interplay between different modes of thinking and ways of communication across cultures.

The concept of cultural translation can be traced to two strands. It has been used in a specific sense as a metaphor for British anthropology in the 1950s. The translation of cultures is the primary concern for determining the perceived effectiveness of cross-cultural communication. It requires not only textual but also contextual knowledge on the part of the translator. The frontal problem is cultural difference, which, instead of being shunned or reduced, must be dealt with squarely, foregrounded, and embraced. Accuracy is important in terms of anthropological representation, and the aim of cultural translation is to reflect a different mode of thinking and understanding the world. Different modes of thinking result in different ways of articulation. In a nutshell, this type of cultural translation emphatically addresses difference rather than similarity. Homi Bhabha's cultural translation is not a conventional concept of doing translation, i.e., involving source or target texts. There are no definite source or target texts. The eclectic nature of "translating" from different sources or source texts is an essential part of cultural translation. In a broader sense, as noted by Waïl S. Hassan, any bilingual writer "who explains one culture to another is necessarily a cultural translator. In the case of a writer of two languages, cultural translation is a two-way activity, since s/he explains each culture to the other" (Hassan 2011: 63). Since the translator addresses a different audience with a different cultural background, they need to negotiate different cultural terms to enable different and diverse cultural experiences to become comprehensible and also sharable.

Admittedly, the concept of cultural translation is somewhat confusing and inconsistent due to different conceptions of it. As noted by Anthony Pym, "the term 'cultural translation' is usually associated with material movement, the position of the translator, cultural hybridity, and the crossing of borders" (Pym 2010: 149). Significantly yet perhaps less noticeably, cross-cultural hybridization that affects the end product of cultural translation may gradually evolve into cosmopolitanism in a transformative process of continuous, selective, and adaptive interaction with different aspects of both cultures involved in translation. In a similar vein, the process of cultural adaptation can be seen as prerequisite for cultural translation. As an important mode of cultural performance, cultural translation is directly linked with the general effectiveness of cross-cultural communication. The epistemology and politics of cultural translation can be analyzed to reveal how it leads to a cross-cultural discourse in a cosmopolitan way. In this metaphorical sense, Chinese American literature is a palpable form of cultural translation without a definite source text to translate from, and the translational use of English is a very interesting phenomenon about Chinese American literary writing. As in the cases of Chinese immigrant writers, most notably Ha Jin, the writing may be directly in English, but the voice is unmistakably Chinese. The same is true of the cultural sources of the material for such writings, which may well be called translational literature because they are a product of cultural translation.

It needs to be said that cultural translation prepares the way for a move towards cosmopolitan translation, and closely related to it is the functioning of cross-cultural psychology with different cultural perspectives brought together. Pym argues that "One of the things that 'cultural translation' theory does best is move beyond a focus on translations as (written or spoken) texts. The concern is with general cultural processes rather than with finite linguistic products" (Pym 2010: 148). The absence of a particular source or target text is the most salient feature of Bhabha's formulation of cultural translation, which takes place in the "third space." In addition, cultural translation can be generalized as being explicitly about the notion of cross-cultural encounter and communication, which not only brings difference into the target language but also, with the full awareness of the cultural difference of the target culture, guides and enables the translator to better negotiate cultural terms in this cross-cultural interactive process of exploring alternative ways of thinking and imagining what it is like to be part of a different community.

Moreover, cultural translation is based on cross-cultural interpretation right at "the heart of interpretation in any intercultural process" (Murphy and Kraidy 2003: 14). It highlights and radicalizes interactions between languages in cultural terms. The critical importance of establishing a methodology for "the translation of cultural language" has been emphasized and demonstrated by many scholars, drawing attention to the inscrutability of the otherness of other cultures. Simply put, to translate the otherness embedded in cultural language invariably amounts to cultural translation, and it engages translation between cultures by incorporating alienness into the target text and introducing the target reader to unfamiliar linguistic idioms and cultural practices. The practice of cultural translation is extensive and made possible by mediating between different worlds with their different cultural values and practices as key components of cultural meaning.

However, the construction and production of cultural meaning are fraught with problems, which vary from age to age and from culture to culture. Evidently, cultural production of meaning or production of cultural meaning requires cross-cultural knowledge and experience pertaining to cultural appropriation necessitated by competing cultural meanings involved in translation. Among others, cultural references, not to mention unexpected vocabulary and concepts, are often not shared and can thus prove to be formidably unfamiliar and enigmatical. Translation needs to address not just linguistic norms but also cultural norms, yet it is precisely the latter that dynamizes interpretation of meaning and significance. In other words, what is involved is not just the translation of words but also cultural meaning, and it also means that the unmediated translation of words with their literal meaning does not normally result in generating the appropriate cultural meaning manifest in different cultural values, codes, expression, and practices.

This is because source and target readers may not have a common "cultural language." For this reason, it is necessary for the translator to make cultural knowledge shared knowledge. As might be expected, without the relevant cultural knowledge to make sense of the unfamiliar or to help the target reader to do so, acts of interpretation are virtually impossible. Wary of any monolithic interpretation of meaning, both Benjamin and Derrida have reiterated the need to bring out multiple potential meanings, including, of course, cultural meaning. Inevitably culturally situated, cultural meaning needs to be contextualized or rather, re-contextualized. For this reason, the recognition of cultural difference requires a form of cross-cultural translation, and the uniqueness of cultural language a clear understanding, which is the source of the theoretical belief in the impossibility of translation. Thus, translation is linked with "the performative nature of cultural communication" (Bhadha 1994: 326). All forms of cultural meaning are open to translation, and in the relentless drive for cultural translation, hybrid sites of meaning open up to reveal how cultural meaning is reproduced and conveyed in the target text. Meanwhile, engagement with globalization has led to members of different cultural communities becoming increasingly aware of each other's cultural rules and standards so that they can understand each other's cultural dispositions and configurations of experience.

Due to the unique nature of many cultural references, they gravitate towards inducing referential anxiety primarily about the resultant impediment to smooth reading but also about the possible loss of signification. Given the relatively exclusive nature of cultural language, the depth of cultural information or content is not often fully experienced. Nevertheless, the range of cultural references needs to be curtailed justifiably only to be restored to varying degrees when necessary because a multiplicity of cultural references is considered to overburden the target reader and destroy the pleasure of reading. While admittedly the fullness of cultural meaning is by no means readily attainable, the manifestation of cultural difference in translation indicates the possibility of understanding cultural meaning. On the other hand, to avoid the risk of deterring and daunting the target reader, the translator may decide to bring out a version devoid of too many annotations. As Wittgenstein sees it in his *Philosophical Investigations*, meaning is not situated at the surface of language but beyond language in particular connection with its cultural use (1958: 43). This cultural use includes interpretation of various meanings.

Given the possible discrepancy between the literal surface meaning and cultural meaning in the source text and their reproductions in translation, it is necessary to understand the intricate networks of cross-cultural engagement and interaction. In this process, however, the multiple layers of textuality with its connotational, affective, collocational, metaphorical, and cultural meaning can prove to be too daunting for the translator to attempt to do justice to the original. Both the immediate and broad implications of negotiating cultural meaning can be imputed to the complexities of cultural performance. To turn untranslatable differences into translatable ones in response to the fact that cultural meaning is difficult to translate because it is not about shared experience. Once again, lack of shared experiences is the root of a variety of translation problems for cultural meaning that is embedded in shared experiences of the community of the source text, and cultural references are potentially problematic largely because they are culturally bound and seemingly exclusive. Only with expert mediation, can cultural meaning be understood by other cultures, particularly if it is adequately explained in the form of "thick translation."

Cross-cultural psychology creates cultural distance in translation, which raises the critical question of cosmopolitan consciousness. In one place of Howard Goldblatt's translation of *Daughter of the River* by Hong Ying, a culturally loaded word in the original *renao* is just translated as "noisy" from the perspective of the other represented by the translator (1998: 225). The Chinese word *renao*, composing of two characters, literally and separately meaning "excitement" and "noise," but the element of noise is only secondary and founded on the supposition that what happens or is going on is pleasant and convivial. In Goldblatt's translation, these are plainly not related to the cultural connotations of noise. Admittedly, a convivial crowd is indeed somewhat noisy, but noise should not be its only or even principal feature. On this occasion, the way noise is perceived seems to show that the translator has unconsciously chosen to be a cultural outsider. In truth, what is missing seems to be a central component of cosmopolitan tolerance, conviviality, and citizenship. Cultural translation is capable of creating an increasingly cosmopolitan ethos of cultural diversity and promoting a celebratory and harmonious version of intercultural relationships.

Cross-cultural paradigms

Cultural translation itself may be called a new paradigm and is fundamentally about bringing out cultural difference expected to be shared by people of different cultural backgrounds. To start with, it is plain that cross-cultural paradigms are in short supply to offer guidance to translators. In any case, cross-cultural paradigms have to be anchored to refer to a set of cultural values and modes of communication associated with both source and target readers. Ineffective cross-cultural communication is ascribed to different cultural assumptions concerning cultural values, norms, and beliefs. People who have had direct experience of studying overseas bring in different cross-cultural paradigms, resulting in paradigmatic competitions and eventually in paradigm shifts in a cross-cultural and functional perspective. Shifting cross-cultural paradigms open up new cosmopolitan vistas to the target reader, constantly exposing them to cross-cultural and intercultural communication and contestation.

In response to different situational needs, more cross-cultural paradigms have been developed as is shown in different versions of the same source text being produced in attempts to represent what has been articulated in the original or to reflect what is intended by different translators. It all boils down to the untranslatability of cultures. The repeated re-configuration of cultural paradigms in different locations and contexts acts as an impetus for paradigm shifts in cross-cultural or intercultural communication. On the one hand, it can be argued that the cosmopolitan frame of translation does not necessarily gesture towards a pristine form of cultural authenticity in terms of reproducing linguistic and formal features manifest in the original. On the other, with regard to the target language and culture, the traditional equivalence-based paradigm is no longer considered of much value or importance. Lu Xun, who had studied in Japan, once questioned the linguistic insularity of the Chinese language: in the obvious absence of equivalence in the target language, in order to foster language change, it was necessary to introduce neologisms and syntactic patterns the Chinese language with or without humility. The outcome of cross-cultural language transfer or production was expected to stimulate vocabulary extensions. Operationally speaking, lack of equivalents or similar words in the target language not only necessitated foreignization for the purpose of facilitating the importation of new modes of expression but also yielded different conceptions of the world, thereby harbingering some cosmopolitan ways of thinking, which were meant to be re-introduced to China. If the concepts articulated in the source text are unfamiliar to the target reader, linguistically and culturally appropriated modes of expression that are appropriate for a particular situation are after all poor substitutions. Lu Xun's advocacy for the necessity to expand the target language in this particular cross-cultural context to expand the Chinese language is grounded on something that is tantamount to a cosmopolitan vision.

Regrettably, the far-reaching significance of Lu Xun's cross-cultural strategy and cosmopolitan vision has not been fully appreciated. But the fact remains that the limited corresponding conceptual resources in the target language are forced to be made conceptually articulatable through translation. Similarly, when new concepts articulated in the source text cannot find appropriate forms to be rearticulated in the target text, they simply force their ways into the target system, thereby forming new methodological and paradigmatic perspectives. Most importantly, this has brought about the generic diversity of paradigms and invited and inspired people to question the entrenched assumption about the worth of the linguistic cultural "pristineness" of the Chinese language. Lu Xun has placed a special emphasis on literal translation of words, which is a mode of foreignization concerning not only lexical or even semantic information but also contextual information.

The cross-cultural mission posited by Lu Xun is both bold and novel not only to his contemporaries but also to many people in China today when traditionalist cultural norms are still strong and constantly reinforced by implicit or explicit references to their cultural superiority and tacit ethnocentrism fed on a long and rich history of civilization in its cultural depth and expansive orientation. While China's cultural heritage is unarguably remarkable, the limitations of the language and culture are also apparent. The supposed linguistic and cultural pristineness of the Chinese language and culture is greeted with adulation and praise, which has spawned reluctance to move beyond narrow and parochial cultural nationalism. Cultural translation invigorates the development of more cross-cultural paradigms while foreclosing self-awareness and a certain cultural narcissism. To capture the fuller implications of this shift of perspective, one needs to under-stand the dialogic and interactive nature of cultural translation by accepting each other's cultural differences to cultivate and promote a non-ethnocentric attitude towards foreign otherness. The various needs of the target culture require para-digm shifts to produce the type of translation needed at different stages of cultural development. Clearly, an awareness of cross-cultural paradigms helps discern dis-similarities in cultures and pertinent approaches to tackling them to adjust to the competing demands of cross-cultural communication in relation to translation.

The inescapable conclusion concerning cultural translation is that a single, so-called standard paradigm, no matter how powerful it may seem, cannot possibly provide all the answers to the problems encountered in bringing a translated text to the target reader. Because of this, alternative paradigms emerge to gain accep-tance, and the emergence of such paradigms is due primarily to translated texts. But sometimes purpose-based paradigms are hard to come by, and frustrated by lack of alternative paradigms, Hu Shi back in the 1920s, though a traditionalist, went as far as to prescribe radical Westernization. Although complete and radi-calized Westernization was to be abandoned as untenable, mounting impatience with China's stagnation and decline permeated many reform-minded intellectu-als and compelled them to explore effective and feasible cultural strategies for improving the lamentable state of Chinese culture.

Cross-cultural contacts are explored and developed to such an extent that an environment of cross-cultural connectedness is created to force different cultures to establish closer links with one another. Although cross-culturality and inter-culturality are often used interchangeably, it has been argued that "intercultural includes cross-cultural movement" (Cosgrove 2005: 4). Alternatively, it can be said that cross-cultural communication precedes and leads to intercultural com-munication, which is an essential prerequisite of cosmopolitan communication. With growing cross-cultural contacts, intercultural interaction is instrumental in creating a network of reciprocal exchange of cultural knowledge and prac-tices. This has involved a subtle but crucial shift of emphasis and direction from cross-culturality to interculturality, signifying the possibility that outsideness can become insideness. Cross-cultural communication necessarily entails mov-ing from one culture to another and is more than just about transmission and reception, whereas intercultural communication refers to interchange between cultures and is therefore more interactive. It is a question of focus and empha-sis. Also, cross-cultural knowledge and awareness are necessary for intercultural understanding to take place.

Interculturality

In Chinese, however, the distinction between cross-culturality and intercultur-ality has never been made clear. Both cross-cultural communication and inter-cultural communication are translated as "跨文化交际," practically meaning the same thing, namely "cross-cultural communication." The lack of lexical precision reflects a rather vague awareness and understanding of the reciprocal possibility and influence during cross-cultural encounters. Moreover, the lack of an appropriate modifier in Chinese belies the overarching trend towards China going out to the world to promote intercultural learning and education. Yet placing an undue emphasis on "cross" rather than "inter" does not seem to yield the implicitly intended outcome. At present, to ratchet up the competitiveness of Chinese cultural products in the world, the Chinese government has financed a large number of research projects to look into how to work out appropriate translation strategies to best serve the purpose of cross-cultural communication. But in the long run, the key to maximizing cross-cultural reach is intercultural communication. Real intercultural communication takes place in and through a third space where cultural hybridization instead of cultural homogenization is generated. The translator produces an internalized language from the "in-between space" of translation and negotiation between two languages and cultures governed by reciprocality and interactive engagements. The eventual result of hybridization is that cross-cultural references eventually overlap with intercultural references underpinned by internationalism. And the move from cross-cultural to intercultural research can be construed as a fundamental paradigm shift. In his book, *A Linguistic Theory of Translation*, J. C. Catford (1965) brings up and discusses "cultural untranslatability." While it is undoubtedly true that untranslatability has always been a serious problem for effective cultural translation, and skepticism towards translation of cultures is commonplace, yet with more cultural exchange and communication, respect for and acceptance of cultural diversity has become inevitable and normative.

Of course, how to make cultural knowledge more transferable remains a challenge. The process of transculturation of other cultures is a complex and haphazard one. Effective cultural engagement requires a multi-dimensional approach to translation. In this connection, Maria Tymoczko repeatedly and emphatically argues for a holistic cultural translation: "Holistic cultural translation facilitates the translation of culture intelligibly and effectively within the larger framework of the goals that the translator has for the translation" (Tymoczko 2014: 248). This "larger framework" is none other than a cosmopolitan one. It is also a framework of a broader, holistic epistemology, which is characteristic of a strong sense of interrelatedness because of the significant heterogeneous nature of cultural translation.

Wolfgang Iser has spoken of "the translatability of cultures" in a positive light (Iser 1996: 248). In terms of the remedy that can be used to address the issue of "a growing awareness of cultural pathology," he argues for "instilling a self-reflexivity into the stricken culture" and further points out, "[t]ranslatabilty is motivated by the need to cope with a crisis that can no longer be alleviated by the mere assimilation or appropriation of other cultures" (Iser 1996: 248). And such translatability, according to Iser, "is to be conceived as a set of conditions that are able to bring about a mutual mirroring of cultures" and the emergence of a cross-cultural discourse "establishes a network of interpenetrating relationships" for this purpose (Iser 1996: 248). To be more precise, in view of the interpenetrating nature of relationships, the discourse in question should be intercultural rather than cross-cultural so as to be in a better position to look into the causes and consequences of these relationships, which "in turn, allow for a mutual impacting of cultures upon one another, and simultaneously channel the impact" (Iser 1996: 248). Active cultural contact and exchange typically lead to mutual impacts and can robustly challenge nationalism, racism, and ethnocentrism.

The rapid acceleration of urbanization in China is profoundly changing its perception of the country in relation to the world. Whether to translate culturally or cross-culturally or inter-culturally indicates a significant shift in perceptions of cultural translation and its function in an increasingly cosmopolitan social environment. Intercultural communication creates an intricate network of mutuality and reciprocality spawned and enhanced by connections. The long-term impact of mutuality on various dimensions of cultural change has profound implications to the target culture. One thing is certain that cultural heritage becomes more sharable through the transformation of local cultural particularity and historical specificity into something general and cosmopolitan.

Cultural untranslatability, in a cosmopolitan sense, signifies an area of difficulty involving potentially hostile situations concerning otherness. A directly related example occurred in the Place de la Concorde, Paris recently, which I happened to observe: an anxious-looking elderly Chinese lady was calling in an overly high-pitched voice in an attempt to find her husband who seemed to have gone astray. A European lady, who happened to pass by, gave the intrusive tourist a long, dirty look. Such instances of spatial violation are unpleasant and annoying, and not entirely harmless to one's eardrums. Admittedly, the psychological process of understanding, or in this case tolerating a different culture is likely to be lengthy and even painful. Yet more urgently and at the same time more significantly, Chinese citizens back home should be encouraged to be mindful of people's welfare whether they are in China or travel abroad. Also, it almost seems too obvious to point out that a resounding lack of cross-cultural understanding is in evidence here. Not surprisingly, cross-cultural incomprehension or lack of tolerance can easily turn into hostility and potential conflict. This instance of cross-cultural "encounter" is disastrous in the absence of appropriation, which is no doubt necessary, although it may seem to be predatory. It is reported that in order to show respect to the cultural other, Chinese tourists are given cross-cultural and relevant contexts provided by their travel agencies, but as can be expected, old habits of thought and action are hard to break. Still, it is absolutely imperative to inculcate cross-cultural respect to other cultural customs and practices and to subscribe to a universal code of conduct. The acquisition of cultural knowledge takes time and is a relatively slow and complex process. To foster universal tolerance of and mutual respect for difference is by no means easy either because what is culturally and socially acceptable in some countries may not be universally shared. It should be noted that awareness of this is important in understanding the nature of cultural contacts.

As the case just discussed indicates, brash and loud Chinese tourists are usually frowned upon when they travel abroad, particularly in Europe. Most of them are far from being world citizens, and their behavior, though based on a cultural norm in China, is not culturally acceptable in a different cultural milieu and thus not so easily tolerated. Curiously, they are just like the culturally insensitive Chinese mothers in the literary works by Amy Tan and Maxine Hong Kingston. The culturally alienated elderly ladies become a constant source of cultural and social embarrassment to their American born daughters, who have to translate for their mothers not the basic semantic meaning, which their mothers can somehow figure out by themselves, but cultural codes of communication with mappings between two different cultural worlds. It is cultural meaning that needs to be translated and proves to be almost untranslatable.

Significant paradigm shifts or changes from closed tradition to a universal modern world can be observed. With high-spending visitors in Galeries Lafayette in Paris and Harrods in London counting out wads of euros being met with mixed feelings, a cultural and psychological reality has emerged. In general, togetherness generates commonality only to reduce the incompatibility of heterogeneous cultural configurations. Due to apparently insufficient exposure to the other world(s), cultural learning is urgently needed. The Chinese government has recently advised travel agencies organizing international tours to "educate" their customers to be "civil" tourists. They are exhorted to avoid making loud noises when traveling overseas. It is apparently understood that such "cultural export" is a far cry from being desirable and can only cause obstacles to cross-cultural communication. This calls for a deeper "cultural introspection" of Chinese culture in the current age of increasing globalization. Massive numbers of Chinese tourists in many parts of the world are going through an intercultural learning process. Their tour guides, who also act as cultural translators, are responsible for explaining the cultural implications of how they behave in a foreign land.

As a result, cultural transformation or hybridization appears gradually on the horizon. How cultural knowledge is conveyed and shared is a matter of great importance. It is fascinating to observe that at least part of a national culture begins to give way to a cosmopolitan culture, in which cultural differences are absorbed, consumed, and transformed into cultural homogeneity. In this connection, cross-cultural psychology needs to turn into intercultural psychology because cross-cultural practices are becoming, more increasingly, intercultural practices. There is no doubt that a shift from cross-cultural experiences to intercultural learning exerts a powerful impact on dynamic intercultural communication concerning cultural attitude.

Cosmopolitanism

Cosmopolitanism embraces and celebrates otherness, rendering conceptual change inevitable, while cosmopolitan translation makes it possible to gain intercultural experience and open up heterogeneous cultural spaces. Part of the interculturally constituted reality is that national culture has acquired some universal significance, and the idea of a cosmopolitan culture and citizenship is closely related to the subtle shifts in cultural attitude. Reciprocal mirroring between the two cultures involved in translation is not only unavoidable but also essential to benefit from the refreshing energies and influences of other cultures. There is no denying that translation is an indispensable cosmopolitan medium, resulting in a redefined understanding of the globalized world. Many translators, consciously or unconsciously, oscillate between nationalist and cosmopolitan perspectives. In fact, cosmopolitan nationalism and nationalist cosmopolitanism are intermingled: each is functional and meaningful in the light of the other. While cultural translation reveals traces of commonality and similarity as well as dissimilarity and difference, cosmopolitan translation increases the infinite possibility of cross-fertilization and hybridization between cultures.

Cultural translation is, in essence, cosmopolitan practice, and it can also be said that cosmopolitan translation is cultural translation with broader intercultural awareness and global perspectives. The centrality of cultural translation to cosmopolitan thinking is beyond doubt, and this mode of thinking entails imagining and envisioning alternative and different ways of life representing different perspectives and worldviews. Cosmopolitan translation can be understood to be a continuation of cultural translation with a high degree of interaction as an integral part of it. It is fair to say that although translation of a cosmopolitan nature cannot be taken for granted, cosmopolitan translation is possible through painstaking incremental progress in finding ways to negotiate cultural differences. Because cultural incompatibilities and misunderstandings are bound to occur, there is a growing need to be sensitive to the nuances of cultural information and knowledge. Essentially, cultural information requires cross-cultural interpretation and representation involving different cultural contexts. Appreciation of cultural diversity is rooted in mutual respect at more than a superficial level and should be based on mutual understanding. Above all, the interactionist perspective is crucial to cosmopolitan translation, which is primarily concerned with exchanging cultural information on equal terms. Through discursive negotiations, creative dynamic reconfigurations of cultural meaning and form can take place without serious obstacles. All this may sound like an idealistic dream, but in reality, cosmopolitan translation, or at least a certain form of it, has become possible, largely due to the fact that increased globalization has unleashed unprecedented cultural energies to empower the interaction of, and demonstrate inter-connection between, different cultures, which is greatly conducive to cosmopolitan dialogue. Moreover, global citizenship breeds cosmopolitan readership. The causal correlation between the two provides the foundation for the possibility of pursuing cosmopolitan translation.

It is noteworthy that China is endowed with a cosmopolitan past, culminating in the Tang dynasty, but lapsed into a persistent state of anti-cosmopolitan domesticity for a long period of isolation from the rest of the world, particularly the West. It was in modern times that Chinese intellectuals began to find a way to recover and revive its cosmopolitan past through relentless search for modernity inspired by reading and translating Western works. In a sense, modernity signifies a radical tendency to renounce tradition and by doing this, to bring China into the modern world in alignment with Western models and values. To modernize China, it was imperative to modernize its people, as in "renewing" them in the words of Liang Qichao (1873–1929), a prominent reformist, who published the journal 《新民丛报》(*New citizen journal*) from 1902 to 1905. For him, the expression "renewing the people" was a renewed concept of part of Zhu Xi's formulation of "新民" (new people), which was meant to be achieved "through universal self-cultivation."[1] An effective way to renew the people was to revamp and modernize their thinking, and subsequently, behavior by introducing to them new foreign ideas.

In the late Qing, translation practice is fraught with tension between tradition and modernity inherent in the transformative nature of the latter. In many ways, translation is a modernizing act to update a text that can be obsolete, out of date or seemingly irrelevant; it prompts a re-reading of a text in existence, resulting in not only an after-life in the parlance of Walter Benjamin but also a new life, or rather, a renewed life. The transformative focus in the late Qing was developing a way to circumvent cultural "untranslatability" by removing or reducing incommensurability and adding new content to the translated text with the aim of creating the impression of conformity and homogenization. Evidently, the reception of cultural products occurs in a different cultural context, appropriation of some kind is necessary from time to time. Appropriation means a somewhat transformed outcome of reading, interpretation, and rewriting, and it is contingent upon a certain form of linguistic and cultural re-contextualization with a view to making sense of cultural meaning for the target reader. In other words, to re-contextualize cultural meaning creates a chance to renegotiate and recover it after its displacement. But it is well known that this practice may be inimical to cross-cultural communication causing the dilution or distortion of cultural meaning.

Clearly, a bridging function is to be established to reconcile exclusion and inclusion to attain a form of cosmopolitan translation as opposed to nationally inflected translation. Contextualization is the key to unraveling meaning. It is often observed that something that makes perfect sense in one language makes no or little sense in a different context after translation, due in no small measure to a lack of contextualization. Nonetheless, the concept of thick translation – known as contextualized translation, though designed by Appiah to enable the target reader to fully understand cultural meaning, is not always the most appropriate strategy or the best way to help the target reader glean cultural meaning. Contextualization considered intrinsic to thick translation insinuates a distrust of translation in its conventional form. It was the deep-seated concern about cross-cultural untranslatability that rekindled a return to the "old-fashioned" practice of translation with its focus firmly on the source text. But in truth, it is more than a simple return; it is a return with a vengeance – the loss of cultural meaning is adequately compensated for by a significant increase in providing detailed contextual information about specific historical and cultural allusions and references. But such an elaborate anchoring of context, valuable as it is in some cases, generates a system of unreadability. The anxiety about the impossibility of reading a foreign literary text also reflects the ontological difficulty of capturing the fullness of cultural meaning from the point of view of cross-cultural communication. The practice of thick translation diminishes the role of the target reader because any indeterminacy is worked out by the translator for them. It is not exactly a practical way to make a text accessible. But as noted earlier, cultural appropriation, especially if it is practiced inappropriately, does not provide the answer to the problem of unreadability either. It seems that this fear of inadequately articulating cultural meaning and desire for access and readability for better reception makes cultural translation a virtual impossibility.

Indeed, in terms of cultural translation, context as a key concept in any form of communication cannot be annulled or bypassed. The act of translation comprises at least a first context, a second context, and also, possibly, a third context. The question is: is translation involved in recontextualizing or decontextualizing? The ideology of translation is known to be closely related to context manipulation, which may lead to a third context responsible for the effects on the reading experience. Translation leads to re-contextualization, whose function, however, is not the same as the recovery of the original context. There are different ways of re-contextualizing a text, the outcome of which is determined by how meaning is interpreted and re-articulated by the translator. Vanessa Leonardi points out: "Translation is a productive activity that focuses on de-contextualization and re-contextualization" (Leonardi 2010: 20). This seems to imply that in order to re-contextualize translation, it needs to be de-contextualized first. But in cosmopolitan translation, it is possible to focus primarily on the de-contextualization part, and to leave the re-contextualization part to the target reader, who may find it increasingly less necessary to do so, given the contemporary reality of globalization and cosmopolitanism.

Furthermore, in order to make sense of cultural meaning, it is necessary to remove cultural meaning from its original cultural context; when this happens, a text goes through a haphazard process of de-contextualization, and then a temporary cultural ambivalence ensues. Cosmopolitanism betokens cultural de-contextualization with a neutralized culture to be abstracted from its historical and societal context that gives it meaning in the first place. Global mobility has prompted cultural de-contextualization. In other words, the original power of contextualization is less limiting and allows the subsequent de-contextualization to neutralize the cultural singularity and make it possible for cosmopolitanism to negotiate cultural boundaries by defusing many of the stereotypes that bedevil cross-cultural thinking about how to bridge differences and foster commonality. The paradox is that in order to contextualize our understanding of a foreign culture, we may need to de-contextualize it. De-contextualization requires negotiation of mitigating cultural particularity; instead of simplistic mutilation, there is still a dialogue, which occurs in polymorphous forms to avoid or reduce unnecessary cross-cultural references or allusions.

A strategic move to disregard such intricate cultural references at this stage proves to be useful. Take Ezra Pound's translation of Chinese poetry, for example. It exemplifies a radical de-contextualization, and one could argue that perhaps it is too radical, and indeed his approach has caused a great deal of controversy. But it serves a purpose, and by reducing the amount of context-dependent information, the "thickness" of cultural translation is thus averted. In any event, it seems that some distance is required to "understand" the foreignness of the source text. In this regard, cultural distance in recognition of cultural difference admits that to fully represent what is embedded in the original is a virtual impossibility. What is originally localized and some specific needs to be transformed into what is universal and normative for the target reader to present a truly holistic and long-term approach to cultural translation. Cosmopolitan translation supposedly high-lights the foreignness of cultural languages, and, at the same time, demonstrates the performativity of translation as the staging of cultural difference so that it is clearly and adequately articulated and reconstructed in the target language.

There is admittedly a profound paradox here. On the one hand, the generation of cultural meaning depends on its context. In reality, to neutralize or interpose the full thickness of cultural translation, nuanced meaning operating at different levels has to be treated with dexterity. On the other, however, the reproduction of cultural meaning is, to some extent, related to a kind of de-contextualization, which is an antidote to re-contextualization. Though often appropriately tailored to ease consumption for the target reader, re-contextualization can ultimately be detrimental to genuine cross-cultural communication, let alone intercultural communication. Indeed, re-contextualization is well espoused by many translation scholars as the ineluctable outcome of translation, but this may well lead to a unilateral cultural situation, in which cultural meaning is seriously compromised. Such a practice can of course be useful to the target culture in many ways but does little to facilitate or promote cultural diversity and pluralism. The relevance and value of cosmopolitan translation should not be difficult to perceive, given its power to shape or transform the entire nature of cross-cultural, or rather, intercultural communication.

National academic space

During the so-called "cultural fever" in the 1980s, after China recuperated from the trauma of the Cultural Revolution and was learning to reintegrate with cosmopolitanism, anything from the West was embraced with gusto by Chinese intellectuals. There was a dire need for fresh ideas and new perspectives. The intellectual starvation was so widespread that it was a matter of great urgency to reopen spaces to foster enlightenment. This, however, resulted in some undesirable repercussions. In the 1990s, Chinese intellectuals, after moving out of their confined space, found themselves unable to engage in intellectual dialogue with Western counterparts. Given that they had been in the state of isolation for too long, they were thrust into an almost standoffish cosmopolitan space. The subsequent frustration and disillusionment could not be avoided. The anxiety associated with "academic nationalism" began to be overwhelming and disorienting. Under the circumstance of Western theories sweeping over China, the term "aphasia" supposedly suffered by Chinese intellectuals following much self-questioning was used by Cao Shunqing to call attention to the grievous situation (Cao 1995: 216). The disquieting question was asked by Cao: "Just imagine this: How can a person with aphasia enter into dialogue with others?" (Cao 1995: 216).

Collective abasement and soul-searching caused some Chinese intellectuals to reflect on an epiphany they had experienced: if everything were borrowed from the West, Chinese scholarship would be undeserving of respect from Western counterparts. Driven by globalization and internationalization, Chinese scholarship naturally sought to become part of the wider international academic community, but its identity seemed to be soon swamped and submerged in the wake of extensive borrowing. It was and still is felt with a grave misgiving that modern and contemporary Chinese culture relies too heavily on Western theoretical knowledge and models while annulling its own discourse. This has formed a breeding ground for academic nationalism. According to the observation of Xiong Yihan:

> "Academic nationalism" is routinely used as a pretext of opposing Western centralism to resist internationalization. Those who maintain this view believe that ideology is often hidden in scholarship. If we become part of the Western-dominated academic production system, we have to accept Western academic hegemony. Chinese scholarship should have "Chinese characteristics," so it is not necessary to be in line with international practice.
>
> (Xiong 2014: 117)

In spite of desultory attempts to de-politicize scholarship, over-emphasis on Chinese characteristics reveals an entrenched distrust of foreign otherness. Cultural politics is epitomized in the issue of cultural identity. Shunning international practice can masquerade as prioritizing Chinese uniqueness, but only to reflect a nationalistic bias. Academic nationalism initiates and countenances cultural protectionism in opposition to cosmopolitan diversity.

Although there is no denying that academic exclusiveness of otherness is irrational and inimical, some Chinese scholars challenge the so-called universal applicability of Western theories. They refuse to engage in a dialogic mode with Western counterparts who are dismissed as knowing nothing about China. Moreover, Occidentalism perceived as patriarchy and Western supremacy was met with apprehension and even hostility. Without a doubt, any pretense of bias-free research or scholarship is problematic and hazardous. The absence of reciprocality between what is Chinese and what is international endangers the future development of scholarship in China. Nationalism and cosmopolitanism are thus dichotomized as a binary division in dealing with "Western academic hegemony." However, a misguided extrapolation of this situation has yielded confusing or misleading results, which is tantamount in many ways to advocating ethnocentrism and narrow nationalism. It should be clearly understood that unless we make sense of the world, we cannot make (better) sense of ourselves. It is important to consider the discursive constitution of academic subjectivity, which is related to authority, legitimacy, and dominance. But it is more important to establish genuinely transcendental intersubjectivity with a view to investigating the relationship between particularity and universality and generating new insights on cosmopolitan mindset in relation to sharing academic space in an intercultural sense.

There has been deep concern about the erosion of Western translation theories in China. In 2004, John Benjamins brought out a collection of essays by Chinese writers and scholars in English translation entitled *Twentieth-Century Chinese Translation Theory: Modes, Issues and Debates*. The title of the volume assumes as a given that there is such a thing as Chinese translation theory. However, even some of the hardcore advocates of this view were not so confident, hence the need to establish it. The prognostic article "论翻译理论的建设" ("On the construction of translation theory") by Dong Qiusi was based on the observation that China still had not established its translation theory, or something that could be called theory. Unfortunately, in the ensuing decade or so, not much progress was made, and then came the Cultural Revolution, which put an end to almost anything of cultural value. After the open-up of China in 1978 which witnessed a resurgence of translation activity, there began an increasing keenness to know about the outside world. The long-standing state of isolation called forth an intense yearning for more cross-cultural spaces. It was against this historical backdrop that Western translation theories together with refreshing main paradigms were introduced to China (Sun 2012: 37).

However, as in other social science disciplines, translation theory still tends to be labeled with the familiar tag of "Chinese characteristics." A striking paradox underlies the anti-cosmopolitan position on thinking about translation. An archetypal example is encapsulated in the scathing criticism of some translation scholars who "belittle themselves and blindly follow suit" (Mao 2003: 5). Similarly, another author can barely move beyond binary thinking. Even-Zohar's polysystem theory is treated dismissively because Yan Fu has already dealt with similar issues (Liu 2001: 43). A self-contained system is advocated to prove the invalidity of Western translation theories. In an article published in 2003, Xu Yuanchong repudiates Nida's concept of dynamic equivalence, with his argument based on his own translation practice (Xu 2002: 52). This is a simplistic and reductionistic approach to translation. A more thoughtful and analytical consideration would contravene the conclusion that has prevented Xu from finding the route to a fecund space for discussing important issues arising from his translation experience.

The cultural location of translation is of great significance, and for some Chinese translation scholars, without considering the context of linguistic and cultural specificity, the relevance of translation theory diminishes, hence the imperative need to champion the establishment of translation theory with Chinese characteristics. This has sparked heated debates. In an article published in 2002, Sun Huijun and Zhang Boran fame a dichotomous question:

> Should the Chinese translation community vigorously introduce and learn from Western translation theories, or use the concepts of traditional Chinese translation theories to create its own translation theories with Chinese

characteristics? In the authors' opinion, this is the most urgent and important issue in contemporary Chinese translation circles, and it is pressing to reach a unified understanding.

(Sun and Zhang 2002: 5)

This either/or mode of thinking epitomizes the attitude of those who espouse "Chinese characteristics." In a sharp riposte to the aforementioned attitude, Zhu Chunshen writes, "This is a politically correct premise but is epistemologically incongruous" (Zhu 2002: 36). Moreover, "a unified understanding" represents a seriously problematic supposition. Why should any understanding be "unified"? Who is supposed to unify all the different understandings?

Zhu Chunshen is troubled by the supercilious remarks and argues that in the context of heteroglossia, no views should be suppressed to be unified because they are different (Zhu 2002: 36). However, some of the problems identified by Sun and Zhang are not chimerical. For instance, "Western translation theories have been painted with an idealistic hue" by some scholars who are seen to be "intellectually subservient to these theories," and due to "a lack a critical attitude" and also independent and innovative research," these scholars are unable to conduct "independent and innovative research" (Sun and Zhang 2002: 6–7). In all fairness, what is observed here is by and large accurate and can be taken as well-intended criticism and a benign reminder. But the overall skeptic view of universalism held by the authors is severely challenged by Zhu Chunshen. The overt emphasis on Chinese uniqueness is a misguided attempt to construct a Chinese translation theory – Chinese characteristics are, in some cases at least, only a thinly veiled euphemism for replacing the so-called Western translation theory.

However, things can change over time, even though almost imperceptibly. Although he used to be one of the arch proponents of "Chinese characteristics," Pan Wenguo's position has softened noticeably. While refusing to abandon his usual standpoint and assailing cultural nihilism as the critical problem of embracing Western translation theory, his recent articles have taken a conciliatory tone. He tries to bypass the theoretical discussion of translation studies with Chinese characteristics by focusing on the practicalities of translation on the grounds that theoretical debates can only result in a stalemate (Pan 2012: 1). He thus argues that because of linguistic differences, translation studies with Chinese characteristics is the inevitable choice (Pan 2012: 2). As he concedes, "It is rather necessary to constantly introduce [to China] new theories and methods from the West" (Pan 2013: 21). To be sure, as a universal cross-cultural activity, translation brings forth and reveals many commonalities. The shibboleth to establish translation studies with Chinese characteristics may well plunge translation research in China into the scourge of narrow nationalism or even ethnocentrism.

The exclusionary definition of translation studies with Chinese characteristics can potentially lead to an impasse. It can be said that striving the intertwined pursuits of territoriality and identity is related to the initial reaction of the nationalist translation scholars to Western translation theories is to carve a snug space in the cosmopolitan world. But if translation research is not transnational, let alone international, it is cause for concern. The irrationality of inflexible insistence on particularism succumbs to the danger of drifting into ethnocentric provincialism, which is self-defeating rather than self-enhancing. For the scholars who crusade for "Chinese characteristics," national academic space is under the threat of being reduced or eliminated. But national academic space can be expanded through a Chinese lens and from a Chinese perspective without necessarily rejecting or ostracizing universalism. As Amanda Anderson has noted, cosmopolitanism traditionally endorses three things: "reflective distance from one's cultural affiliations, a broad understanding of other cultures and customs, and a belief in universal humanity" (Anderson 1998: 267). To buttress the claim of more commonality which underscores the underlying universalism, it is necessary to investigate both the possibility and limits of reciprocality. In Bakhtinian terms, translation is dialogic, and it is thus difficult to imagine Translation Studies devoid of a cosmopolitan dimension. The growing cosmopolitan nature of humanities and social sciences is a reflection of international connectedness and insight. National academic boundaries can no longer be guarded, and there is an unmistakable trend to move towards a convergence of different academic traditions and cultural backgrounds. And undeniably, cosmopolitan translation can be a powerfully enabling concept to encapsulate translation practice and account for dialogic, interactive approaches within the framework of cosmopolitan thinking.

Conclusion

The growing relevance of cosmopolitanism to Chinese cultural reality concerning translation is well illustrated by an impassioned eagerness to reach out to the world. The increasing transnational experience of many ordinary Chinese makes world cultural citizenship a not entirely remote possibility. The traditional boundary between national identity and cosmopolitan openness is constantly transcended, yet the cosmopolitan potential of translation is yet to be realized. The concept of cosmopolitanism is both broad and multifaceted, and its relevance to translation is not always easy to observe. Yet what is clear is that cosmopolitanism is driven by the practice of cultural translation characterized by interactive complexity, which provides a significant nexus of nationalism and cosmopolitanism and underscores experiential commonalities. Although different versions of cosmopolitanism are represented in literary and theoretical works, cultural translation concerning cosmopolitanism satisfies the necessary condition of dialogue and reciprocality. Cosmopolitan translation entails transformation, which starts a movement from unawareness to awareness and from exclusiveness to inclusiveness. Experiential referents of various kinds are minimized not to be exclusive but to be inclusive in a more general way. This assumed connection between particularity and universality has not hitherto been adequately accounted for, and instead of shunning or erasing difference, cosmopolitan translation places a greater emphasis on similarity or commonality while also acknowledging the asymmetry between languages and cultures that does exist. Respecting difference and diversity, it consciously fosters and is fostered by the practice of producing more accessible and acceptable, but also dynamic, interactive translation.

Note

1 Zhu Xi (1130–1200) was a Song Dynasty Confucian scholar who devoted his life to the propagation of Confucianism. A great neo-Confucianist, educator, and thinker, Zhu Xi has had an immense influence on the development of Chinese philosophy.

References

Anderson, Amanda (1998) "Cosmopolitanism, Universalism, and the Divided Legacies of Modernity," in Pheng Cheah and Bruce Robbins (eds.) *Cosmopolitics: Thinking and Feeling Beyond the Nation,* Minneapolis: University of Minnesota Press.

Bhadha, Homi K. (1994) *The Location of Culture,* London: Routledge.

Cao, Shunqing (1995) "21世纪中国文化发展战略与重建中国文论话语" (The Development Strategy of Chinese Culture in the 21st Century and the Reconstruction of Chinese Literary Theory Discourse), 《东方丛刊》 (*Oriental Studies*) 13(3): 213–227.

Catford, J. C. (1965) *A Linguistic Theory of Translation: An Essay in Applied Linguistics,* London: Oxford University Press.

Cosgrove, Charles H. (2005) "Cross-Cultural Paul: Journeys to Others," in Herold Weiss and Khiok-Khng Yeo (eds.) *Journeys to Ourselves,* Grand Rapids, MI: W. B. Eerdmans Publishing.

Hassan, Waïl S. (2011) *Immigrant Narratives: Orientalism and Cultural Translation in Arab American and Arab British Literature,* New York: Oxford University Press.

Hong, Ying (trans. by Howard Goldblatt) (1998) *Daughter of the River,* New York: Grove Press.

Iser, Wolfgang (1996) "The Emergence of a Cross-Cultural Discourse: Thomas Carlyle's *Sartor Resartus,*" in Sanford Budick and Wolfgang Iser (eds.) *The Translatability of Cultures: Figurations of the Space Between,* Stanford, CA: Stanford University Press.

Leonardi, Vanessa (2010) *The Role of Pedagogical Translation in Second Language Acquisition: From Theory to Practice,* New York: Peter Lang.

Liu, Airong (2001) "建设有中国特色的翻译理论体系" (Establishing a Theoretical System of Translation with Chinese Characteristics), 《中国科技翻译》 (*Chinese Science and Technology Translators Journal*) 14(4): 42–45.

Mao, Ronggui (2003) "翻译与美学" (Translation and Aesthetics), 《上海科技翻译》 (*Shanghai Journal of Translators for Science and Technology*) 17(3): 5–9.

Murphy, Patrick D., and Marwan M. Kraidy (eds.) (2003) *Global Media Studies: An Ethnographic Perspective,* London and New York: Routledge.

Pan, Wenguo (2012) "中国译论与中国话语" (Translation Theory and Discourse of China), 《外语教学理论与实践》 (*Foreign Language Learning Theory and Practice*) 31(1): 1–7.

Pan, Wenguo (2013) "构建中国学派翻译理论: 是否必要? 有无可能? " (Translation Theory with a Chinese Brand: Is It Necessary or Possible?), 《燕山大学学报 (哲学社会科学版)》 (*Journal of Yanshan University [Philosophy and Social Science Edition]*) 14(4): 20–24.

Pym, Anthony (2010) *Exploring Translation Theories,* London and New York: Routledge.

Sun, Huijun, and Zhang Boran (2002) "全球化背景下对普遍性和差异性的诉求: 中国当代译学研究走向" (Universality vs. Difference: On the Development of Contemporary Translation Studies in China), 《中国翻译》 (*Chinese Translators Journal*) 23(2): 4–7.

Sun, Yifeng (2012) "The Shifting Identity of Translation Studies in China," *Intercultural Communication Studies* 21(2): 32–52.

Tymoczko, Maria (2014) *Enlarging Translation, Empowering Translators*, London and New York: Routledge.

Wittgenstein, Ludwig (trans. by G. E. M. Anscombe) (1958) *Philosophical Investigations*, Oxford: Basil Blackwell.

Xiong, Yihan (2014) "中国社会科学的国际化与母语写作" (The Internationalization of Social Sciences and Native Language Scholarly Writing in China), 《复旦学报 (社会科学版)》 (*Fudan Journal [Social Sciences]*) 4(4): 116–123.

Xu, Yuanchong (2002) "谈中国学派的翻译理论: 中国翻译学落后于西方吗?" (On the Translation Theory of Chinese School: Does Chinese Translation Studies Lag Behind the West?), 《外语与外语教学》 (*Foreign Languages and Their Teaching*) 23(1): 52–55.

Zhu, Chunshen (2002) "'特色' 抹不掉, '特色论,' 不必要: 读孙会军、张柏然论文有感" (Let It Be, and Let It Lie: A Response to Sun and Zhang), 《中国翻译》 (*Chinese Translators Journal*) 23(6): 36–39.

4 Translation and world literature

Introduction

World literature has continued to draw attention to humanities research. Since the possibility of world literature rests on international circulation, translation has a pivotal role to play. However, in recent years, serious doubt has been cast on the meaningfulness of this role, foregrounding the chronic issue of untranslatability that is seen to undermine the chance of world literature. There is no denying that if the role of cross-cultural communication is played inadequately or unsatisfactorily, the circulation of national literatures is impeded to become world literature. Through the heterogeneity of different context dimensions, cross-cultural interpretations, and forms of mediating cultures in various manifestations are brought to the fore about the essential need for further investigation and research. This chapter attempts to frontally address the issues raised by scholars working in the field of world literature in relation to renewed challenges to translation and for that matter, Translation Studies. Translation happens at a specific location and time, which in turn govern and determine what happens to and in translation. The quality, or rather acceptability, of translation for the purpose of enabling the circulation of literary texts across national boundaries will be re-examined in connection with world literature, the success of which necessitates cross-cultural transformation as exemplified in inscribing the putative literary value into translation.

Translation and circulation

Much has been written about the key role of translation in cultural development and nation-building as well as in the promotion of world literature, among many other things. But some more fundamental questions remain either open or unanswered as to what exactly constitutes the role and how and to what extent that role is understood and subsequently performed. It is an existential fact that in the American academic world translation studies has been overlooked for a long time. Recalling her experience at the World Literature Institute Summer School program at Harvard in 2014, Susan Bassnett was made, together with Lawrence Venuti, to palpably feel the "abyss between the study of world literature and the study of translation" (Bassnett 2019: 1). This situation is somewhat surprising and unfortunate. It seems that scholars working in what should be two contiguous disciplines do not talk to each other. However, while some scholars question the pivotal role of translation in promoting world literature, there seems to be a modest revival of interest in Translation Studies because of world literature. Now that translation studies can no longer be bypassed in discussing world literature, it is time for the two disciplinary spaces at least to correspond to each other.

There is little doubt that world literature rests on global circulation, but because the challenges of untranslatability remain largely and fundamentally unaltered, it is necessary to examine the theoretical underpinnings of the nature and complexity of untranslatability. Emily Apter's provocative title of her *Against World Literature* is clearly meant to problematize the concept and practice of world literature in view of the fragility of translatability. Despite her almost fatalistic attitude to the crippling effect of untranslatability, as observed by David Damrosch, in her *Against World Literature*, Apter has little engagement with translation studies and "neglects major figures whose work could enrich her argument at many points" (Damrosch 2014: 506–507). He further points out that the book

> nowhere discusses or even mentions such seminal figures in the "cultural turn" of contemporary translation studies as Susan Bassnett, André Lefevere, Gideon Toury, Harish Trivedi, or Lawrence Venuti, even though from the 1980s onward these theorists revolutionized a previously formalist field to address issues of power, inequality, and the thorniness of language.
>
> (Damrosch 2014: 507)

Thus, a singular lack of interaction between different but closely related disciplinary spaces is rather puzzling. Ironically, in an interview, Apter claims that "*Against World Literature* used translation theory to redress power imbalance in cross-cultural and cross-lingual comparison" (Bertacco 2016: 10). It is clear that the "translation theory" mentioned earlier is exclusionary and cannot be said to reflect the important progress made in translation studies. In light of the dearth of transdisciplinary engagement, there is need to create discursive spaces for dialogic perspectives.

Apter's stance about untranslatability seems to be intransigent, and the contentious argument against the validity of world literature has caused considerable pain to translation scholars. How seriously should her argument be taken? She has certainly succeeded in shocking people into an awareness of the complexity of translation, out of their comfortable assumption of transferability across languages and cultures. It seems that untranslatability deeply rooted in incomparability as represented by alterity cannot be dismissed as an already demolished notion, which has survived into the present day through different times and spaces. Serious rethinking and revisiting are thus necessitated. If what is at stake is untranslatability, the success of translation becomes uncertain. Meanwhile, inadequate or failed translation, which is ordinarily ascribed to untranslatability, seems to be inevitable and constitutes a necessary part of translingual practice.

As claimed by Derrida, there is no absolute untranslatability and, for that matter, absolute translatability. Either direct or indirect translation vacillates along a spectrum of these two possible extremes in search of solutions to manifold problems of untranslatability or lack of translatability. We need to tackle head-on the various possibilities of representation in translation by examining uncertainty and contingency potentially associated with interactive changes to enable better understanding of the multi-dimensional nature of translation operating at different levels and in different spaces.

World literature is customarily a singular concept. Yet the dissemination of world literature, as is patently obvious, depends on translation into various languages. Readers of different nations can encounter each other's literature only through translation, and reading world literature simply means, in most cases, reading a translation. This may well seem to be self-evident or even trivial but should not be dismissed lightly when the value of translation is subject to severe limitations.

In the context of world literature, the common target language is English, which is undisputedly the prominent, if not dominant, international language. There is an implicit assumption that English is widely used as a world language, representing Western-centric universalism. However, the number of people reading English is not predominantly large. To be real world literature, more languages must be involved. While there is an increasing awareness of the hegemonic role of English, other so-called world languages, in the words of Kathleen Shields, "such as Arabic, Hindi, French, German, Chinese, and Russian are all yielding to English in the hierarchy of translations" (Shields 2013: 4). Nevertheless, it is still necessary and indispensable to translate into other languages for world literature to come into being and become influential. World literature consists of selected literary texts in translation to reach a heterogeneous international readership. It is safe to hypothesize that world literature exists mostly, if not only, in translation, without which, the concept of world literature is of little use. It is only meaningful to study world literature in translation and how it is shaped and enabled or inhibited by the latter. In this regard, it has to be recognized that literary translation necessarily operates across cultural spaces.

World literature is basically composed of the literatures of the world while national literatures move from national circulation to global circulation. They either become international or transformed from national into international. It can also be said, however, that central to the core of world literature is variety and heterogeneity. World literature can be typified by a tacit assumption of the one-world system, which is deeply problematic because there is little ground for confirming or supporting it. A related question would be how translation in its multifarious forms and ramifications, while bringing into existence of world literature, can challenge and possibly change the one-world system.

Sure enough, world literature is critically contingent on international circulation. How is an international readership acquired and developed? Invariably, whether one likes it or not, "[t]ranslation into English and into other major languages such as French and Spanish has been for some a condition of publication and for many a path to translation into subsequent national editions" (Walkowitz 2015: 11). With a firm reference to the preponderant role of translation, especially into English, we examine how literary texts are made available to an international readership. Given the changing nature of translational activity in different cultural contexts and historical periods, it is all-important to carry out substantial engagement with translation practice by examining how national literatures become internationalized with diverse perspectives and literary traditions being brought together. One may say that unless a translated text travels well into the target language, something valuable to be called universal cannot be reliably measured for it to resonate with the target reader. The trouble in gaining access to international circulation is that to determine the precise composition of the target reader can be difficult. Likewise, it is not easy to aim at a target that is out of sight – the sheer range of variables makes it difficult to identify, let alone aim at a specific target. After all, it is not always clear for the writer or, indeed, the translator as well to know and satisfy the expectations of the international audience whose background and worldview are probably little known.

International circulation is subject to a multitude of factors, which may generate considerable uncertainty and disagreement as to what may constitute and be accepted as world literature. In general, a readable translation is preferable, thus increasing its capacity for reception. However, what if some novels that have been written ostentatiously not for translation, is there a chance for them to be read as world literature? Literature is normally produced for a limited audience (local audience) rather than for global consumption, although this situation has been changing rapidly in recent years. Unless something is written with an international readership in mind, the task of translation can be more challenging. Since under most circumstances, the source reader is different from the target reader, to be of interest to an international readership is a prerequisite for international circulation. In this regard, whether specificity in translation as exemplified in national literature is good or appropriate for world literature is something that should be thought out.

Yet it is precisely the specificity that is vulnerable to loss in translation for assorted reasons. In response to Damrosch's reference to gain as opposed to loss in translation, Harrison expresses undisguised skepticism, claiming that without the knowledge of the source language, it is dubious to speak of gains and for that matter, losses. Thus, he challenges the validity of Damrosch's approach: "When Damrosch reads or teaches a text written in a language he doesn't know, how can he tell that it has gained in translation? And how can his students tell?" (Damrosch 2014: 412). This, however, is not strictly impossible. For instance, comparing different translation versions of the same source text can yield revealing insight. Damrosch has demonstrated this by comparing two different translation versions of Bei Dao's famous poem "The Answer" (Damrosch 2003: 22). In so doing, he has created a functional space to measure the literary aptness of different translation versions. There is no doubt that translation warrants various levels of scrutiny, and this can be done even without referring to the original. Aside from accuracy, which is prioritized by Harrison, what about nuance, literary merit, and cultural implication? Translation is a relational, referential, and transformational activity, and despite shortcomings at the lexical-semantic level, the translated text can still be enjoyable, which makes it possible to introduce world literature to a global audience.

For Harrison, however, it is apparently not enough to examine two translation versions without going back to the original. While acknowledging the value of the exercise championed by Damrosch, he insists that "it still has to be better if you can read the original too, if only in the minimal sense that it is one more version" (Harrison 2014: 414). He even argues "that anyone who is serious about world literature should also be serious about making their students learn foreign languages" (Harrison 2014: 412). Not only is this an unattainable expectation, but it may not even be a desirable one. Franco Moretti stresses that "we are talking of hundreds of languages and literatures here" (Moretti 2000: 55). Moreover, world literature cannot possibly rely on a small group of students for international circulation, and even though it is possible for them to learn all the foreign languages required for reading world literature, it is unlikely for them to develop a sufficiently advanced level of linguistic proficiency in and relevant cultural knowledge of original texts. Such a reading practice would only entail a seriously compromised undertaking. And above all, it will almost certainly fail to promote the circulation of world literature.

World literature and untranslatability

At the heart of the contention is untranslatability. For Bassnett however, renewed concern about lack of translatability regarding world literature seems misguided, and as she sees it, untranslatability has always been an integral part of translation practice (Bassnett 2019: 5). Yet admittedly, the untranslatability problem has not been really solved, either in theory or in practice. It undeniably is an old notion, as pointed out by Trivedi, and according to him, untranslatability, as is mostly manifest in culture-specific words, should be put into perspective, as "they are soon enough assimilated as such in other languages" (Trivedi 2019: 24–25). While Apter may have overstated its import, Trivedi seems to downplay the erosive hazard created by untranslatability, which however cannot be glibly dismissed as negligible. In any event, untranslatability is by no means confined to culture-specific words, as he stoutly insists.

As asserted by Lucas Klein, world literature, "however defined," must build itself on translation (Klein 2016: 611). The prime threat to its existence is untranslatability, or more specifically, cultural untranslatability. Untranslatability is a general overarching concept that can be related to any aspect of incommensurability between languages and cultures involved in translation. There are many stumbling blocks that obstruct cultural encounter, not to mention engagement. Translation results in a text reproduced in a different historical and cultural context, and thus the process and the associated hazards of reproduction must be considered in a different cultural context. Apter may be right in insisting that borders between cultures cannot be crossed as easily as often assumed, even though they seem to be crossed or claimed to be crossed all the time. This is analogous to repeated references to untranslatability, yet the untranslatable seems to get translated all the time. The ensuing question is: What, exactly, is untranslatability? As a violent act, translation is known to be capable of causing damage to the original in the process of overcoming untranslatability. This practice is described by Tim Parks (2010) as "changing everything in order that it remains the same, or as close as possible to [the translator's] own experience of the original." Nevertheless, how cultural borders can be crossed or whether they are crossed felicitously is an inevitable part of translation. Untranslatability can be broadly divided into two types: something can be either tangibly untranslatable or inadequately translatable, and depending on the nature of untranslatability, the coping strategies can range from linguistic, stylistic and cultural domestication. However, any practices barring direct access to signifiers of the original may prevent these signifiers from functioning in an organic way.

The correlations between the fragility of translatability and the dissemination of literature are indicated in empirical observations that untranslatability potentially inhibits world literature, and thus there arises the renewed necessity to look at the complex notion of rewriting as a manipulatory process concerning translation and the literary fame of the translated text. To start with, world literature results from rewriting national literatures and involves transposition from one cultural context to another for a different readership. Both despite and because of rewriting, national literatures are recreated and reshaped through translation to re-emerge in a different guise. Marked by contacts and intersections, translation is founded on convergences and divergences – in ever varied forms of rewriting, which is generative and innovative in character. How national literatures are rewritten to become integral parts of world literature is riveted on untranslatability, and more significantly, how effectively it is tackled.

Translation is typically blamed for obscuring the artistic value and intention of the original. When Gayatri Chakravorty Spivak, in her *Death of a Discipline* (2003) and other writings, admonishes students of world literature for not learning other languages, she is principally concerned about the essential untranslatability of different political and cultural contexts. Similarly, for Apter, the problem of untranslatability, especially in a cultural sense, is serious enough to undermine any attempt to establish world literature as a valid concept. In this regard, Apter's *Against World Literature* (2013) acts as a somber reminder of the virtual impossibility of translatability and, correspondingly, the impracticality of world literature. From her point of view, the pathological dependence of world literature on translation can only conclusively mean that if the reliability of translation is questionable, the validity of world literature cannot be upheld. Undeniably, linguistic ignorance of the source language is further aggravated by insufficient attention to cultural differences, and the combination of them gravitates towards demoting the diversity of world literature in favor of some sort of universalism. The resultant literary universalism, which sees literatures of different countries as an interrelated one system, will almost certainly nullify world literature as we know it.

World literature tends to be impoverished by lack of transcultural translatability, and because of this, untranslatability has been viewed as a troublesome impediment to world literature. Rebecca Ruth Gould points out, "Untranslatability is in vogue these days, thanks to its promotion as an antidote to the homogenizing excesses of world literature" (Gould 2018: 2). However, instead of diluting or concealing untranslatability, homogenization cannot obscure the deep-rooted demand for proper translation. Apter may seem to argue for the virtual impossibility of world literature by foregrounding untranslatability, which is held decidedly responsible for this lamentable state of world literature. It is true that the assumption of facile translatability is flawed and cannot be consistent. Thus, she poignantly reminds us that incommensurability between languages and cultures must not be underestimated. What she particularly stresses is the real function of translation, and any distorted or diluted form can seriously impair that function. Ultimately, the genetic vulnerability of world literature is demonstrated by translation that fails to render justice to the source text. Whether this argument is seen to be defeatist or realistic depends on how untranslatability is perceived and processed in translation practice in particular situations and contexts.

By implication, Apter is ultimately concerned about the existential and functional irreducibility of translation in relation to world literature. If what originally appears to be different and alien turns out to be diluted or distorted in translation, world literature suffers, sometimes even fatally. The linguistically and culturally ineffable in the target language is most conducive to seeming untranslatability. Because cultural practices and articulation vary markedly, Apter questions "cultural equivalence and substitutability" (Apter 2013: 2). The ideas of equivalence and substitutability involved here are essentially related to irreducibility, without which, as posited by Apter, there is not much point in talking about world literature (Apter 2013: 2). The thinking behind the insistence on complete irreducibility is all-inclusiveness, but complete irreducibility of anything creative is barely possible. Moreover, if absolute irreducibility is prerequisite of translation, then untranslatability will become absolute. Thus, it would be futile to concentrate on the transfer of surface meaning, and for this reason, it is perhaps more meaningful to think of the complexity of translation as irreducible rather than as confined to tackling the practically impossible. It is true that in contemplating the vastness of the concept of world literature, one may fail to give due consideration to irreducibility. But it is also worth noting that an undue emphasis on irreducibility does not help to address untranslatability.

The superficially translatable belies ingrained unsubstitutability, and a diluted translation shows telling signs of untranslatability. As a matter of fact, it is not always easy to know exactly what gets lost in translation. To be all-encompassing in an exhaustively explanatory form as in thick translation invariably destroys the literariness of literary translation. Yet linguistic strangeness and cultural alienation pose serious obstacles to reading world literature in translation. In this connection, however, traditional domestication, which threatens to erase specificity, is not the definitive answer, which explains why the focal point keeps shifting back to untranslatability. For Benjamin, untranslatability refers primarily to linguistic incommensurability and poetic forms without any mention of cultural difference, which further compounds the crucial dimensions of untranslatability. For this reason, literal translation, instead of reducing the sense of strangeness and alienation, creates the possibility of incomprehension, hence the pandemic disapproval of it among translators and readers alike. The language of translation is a somewhat artificial language, and because it can be devoid of naturalness, it needs to be reinvented from time to time to make cross-cultural shareability possible. Against this background, constant efforts are underway to make the target language more flexible and adaptive. As it happens, optimality in translation can also be increased by virtue of finding ways to expand the target language. The truth is that while "absolute equivalence" is out of the question, as argued by Ali Darwish, it is possible "to achieve optimal approximation between the source and target versions of text in terms of utility and appeal" (Darwish 2008: 115). There is no compelling reason to impugn the legitimacy of world literature due to the absence of absolute equivalence and substitutability, the requirement of which would be apparently unreasonable and even unjust.

Mistranslation and failed translation

The bad reputation of translation is usually and rightfully ascribed to inadequacy and unreliability, hence the association with its putative inferiority to the original. However, adequacy is intrinsically at odds with acceptability. Gideon Toury has noted the dichotomy between adequacy and acceptability in discussing translational norms in relation to cultures (Toury 2012: 70). The binary oppositions are an indication of predominance. It is noteworthy that either inadequacy or unacceptability verges on failed translation to a certain extent at least. Translation enables and facilitates the interconnection of different cultural and literary spaces, but these spaces are not easy to reconcile, especially if they seem to be alien to each other. It is therefore only too natural to encounter exempla of failed translation.

What is exactly failed translation then? It has to be said that mistranslation is not always tantamount to failed translation, even if the original is transfigured. There are numerous instances of mistranslation attributable to a multitude of factors, not the least of which is related to the interpretation of the source text. Arguably, there are different or equivocal ways of reading, and misrepresentation in translation may result from different ways of engaging and interpreting the source text. It is axiomatic that mistranslation can be deliberate due to censorship or other causes, ideological, cultural, political, and even aesthetic. Machine translation is notoriously prone to mistranslation, although the technology involved is making impressive progress. An inordinate reliance on machine translation is dangerous in view of its unreliability and uncertainty of references. Some translators feel tempted to make improvements over the original, the reading of which can be skewed by personal preference or inclination. While it is not always easy to discern whether this constitutes mistranslation or misrepresentation, this practice is generally seen as controversial and can be potentially misleading. After all, accuracy and reliability traditionally occupying a central role in the concept of fidelity cannot be altogether disregarded, since this may have a negative impact on the quality and identity of translation. Nonetheless, what is supposed to be good for world literature remains a primordial aspect of translation. It is still impossible to remove the fundamental dichotomy between accuracy and acceptability.

Notwithstanding that mistranslation or misrepresentation in translation is sometimes perceived to compromise world literature, umpteen cases have proved otherwise. Ezra Pound has mistranslated many parts of classical poetry in *Cathay*. In this case, significantly, word-for-word accuracy does not appear desirable. Wai-lim Yip argues that the real problem for translators of classical Chinese poetry is "not so much their ignorance of the Chinese language or text" than through "their failure, as translators, to see the special mode of representation of reality constituted or made possible by the peculiarity of the Chinese language itself" (Yip 1969: 12). The cultural importance of Pound's translated work is significantly greater than semantic accuracy. Similarly, Lin Shu, the most famous translator in the late Qing dynasty, who translated an astonishing array of Western literary works into Chinese, is well-known for producing mistranslations. Like Pound, he had no knowledge of the source language(s). Despite vigorous animadversion being raised against his translation practice, Qian Zhongshu, who had been a research student at Oxford, was acutely aware of the countless errors in Walter Scott's novels in Lin's translation, but still felt most fascinated, and developed a theory of 訛 "error." Indeed, it can be argued that boundless energy can stem from mistranslation. By referring to Lin's translation of Dickens's novels, Qian asserted: "He must feel that Dickens's descriptions are not sufficiently consummate and hard-hitting, hence the necessity to translate in a hyperbolic manner by exaggerating the absurdity of the characters and situations" (Qian 1981: 25). Such is the effect of "erroneous" treatment of the original through Lin's (mis)translation. This type of indirect translation, without direct access to or contact with the source text, proved to be phenomenally successful at the time. Rather surprisingly, to strategically mistranslate for a particular reason or purpose can sometimes perform miracles. From Qian's point of view, there seem to be instances of good mistranslation in Lin's case: paradoxically, mistranslation was his effective mode of communication.

As opposed to faithful but bad translation, the anomalous cases cited earlier are emblematic of semantic and stylistic loss and gain, which typically feature in literary translation. Apart from the translator's personal inclination to improve on the original, more often than not, it is the lack or absence of reproducibility that prompts deviation and variance. Although it can well be said that a poor translation spoils what is interesting and significant in the original and can even tarnish the reputation and influence of the original author, a mistranslation, however, may not always be so damaging. Put another way, a mistranslation is not necessarily a poor translation, which causes the lowering of the literary value of the original, since a mistranslation can sometimes produce the opposite effect. Strictly speaking, any improvement on the original borders on mistranslation. Moreover, there is no denying that "improvement" can be subjective and hard to ascertain. Intimately related to it is gain in translation, which can offset loss with respect to "damage," although improvement is not guaranteed. Moreover, even if gain outweighs loss, the accuracy or reliability of translation is still at stake because of the haphazard nature of gain.

Lack of accuracy is typically found in mistranslation, distortion, and errors of various kinds. Moreover, the extent to which the style of translation is unrelated to its original is a serious concern for Apter. However, it is worth noting that mistranslation should not be simplistically identified as failed translation. It is always possible that something is gained in translation, but if so, is it analogous to mistranslation? It is still distinctly different from failed translation. Admittedly, a simple translation flaw, be it referred to as mistranslation or failed translation, can derail or mislead the target reader from what the author has originally intended.

As a literary icon, Lu Xun published a famous short story in 1921 entitled "归乡" ("My Native Place"). A comparative study of four English translations of the original attests to the fact that different reading experiences can be created. In a sense, these versions were produced in different spaces. Even the title is variously translated as "My Native Heath," "Hometown," and "My Old Home," with the last being shared by two translation versions. Any mistranslation or failed translation? Ironically, a technically failed translation can be regarded as a successful one.

For the sake of exposition, a literal translation is hereby provided: Ah! This could not have been my native place I had remembered for the last 20 years.

1) Ah, this could not be the countryside that had been *constantly in my thoughts* for the past twenty years!

       (Wang Chi-chen 1941; my italics)

2) Ah! Surely this was not the old home I had *remembered* for the past twenty years?

       (Yang Hsien-yi and Gladys Yang 1963; my italics)

3) No! This was not the countryside I had *recalled* time and again for more than twenty years.

       (Lyell 1990; my italics)

4) Was this the place I had *kept nostalgically alive in my thoughts* these past two decades?

       (Lovell 2009; my italics)

I have recently done a little experiment in an MA literary translation course. The students almost unanimously voted for version 4 as their favorite version. Either "remembered" as in version 2 or "recalled" as in version 3 would be undisputedly the right word for "记得" in the original. But they are both somewhat lackluster, even though there is nothing inept about them. Even without referring to the source text, it is not difficult to discern the superiority of version 4. Despite deviating somewhat from a close translation of "remembered" or "recalled," it stands out to the reader, bringing to mind the way in which the narrator reacted to his home journey. Surely this cannot be classified as mistranslation. The given situation warrants an appropriate level of dramatization. Other versions are not cases of failed translation, although they appear to be less successful. These four versions can be considered to be an exemplar of how different translation spaces are played out in relation to authenticity and adequacy. The juxtaposition of different translation versions of one source text brings to prominence several sites of translation production and dissimilar spaces in which these versions were created.

As the previous example suggests, it may well be a simplistic way of looking at translation if it is thought to carry such labels of foreignization and domestication. However, it can still be said that if domestication is prone to mistranslation, foreignization can be attributed to at least one type of failed translation, namely failing to communicate the intended meaning embedded in the source text. Moreover, cultural mistranslation is integrally rooted in cultural misunderstanding and misperception. Therefore, cross-cultural knowledge is of crucial importance, lack of which can easily result in either mistranslation or failed translation. The latter can refer to, in relative terms, inadequate or lackluster translation. More to the point, it is the polysemy of meanings that is most likely to be lost in translation, leading to what is regarded as failed translation. In truth, there is no way to rule out deliberate failure of translation. Moreover, due to the plurality and polysemy of cultural meanings and forms, mistranslation or failed translation is something of an inevitable consequence of attempting to attend to everything at the same time. The practice of creative translation, championed by many translation scholars, may come at the risk of mistranslation as well. In sum, mistranslation can be variously motivated and manifested to different degrees and at manifold levels. Sometimes the politics and poetics of mistranslation are enigmatic and paradoxical and too intertwined to be distinguishable from each other.

Authenticity and reliability

The notion of translational authenticity is irretrievably related to reliability. Authenticity and reliability are the presiding concern of Apter, who presumes that untranslatability is a formidable impediment to successful literary translation. In many ways, notably in reference to culturally distant language pairs, such as English and Chinese, the attempt to establish authenticity can be easily thwarted by untranslatability. The validity or legitimacy of world literature must be bolstered by generic diversity that is ingrained in authenticity; its conceptualization and perception are consistent with a general need for reliability in translation practice. As Apter sees it, "Translation is haunted by the anxiety that it is unoriginal or illicitly appropriated intellectual property" (Apter 2013: 126). Indeed, its unoriginal status signifies that translation is deprived of authenticity. Thus, in the context of translation, it is necessary to delink originality from authenticity. And whether the original is licitly or illicitly appropriated is a different matter; it is sometimes up to the original author to decide. Moreover, the question of ownership is a murky one and depends on how translation is done and can be done, and also on how the nature of the activity is understood. Translation entails rewriting accompanied by an act of repossession and arrogation. This rewriting is often based on interpretations that invariably give rise to variations, which calls for a new understanding of authenticity given the fact that there are various ways of expressing authenticity other than just imitation of the original in all its aspects. Needless to say, if parts of a source text are misinterpreted by the translator, they are not authentically translated. Authenticity can be under threat of appropriation, which subsequently leads to hybridity, and this can only be exacerbated by indeterminacy and subjectivity. Translation is something of a hybrid, and consequently, the language of translation is a somewhat hybridized one.

It is worth pointing out that authenticity is never static and should be viewed as a dynamic process involving cultural integration and hybridization. Authenticity can be under the serious threat of appropriation, which can lead to hybridity, which can be exacerbated by indeterminacy and subjectivity. Even indirect access to the original does not warrant disregard of details, whose meticulous restoration is a credible and reliable testimony to authenticity. After all, cross-cultural reproduction is defined and appropriated by access and configuration, even though appropriation purports to undermine authenticity. In addition, a given cultural attitude determines how translation is perceived. For instance, Chineseness has been jealously guarded and defended by some Chinese scholars, who have displayed little tolerance towards any signs or evidence of domestication that is seen to attenuate the so-called authentic Chineseness when Chinese literature is translated into other languages, particularly English. Domesticating strategies can be broadly categorized as linguistic domestication, cultural domestication, and stylistic domestication for the overarching purpose of reducing alienation and lifelessness. Yet all of these may compromise translational authenticity in one way or another and to one degree or another.

In reality, authentic reproduction is more about reliability in terms of accuracy and adequacy. Yet this is not unproblematic and may indeed be the root cause of failed translation, for systematic search for authenticity compromises translatability or even leads to untranslatability. Moreover, translation necessitates appropriation of native cultures, the result of which is that sometimes the absence or diminishing of authenticity cannot be avoided. This must be a cause for concern, given the possibility of the negative impact of literary globalization (Western-centric) that tends to homogenize or standardize native cultures, thus threatening to diminish or annihilate authenticity that is supposed to represent cultural diversity buttressed by authentic indigenous cultures and literatures. Put differently, if and only if translation is meant to be genuinely representative of national cultures and literatures can cultural and literary diversity be retained when treated as part of world literature.

It is the competing cultural or literary values that provide excitement and motivation towards learning about different experiences. As noted earlier, authenticity is linked to reliability. The target reader wants to read world literature for some sort of authentic cultural values because it is cultural authenticity that brings vitality to world literature. In this connection, authentic representation is of crucial importance and must be addressed seriously. It is cultural authenticity that gives vitality to world literature. However, the notion of authenticity concerning translation must be treated with caution and should be viewed as dynamic rather than static. If one says that national literary texts should be translated in authentic ways, it is not always clear what exactly constitutes authenticity. The challenge or dilemma of authenticity can be attributed to its adaptive or transformative nature. Furthermore, translational authenticity as a contested term is relational and relative. Moreover, the discourse of translational authenticity is capricious with variable referents. One source text may receive multiple translations into the same target language. And it is not always easy to conclude which version is more authentic.

Even appropriated authenticity can still make up and even underscore linguistic and cultural difference to be registered in the target text. In an ultimate sense, authenticity is closely linked to untranslatability, and if anything, can compound the latter. Therefore, translation, especially literary translation, needs more dynamic spaces to transcend cultural boundaries and open up new possibilities. In analyzing two different translation versions, among various others, of one of Bei Dao's poems, "The Answer," David Damrosch praises the "poetic eloquence" of one version, which is also attributed to readability (Damrosch 2003: 23). The other version, however, is blighted by an "unpoetic" stiffness because it "tries to convey an underlying word play in the original" (Damrosch 2003: 23). There seems to be a price to pay when "authentic" translation is attempted. When a given text is variously translated, many possibilities arise for the translator to explore various levels of fullness or effectiveness. There exists an apparent discrepancy between the inherent poetic qualities and literal meaning of the original. The "inferior" version is concerned with reproducing a world play, which is notoriously difficult to translate. But once done, and done properly, it can become generative in conjunction with what something foreign can do, even if a given translation verges on the unpoetic. Authenticity or foreignness does not have to be confined to formal representations so that poetic constraints can be reduced or eliminated. In addition, the shaping or hindering force of the local context can be a defining factor in allowing or disallowing authentic modes of expression in translation.

In the view of Benjamin, literal translation of poetry never works, and a certain amount of creativity is necessary. Simply put, if something is not fully replicable, it must be recreated. In so doing, some deviation from the original meaning or form is unavoidable. Moreover, literariness in poetry translation is given precedence to the content, which recurrently points to the poeticity of language. A significant literary text is a cultural event, often innovative and refreshing, and its cultural singularity must not be treated lightly in translation. Yet the poeticity of language does not come easily in translation. Furthermore, its transfer or recreation may cause some discomfort to the target reader, who is expected to make a certain amount of effort in decoding the poetic message. Lu Xun once championed a commitment to the reader's labor of interpretation in his translation practice: "instead of translating in order to give people 'pleasure,' I often try to make them feel uncomfortable, or even exasperated, furious and bitter" (Lu 1980: 78). This "hard translation" disallows the reader to passively consume a text, with the overt goal of enriching or expanding the Chinese vocabulary and syntax and also of presenting conceptual underpinnings of aesthetic experience. Both linguistic and cultural authenticity is predicated on this translation strategy.

In a practical sense, authenticity is about rewriting in a relatively undistorted form. Some ten years ago, when Gao Ertai was a visiting scholar at the University of Nevada-Vegas (UNLV), he was approached by an editor of Harper Collins to publish his autobiographical novel *In Search of My Homeland*, and subsequently, he signed a publication agreement. However, perhaps due to editorial consideration, the narrative of the text was restructured with certain deletions and additions. Gao found this unacceptable, and he stated: "what I wrote in my own work is not to be found in the translation, which also contains what I did not write in the novel." This was followed by a strongly worded protest: "The so-called deletions are practically tantamount to castration" (Gao 2012). He further remarked:

> I think the life of a work is not in itself, but in the reading of it. A misunderstood work does not exist, just as a work that is no longer read is akin to death. To allow misleading [translations] is almost like a masquerade ball, although I know that a masquerade is good for both fame and money.
>
> (Gao 2012)

The thrust of the previous argument is to underline the value of authenticity, although to claim that a misunderstood work does not get read is unsubstantiated. According to this line of argument, an unreliable work can easily be a misunderstood one. Two related and more central questions are: Is this translation approach good for world literature, and if so, should this text be accepted as such?

Gao's more detailed account of what has happened to his novel after translation sheds light on how the "rearrangement" of certain parts of the story can harm the integrity of the narrative:

> "Drum in the Movie" is about the Anti-Rightist Movement. The story ends with me returning to Lanzhou twenty-one years later and bumping into a meek and acquiescent former colleague, who had followed everyone in backstabbing me. I was invited for a drink in his dorm room on the top floor of his school building. He told me that after I was dealt with (re-education through labor), his wife and child back home died in the Great Leap Forward (and starvation) period. As he was homeless, he still lived in the old school in his old age . . . The scenery outside the building remained the same, with the gloomy cold sun setting in the west silent. This ending is absent in the translation. Without it, there is no historical diversity as reflected in individual experience, no epitome of the fate of "people" other than the "rightists," no contrast between the despondent ending and the

sprightly start, and no structure of tension between comic and tragic inter-woven. What remain [in the translated text] are the political movements that have been repeatedly narrated by thousands of people, which has become a formula. Is it still worth writing about?

(Gao 2012)

The translator, or rather the editor, probably had in mind the expectations of the western reader. But more generally, for multiple audiences who are culturally or ideologically heterogeneous, the authentic representation of otherness is crucial in reflecting different perspectives on the world and on human experiences.

The underlying universal deep structures corresponding with specific narra-tives and references are what is required for a text to be accepted internationally. Thus, to recreate an authentic narration in translation is the common expec-tation. Likewise, how to translate the authenticity of suffering is an emotion-ally charged and culturally sensitive issue. The experiential effect of authenticity needs to be accurately reflected in translation, which cries out for solutions to the problem of irreducibility concerning what has been recorded as part of human misery and suffering. What is missing or deleted, in this case, is precisely what the original author intends to foreground and seek attention. Nevertheless, to avoid reductionism or downright deletion is patently not always possible, even though sometimes necessary.

There is always a potential opposition between authenticity and functional-ity, for cultural authenticity can risk alienation or even hostility. The desire for international recognition may be so overwhelming that indigenous specificity is at stake. Specific cultural signifiers can be treated as dispensable for the sake of easy access and readability. Translation must enable world literature to pro-vide something that can be understood and appreciated internationally. In this regard, Damrosch offers a way of looking at specificity in the original: "To read Bei Dao's poem in English we should be alive to relevant aspects of the context of their production, but we don't finally need the Chinese context in all its par-ticularity" (Damrosch 2003: 22). This disengaged reading strategy attaches less importance to specificity and echoes Moretti's notion of distant reading, which implies that at the end of the day authenticity underpinned by particularity is not of cardinal importance in the transcultural sharing experience. Moreover, because of untranslatability, specificity is subject to change and transformation. Despite Apter's adamant insistence on unsubstitutability, translation forces its way into existence by means of violence, thus compromising authenticity.

Translation provides a new language to house the source content. Whether it works or not may not be determined by authenticity because efforts to preserve it can result in reducing readability or even intelligibility. Since one source text can be variously translated, comparing these different versions reveals the conflict-ing roles of authenticity. "Stylistic losses," in the words of Damrosch, are barely avoidable. (Damrosch 2003: 289) But such losses can be costly in translation for impugning on the full function of the original. In a letter to the review editor of *The Byron Journal* regarding Gilles Soubigou's criticism of his translation into

French of *Manfred, The Prisoner of Chillon* and *The Lament of Tasso*, Davy Pernet has the following to say:

> The quality that I claim for my translations is precisely the reason I did not use Benjamin Laroche's version, which is copyright free. Though it is not the worst, Laroche's translation lacks precision, tending to a Voltarian phraseology which is not Byronic at all. Furthermore, it tends in my view to deaden the verse, systematically destroying images and unique qualities of expression. I thought Byron deserved better.
>
> (Pernet 2009: 170)

A more nuanced understanding of authenticity in translation is clearly needed. If poetry is not translated poetically, authenticity is put at risk. As an intrinsic dimension of translation, especially literary translation, authenticity is not to be disregarded. On the other hand, translation should not be dichotomized as either authenticity or inauthenticity.

Literary value through translation

Literary value defies definition or even description and has proved to be very elusive and intangible. But it can be noted that its absence in translation diminishes literature's dynamism to be accepted as world literature. Losing much of literary value through translation is a price that the literary translator can ill-afford to pay and is mainly responsible for poor reception and appreciation. The devaluing of translated literature is common when compared with the original, which explains why it occupies a peripheral position. Moreover, the translator is torn by what seem to be conflicting demands when it comes to literary translation, particularly the translation of poetry. As early as 1921, Amy Lowell lamented: "Chinese is so difficult that it is a life-work in itself; so is the study of poetry. A Sinologue has no time to learn how to write poetry; a poet has no time to learn how to read Chinese"; in 1958, George Kennedy, referring to Ezra Pound, commented: "Undoubtedly this is fine poetry. Undoubtedly it is bad translation"; drawing a distinction between the "poet-translator" and "critic-translator" (Quoted by Lucas Klein 2014: 57). Paradoxically, this is somewhat akin to suggesting that even if you want to be a good translator, you may well end up producing bad translations.

How to avoid bad translations is an enduring conundrum. It has been stated by Anna Sun that "[t]he language of Mo Yan is repetitive, predictable, coarse, and mostly devoid of aesthetic value" (Sun 2012). If the scathing attack can be justified, how is the translator supposed to react? The language of Shakespeare can also be said to be coarse in certain places. Does this give the translator the right to alter or delete "repetitive" or "predictable" parts? To start with, repetition can be a part of rhetoric and is thus completely different from redundancy. Predictability is often seen as a demerit. But even so, does it deserve retention in translation? Predictable to whom? If it is to the source text reader, it may not be so to the target reader. This is the abstruse and esoteric part of translation or mis-translation. Besides, what exactly constitutes "aesthetic value" is a transcultural conundrum. Setting out to improve on the source text often leads to domestica-tion, which easily lapses into mistranslation: as it fails to capture or represent the intended meaning or rather, effect in the source text.

The literary success of one work may not be repeated in translation. Instead of creating an after-life, translation can put an end to the life of the original. In a related vein, since inauthenticity and untranslatability are bona fide reasons for the doubt on world literature, the concept of cosmopolitan translation is of paramount relevance here. In the context of cultural globalization, for a text to win international recognition and appreciation, translation is squarely con-fronted with asymmetrical modes of cultural exchange. It is increasingly clear that a reduced multiplicity impairs diversity, defying the gnawing essence of world lit-erature. The simultaneously local and cosmopolitan character of world literature is the very embodiment of what cosmopolitan translation can offer. In translating world literature, the translator cannot take lightly the irreducible other, which helps protect and foster diversity. It can be said that, without diversity, world lit-erature would lose its legitimacy and eventually be "confined to the Anglophone realm" (D'haen 2012: 144), and if devoid of the claim to universality of narra-tion, the so-called world literature is unlikely to be recognized as representing the world literary practice. Undeniably, international appreciation and publicity of the widest possible range of national literatures are indispensable prerequisites for there to be world literature.

As has been repeatedly argued, the very existence of world literature depends on translation, and the presumed impossibility of world literature is inextricably bound up with the inherent impossibility of translation. If translatability is in doubt, universality is out of the question. It is unmistakably true that transla-tion entails transformation, but transformation is such a complex concept and should not be treated in a homogenizing manner. As such, translated literature as the prerequisite and underpinning of world literature must attest to hetero-geneity and diversity, whereas translation is very prone to erasing multiple local and national differences. By contrast, foreignization strategy in translation rec-ognizes and celebrates difference that paradigmatically represents foreignness in the source text. However, as we all know, rigid or uncompromising adherence to foreignization strategy would render translation barely communicative, which ultimately precludes the possibility of world literature. It is therefore essential to find an optimal balance between manifesting foreignness and aiming at intel-ligibility and readability. In sum, world literature requires translation to provide the basis for greater appreciation of great literatures all over the world. How is it possible to do so? The notion of cosmopolitan translation may be an answer.

We may consider the possibility of creating a unified perspective on world cul-ture. It can be argued that if there is such a thing as one world culture, it must logically be a unified one, which is substantially different from a homogenized culture. Such an assumption, however, is probably too simple and generalized, given that, although it is singularly convenient, the view can be bedeviled by the heightened awareness of untranslatability. In a discussion of Virginia Woolf and her reception in Sweden, Catherine Sandbach-Dahlstrom points to the cultural identity of the target reader:

> The reader from a different country will, of course, always already be an Outsider displaced from the type of understanding that characterizes a national interpretive community. In other words, lacking the kind of cultural coding engendered by class and national affiliation, certain aspects of Woolf's life and writing may be opaque to them.
>
> (Sandbach-Dahlstrom 2002: 148–164)

As cultural outsiders, it is not uncommon that the target reader is denied complete access to certain parts of the translated text or the source text. Despite the underlying commonality, the displacement caused by reading a culturally unfamiliar text can be significant enough to alienate the target reader who does not belong to the appropriate "interpretive community." We should be reminded that it is for this community that the text is written in the first place.

In many respects, the resultant cross-cultural implications are manifold. If basic comprehension is equivocal, the inherent literary value will almost certainly elude the target reader. A central question to be explored here is literary value in this transcultural context concerning translation. It is thus vital to cultivate a cosmopolitan literary culture by clearly illustrating the manifold interconnections of transcultural references. Moreover, these references are not exactly insurmountable obstacles to communication. A literary text is about a part of the world, which can be shared and indirectly experienced through translation. In the view of Mazhar Hayat, "Works of world literature have immense potential to outlive historical and cultural boundaries of their local frames of reference to pave way for international literary culture" (Hayat 2016: 16). The unquestioning acceptance of untranslatability means acknowledging the impossibility of knowing others. It should be said that since nothing is completely untranslatable, it is still possible to know something about others. Local and global, as well as specific and universal, are intertwined and to some extent inseparable, in the process of cross-cultural encounter and hybridization, the result of which can widen international appreciation

Still, how can aesthetic pleasure that is taken to be sharable and derived from reading translated literary texts find a true channel in translation? What exactly constitutes the so-called literary merit of a translation? These are related to the consideration of the formation of world literature. To create an equivalent or comparable literary value in translation by exhibiting the universal character of the original is key to the success of a translation. The legendary translation practice of the late Qing translator Lin Shu is a case in point:

> The Chinese translation of Scott's *Ivanhoe* by Lin Shu was treated and transformed in such a way that is unacceptable from today's point of view. Since it [this practice] is taken as a historical occurrence, there is no need to get

into it. Yet looking at it from a different angle, even though this translation suffers from the defect of "unfaithfulness," his deep literary knowledge made it a great artistic accomplishment.

(Han 2006: 24)

When editing this translation, Mao Dun specifically pointed out that this translation was "staggeringly varied and beautiful, more or less matching the original style" (Mao 1981: 199). In terms of aesthetic judgment, the role of the translator's subjectivity is pivotal in determining the appeal and quality of the translated text. In general, the goal of translation is to maximize the value of great literature, which deserves proper representation in a different cultural setting. It is noteworthy that it is entirely possible to be semantically unfaithful yet stylistically faithful, especially in the case of reproducing references and allusions across cultures, just as accuracy or authenticity can be achieved at the expense of literary value.

But aesthetic interest in and curiosity about otherness and its various life experiences can be blurred by poor translations. Literature is both contemporary and enduring (historical), and both local and international (cosmopolitan) and literary value is concrete and uncannily universal. As observed by Stephen Owen, "The most interesting aspect of the Nobel Prize for literature, however, is that it is commonly given for literature in translation" (Owen 1990: 28). He further asserts: "When the Nobel Prize is awarded to a poet, the success of that poet's work in translation is inevitably an important, perhaps even a deciding, factor" (Owen 1990: 28). While literary value may not be directly linked to readability, unreadability can vitiate literary value, and since translation can easily lead to unreadability, it is necessary to focus directly on what makes translation unreadable and then on what can be done to make it less unreadable or even readable. On the other hand, what seems to be alien, thus perhaps unreadable, can also be resplendently exotic, the concomitant unreadability becoming to be acceptable and even attractive to the target reader. It is new modes of expression engendered by translation that enrich and expand the target language. The truth is that many new modes of expression are invented out of necessity as the translator struggles to find a way out of untranslatability; or something just comes out "naturally" as an unnatural language associated with translation. Or innate strangeness embedded in the original is displayed as new modes of expression. Also, even a mild violation of the norms of the target language contributes no less significantly to the appeal of the language of translation.

Conclusion

World literature is intimately linked with acceptability as governed by transcultural understanding and appreciation, and it must circulate beyond a national audience to win international recognition. It reinforces the trotted-out truism that this circulation, to a large extent, is activated and facilitated by translation. As an important part of international cultural exchange, the canon of world literature is repeatedly subject to renewal, change, and expansion. Local traditions from around the world and global influences on them, as characterized by convergences and divergences, bring together and reconcile local and global perspectives, which should be genuinely complementary to each other. Consequently, a new sense of cultural belonging or identity is developed in shaping and reshaping world literature, thereby rendering the situation of world literature seemingly untenable and indefensible. So far scholars have mainly focused on the role of translation in making world literature possible, but how exactly that role is played in terms of translation requires more investigation. At the heart of transcultural experience is whether acceptability can be extended beyond national boundaries, despite untranslatability or lack of translatability. For international circulation, literary untranslatability canvassed by Benjamin has continued to evince an overriding concern. Closely related to it is cultural translatability in the current context of globalization. World literature is afflicted by not only cultural untranslatability, but also literary untranslatability, and their combination increases the difficulty of transcultural negotiation, involving many nearly insuperable difficulties.

Curiously enough, literary translation has been systematically undervalued and undertheorized about world literature. This general lack of attention to and recognition of the central importance of translation is unfortunately prevalent, which is potentially inimical to international circulation and thus causes profound repercussions to the development of world literature. Given this concern, the limits of translatability must be fully understood, and the challenge involved confronted unremittingly. Among other things, the distinction between local readability and global readability is an inescapable consideration in translating world literature. Translatability is intrinsically related to the possible reproducibility of the original meaning. The aesthetic of authenticity has provoked further thinking on the nature of transcultural communication. Artificially constructed signifiers as a result of translation may indeed compromise the reading experience of the target reader, and for this reason, it is critically important to promote sustained engagement with the source text, which will then benefit from effective and dynamic translation. Regarding cross-cultural translation, it remains meaningful to underlie the concept of authenticity. After all, it is a genuine world literature rather than a spurious one that can create enduring value. Reductive as it may be, translation plays an indispensable role in making world literature viable, and by providing an effective perspective for understanding how that role is or can be played, it becomes possible to move from a mono-cultural to a cross-cultural perspective so as to increase the "shareability" of a foreign text as part of the endeavor for international canonization. It is also important to transcend the confining spaces of related disciplines with their perceptions and practices to work out a multi-dimensional approach to problems encountered in translating and understanding world literature.

References

Apter, Emily S. (2013) *Against World Literature: On the Politics of Untranslatability*, London and New York: Verso.

Bassnett, Susan (2019) *Translation and World Literature*, London and New York: Routledge.

Bertacco, Simona (2016) "An Interview with Emily Apter," *The New Centennial Review* 16(1): 9–27.

Damrosch, David (2003) *What Is World Literature?* Princeton: Princeton University Press.

Damrosch, David (2014) "Review of *Against World Literature: On the Politics of Untranslatability*," *Comparative Literature Studies* 51(3): 504–508.

Darwish, Ali (2008) *Optimality in Translation*, Patterson Lakes, Vic.: Writescope Pty Ltd.

Derrida, Jacques (ed. and trans. by Joseph F. Graham) (1985) "Des Tours de Babel," in *Difference in Translation*, Ithaca, NY: Cornell University Press.

D'haen, Theo (2012) *The Routledge Concise History of World Literature*, London and New York: Routledge.

Gao, Ertai (2012) "文盲的悲哀 – 《寻找家园》译事琐记" (An Illiterate's Regret–On the Translation of *In Search of My Homeland*),《财新新世纪周刊》(*Caixin New Century Weekly*) 525: http://magazine.caixin.com/2012-11-02/100455577.html.

Gould, Rebeca Ruth (2018) "Hard Translation: Persian Poetry and Post-National Literary Form," *Forum for Modern Language Studies* 54(2): 191–206.

Han, Hongju (2006) "《撒克逊劫后英雄略》的文学价值和影响" (Literary Value and Influence of *Ivanhoe*),《浙江师范大学学报 (社会科学版)》(*Journal of Zhejiang Normal University [Social Sciences Edition]*) 31(5): 23–27.

Harrison, Nicholas (2014) "World Literature: What Gets Lost in Translation?" *The Journal of Commonwealth Literature* 49(3): 411–426.

Hayat, Mazhar (2016) "Conflict between Internationalist Cultural Exchange and Market Realism in World Literature," *NUML Journal of Critical Inquiry* 14(1): 16–30.

Klein, Lucas (2016) "Review: Addressed and Redressed: World Literature and Reading Contemporary Poetry in Translation," *Comparative Literature Studies* 53(3): 611–616.

Lovell, Julia (trans.) (2009) *The Real Story of Ah-Q and Other Tales of China: The Complete Fiction of Lu Xun*, London and New York: Penguin.

Lu, Xun (trans. by Yang Xianyi and Gladys Yang) (1980) *Lu Xun: Selected Works*, Beijing: Foreign Languages Press.

Lyell, William (trans.) (1990) *Lu Xun: Diary of a Madman and Other Stories*, Honolulu: University of Hawai'i Press.

Mao, Dun (1981)《我走过的路》(*The Way I Have Walked Through*), Beijing: People's Literature Press.

Moretti, Franco (2000) "Conjectures on World Literature," *New Left Review* 1(January–February): 54–68.

Newmark, Peter (1989) *The Translator's Notebook*, London: Aslib.

Owen, Stephen (1990) "What Is World Poetry?" *The New Republic* (November 19): 28–32.

Parks, Tim (2010) "Why Translators Deserve Some Credit," *The Observer*, April 25.

Pernet, Davy (2009) "Letter to the Reviews Editor," *The Byron Journal* 37(2): 170.

Qian, Zhongshu (1981) "林纾的翻译" (Lin Shu's Translation), in Qian Zhongshu et al. (eds.)《林纾的翻译》(*Lin Shu's Translation*), Beijing: Commercial Press, 18–52.

Sandbach-Dahlstrom, Catherine (2002) "'Literature Is No One's Private Ground': The Critical and Political Reception of Virginia Woolf in Sweden," in Mary Ann

Caws and Nicola Luckhurst (eds.) *The Reception of Virginia Woolf in Europe*, London and New York: Continuum, 148–164.

Shields, Kathleen (2013) "Challenges and Possibilities for World Literature, Global Literature, and Translation," *CLCWeb: Comparative Literature and Culture* 15(7): http://dx.doi.org/10.7771/1481-4374.2381.

Spivak, Gayatri Chakravorty (2003) *Death of a Discipline*, New York: Columbia University Press.

Sun, Anna (2012) "The Diseased Language of Mo Yan," *Kenyon Review* (Fall): https://kenyonreview.org/kr-online-issue/2012-fall/selections/anna-sun-656342/.

Toury, Gideon (2012) *Descriptive Translation Studies and beyond*, Amsterdam and Philadelphia: John Benjamins Publishing.

Trivedi, Harish (2019) "Translation and World Literature: the Indian Context," in Susan Bassnett (ed.), *Translation and World Literature*, London and New York: Routledge, 15–28.

Walkowitz, Rebecca L. (2015) *Born Translated: The Contemporary Novel in an Age of World Literature*, New York: Columbia University Press.

Wang, Chi-chen (trans.) (1941) *Ah Q and Others: Selected Stories of Lusin (Chou Shu-jen)*, New York: Books for Libraries Press.

Yang, Hsien-yi, and Gladys Yang (trans.) (1963) *Selected Stories of Lu Hsun*, 2nd ed., Beijing: Foreign Languages Press.

Yip, Wai-lim (1969) *Ezra Pound's Cathay*, Princeton, NJ: Princeton University Press.

5 Spatial translatability

Introduction

Translatability is as old as translation itself and also at the very foundation of the possibility of translation. The concept is a well-trodden ground but still remains central to Translation Studies and beyond. Translatability is reputed to be haunted by the apparition of untranslatability, which stipulates and defines the limits of translatability. In practical terms, the main task for translators is to identity translatability and be aware of its limits and then develop appropriate strategies concerning what works best to expand such limits. Whether something can be translated or not depends on a host of factors, the most important of which is no doubt meaning. But meaning in different cultural discourses is problematized. The act of translation entails the interpretation of meaning, which is then to be produced in the target language. One may argue that if something is interpretable, it is translatable. An interpretative space gives rise to the necessary space(s) for translation. However, to be sure, translation is much more complicated than the transfer of meaning, and it is also concerned with the transfer of form. Meanwhile, the question of the transferability needs to be explored because it is not something that can be taken for granted in relation to translatability. If translation is acknowledged as possible, translatability is inherently implied.

A historical overview

Translation theorists and practitioners alike have long been tormented by untranslatability while searching for optimal translatability. The possibility of translation has much to do with the inherent translatability or the degree of translatability. There is of course no such thing as absolute translatability, and thus the success of translation is not defined by its translatability but the degree of its translatability. It is safe to say the translation is predicated on various degrees of translatability, and at the same time hampered by various degrees of untranslatability across and within multiple linguistic, historical, and cultural spaces. Despite the presumed optimism about translatability, untranslatability has been a perennial concern of translators, primarily due to lack of freedom, which characteristically underlines translation. Frustrated by and in recognition to untranslatability, over the centuries, people have discussed different types of translation, including loose or rough translation or explanatory translation, all of which can be viewed as attempts and efforts to overcome the otherwise untranslatable.

Untranslatability suggests the impossibility of translation, or adequate translation. The continuous divide between translatability and untranslatability has a constant source of tension and anxiety. Kum raj va, who contributed to Buddhism and Buddhist philology, was not entirely sanguine about translatability and offered his observation: "To translate the [sic.] Sanskrit into Chinese is to lose the style of the original. Though the message can be conveyed, the effect might be of a quite separated style. It is like chewing tasteless rice which grosses [sic.] people out" (Quoted by Cao 2014: 110). But Kum raj va was "known for his heavy excision of the source" (Cheung and Lin 2014: 95). Multiple reasons can be postulated, one of which may well be out of stylistic consideration, to explain the apparent contraction of the space as compared with that of the original. In reality, translatability has always been met with demurral. And a reluctance to embrace translatability takes many forms, and it has always been difficult to look beyond the simple dichotomy between translatability and untranslatability.

It has to be pointed out that both translatability and untranslatability can be and are indeed understood differently during different historical periods and in different cultural settings and by different groups of people with different perspectives. Since the eighteenth century in Europe, untranslatability has been the focus of debate. In China, discussions about untranslatability have continued, albeit intermittently, since Buddhist translation in the third century. In view of the fact that people of different periods perceive translation differently, different approaches to translation problems have been explored, and not surprisingly, the effectiveness of such approaches is evaluated somewhat differently. Fully aware of the problem of untranslatability, Schleiermacher proposes a solution in the form of what appears to be a fundamental dichotomy: "either the translator leaves the author in peace, as much as possible, and moves the reader towards him; or he leaves the reader in peace, as much as possible, and moves the author towards him" (Quoted by Lefevere 1977: 74). In response to the intrinsically untranslatable nature of literary translation, Schleiermacher solicitously ponders the best way to secure translatability without forcing a conclusion, although his predilection is clear enough in light of his cultural strategy at the time.

In "The Task of the Translator," Walter Benjamin speaks of producing "the echo of the original" in the translated text (Benjamin 1969: 258), which in a sense connotes dynamic translatability. This can be construed as a way to achieve translatability by freeing translation from the constraints placed by the so-called need to adhere too closely to the original. J. C. Catford investigates the nature of linguistic and cultural untranslatability and discusses them in relative terms. Without specifically addressing translatability, Gramsci sheds light on its restrictive nature: "translatability is not 'perfect' in every respect, even in important ones (but what language is exactly translatable into another? what single word is exactly translatable into another language?), but it is so in its basic essentials" (Gramsci 1995: 309). In any event, the possibility of overcoming untranslatability is a positive sign that the otherwise stringent limits of translatability can be expanded to varying extents.

How the limits of translatability can be expanded has been the consideration of translators. An increasing number of approaches have been brought to bear on taking more perspectives into account. To a large extent, more perspectives denote more translational spaces. Increasing global interconnectedness has generated a higher demand for the quality of translation in terms of both adequacy and readability. On this account, dynamic resourcefulness in making translation possible and effective is in dire need of being enhanced.

When a translation problem arises, the initial response is normally to search and obtain an equivalent or comparable space, which tends to limit the underlying translatability. Under spatial restrictions, it is difficult to overcome untranslatability. Yet if a different space is configured where such restrictions are not present or severe, there is a chance to enable translation to function. Once the equivalent or comparable space is transcended through performative engagement with what essentially needs to be dealt with, it becomes possible to demystify and evade the potential impasse of unstable translation. All this explains why the traditional prescriptive approach to translation is infelicitous and can even be misguided.

Critical issues and topics

In response to the inept prescriptive approach, descriptive translation studies was developed in the 1980s and has since been influential in recent decades, with a firm emphasis on the target system. Its target-oriented approach to translation means that less importance is attached to any detailed comparison between the source and target texts, and since the focal point has shifted to translational norms, it seems that the relevance of translatability has diminished if not vanished altogether. Translational norms, it seems to be, are products of the social and cultural spatial environment. As a result, at least in a relative sense, translation becomes untrammeled and free of the constraints of adhering tightly to equivalence. In a nutshell, the common concern is whether the translated text functions in the target system. And translational norms are primarily related to the target language rather than the source language. It seems that equivalence and faithfulness have been forced out of the central concern, together with the original spatial entanglement. Nevertheless, the endurance and continued relevance of translatability can barely be annulled and as such, concern and engagement with the concept of translatability have persisted: it has proved to be impossible to circumvent untranslatability altogether. The centrality of translatability to the possibility or success of translation makes it essential to revisit the concept in the current context of globalization, in which intercultural communication has become increasingly more prevalent, thus rendering it a more relevant topic for the modern world.

Even if a text is presented and regarded as translation, it does not mean that focusing exclusively on the target text is enough. The epistemological assumptions of translatability have not changed in any substantive way: it remains an overriding concern for translation is under explicit threat of unintelligibility or a lower degree of translatability. Equivalence and faithfulness have seriously strained the concept of translatability, while in many ways translatability depends on the availability of equivalence, whose absence or notable lack leads to, as is commonly held, untranslatability. But it is a far cry from truth. Translatability is not static with readily available equivalents but concerned with a performative potential as a means to create space to explore possibilities. The whole process is a matter of contingency. By the same token, it should be said that untranslatability is never fixed but only temporal or situational.

Derrida's assertion that translation is both necessary and impossible (2001: 170–172) virtually signals the impossibility of exact or full translation, and a certain level of tolerance of partial translation should be considered in light of the varieties of interaction between two languages and cultures. Translation functions at different levels, and some levels are more irreducible than others. So sometimes we can only talk about the selectively translatable as well as partially translatable, depending on the particular level(s) at which translation can be performed in a practical way. This is a common translation strategy of singling out the most important parts that are thought to be part of the essential quality of the original. The functionalist approach to translation, for instance, has greatly expanded the notion of translatability by moving well beyond its normal limits and also by minimizing its dominance in considering ways of what might work to match the original. In truth, the functionalist approach to translation is not so interested in seeking to grasp the perceived commonality between the two cultures involved in translation.

It appears that translating inadequately is not uncommon, reflective of how translation is defined by Derrida: both necessary and impossible. Of course, the impossibility of translation is accepted only in absolute terms. Inasmuch as translatability and untranslatability are and can only be relative, the dichotomy between them is often false. Still, translatability cannot be meaningfully discussed without reference to untranslatability, which requires an attempt to bring to light the supposed opposition between translatability and untranslatability, and the related space between universalism and relativism by examining the changes in the awareness and perception of the limits and also elasticity of translatability. How to go beyond the limits of translatability concerning denotation, sense, and reference, among other factors, remains the key determinant of whether translation should be properly theorized and understood. The modern Chinese almost excessive preoccupation with authenticity in translation has further challenged the limits of translatability as a contextualized cultural practice, thus drawing attention to different degrees and types of translatability. The nature of the reality of translatability and untranslatability is such that it calls for the development of heightened understanding and awareness of them as interactive and relative and can also be seen as interrelated and presupposing each other.

Failing to understand the nature of untranslatability would make it impossible to entertain the possibility of translation. Meanwhile, it is also useful to develop a heightened awareness of the limits of translatability. Numerous lexical gaps and cultural lacunas need to be filled, although it is known that this is not always possible. In a letter to A. W. Schlegel, Wilhelm von Humboldt makes it quite clear: "All translation seems to me simply an attempt to solve an impossible task" (Quoted by Wilss 1982: 35). In other words, all translations are apparent attempts at finding solutions to some insoluble problems. Various problem-focused coping strategies have been developed to stretch the limits of translatability, including semantic extension, paraphrase, and creating neologisms when such needs arise. It can thus be said that the assumed commensurability might not necessarily be a vital precondition for translatability. In short, if a translation is done in a somewhat loose rather than strict way, translatability increases correspondingly.

Translatability is intrinsically concerned with accessibility and shareability. It is known that lack of cultural proximity debilitates translatability, and translation veers disconcertingly between cultural proximity and cultural distance. A certain commonality between the source and target texts is to be embraced because it enables translation to be functionally operational. To varying degrees, the interconnectivity and commonality can be presupposed, and it seems that the unintentional assumption of commonality tends to erase the fundamental cultural differences. Cultural universalists may argue that cultural experience can be widely shared, but universal translatability is illusory, and commonality cannot possibly avoid the reality of untranslatability. The translator agonizes over cultural universals and particulars in assessing whether the shareability conditions are favorable. Given that one of the tasks of translation is to create a shareable cross-cultural experience, the translator must take into account the response of the target reader, which effectively means that translatability has to include cross-cultural readability with a view to ensuring acceptability. Intelligibility is a precondition to comprehensibility, which in turn should also be a precondition to readability, all of which may create different dimensions of translatability.

Moreover, the process of meaning being produced and reproduced in cross-cultural communication introduces contingency and uncertainty. For this reason, the distinction between universals and particulars needs to be made all the time to discern what is realistically shareable and what is not. The presence of constraints on the sharing of cultural knowledge and reading experience reveals the vulnerability of translatability. It is therefore important to evaluate the effects of different levels of commonality and universality in relation to recontextualization, which provides somewhat different contextual frames of reference and focuses predominantly on reinterpretation to provide the desired translation. This is a crucial process of selecting and filtering in overcoming translation difficulties, and perhaps also in employing self-censorship. What gets translated and what gets untranslated shows what is valued and what is perceived to be less important.

It can perhaps be argued that literalness is the ultimate manifestation of translatability. However, not much is directly transferable in translation, which requires a modification of many aspects of the source text, including its formal features. The literal transfer tests the limits of translatability, and if no appropriation is made, translation rarely works in real situations. Transferability means that something is literally translatable without the need to change the literal wording in the original. The absence or impossibility of transferability calls for appropriation strategies in order to promote translatability. Translation, particularly in a cross-cultural sense, must necessarily be an act of appropriation, although sometimes there seems to be a thin line between adaptation, reinvention, and appropriation in terms of making adjustments, major or minor, as required by the actual situation, to make translation possible. Typically, when untranslatability is difficult to negotiate, indirect translation is proposed as an alternative strategy (Newmark 1998: 17). Likewise, to make translation manageable, appropriation is the effort to make modifications, adjustments, and alternatives. At the same time, to avoid overtly radical acculturation cause undue damage to the source text, painstaking negotiations are in order. More specifically, being able to translate cultural references is an essential prerequisite for cross-cultural communication. And if no serious attempts are made to capture or reproduce to some extent cultural references, including explicit and implicit intertextual ones, the cross-cultural experience of reading translations will be seriously compromised.

Although cultural references are notoriously difficult to translate, they are, without any doubt, of particular importance, since they influence sense and comprehension, as well as aesthetic complexity and appreciation. Thus, the probing of the dual limits of intelligibility and referentiality is the most challenging aspect of translation. Perhaps for simplicity's sake, translation tends to obscure the recognition of intertextual references. The underlying reason rests on the apprehension that intelligibility may be compromised as a result of interactions between cultures. This can be understood as cultural references being extensively transformed in the translated text. The functionally similar approach is common enough to functionally substitute the potentially untranslatable references or allusions. In general, the specificity of a particular culture embedded in the original cannot be reproduced in translation without generating awareness of and concern about translatability in terms of functionality. Translational endeavors include appropriating intertextual references and allusions, which are otherwise beyond the knowledge scope of the target reader.

Metaphor translation poses a similar challenge, which also makes it necessary to foreground and explore what is common and sharable but more importantly, to address the lack of translatability when referents turn out to be alienating. It is plain that metaphors and puns, if they are to be exactly translated, blatantly resist translatability. Douglas Robinson, reviewing the strict practice of translation in ancient Rome, revisits the traditional definition of translation: "If 'translation' is defined narrowly as the exact rendition of everything in the source text, including meaning, syntax, and mood, then translation itself becomes impossible" (Robinson 2001: 15). In modern times, perhaps no one would define translation in such an unrealistic way because it would surely guarantee absolute impossibility. The translator cannot be and is indeed no longer expected to stick slavishly to the original. Strict literalism is a sure recipe for untranslatability, for its inevitable outcome is inaccessibility. Nevertheless, we may consider Ali Darwish's definition of translatability as "the degree or extent to which the translation of a text is possible without loss of meaning and with relative ease" (Darwish 2010: 75). "Without loss of meaning" may seem misleading and unhelpful for the purpose of making translation operational. But once again, this is meant to be achievable only in relative terms. It is just possible to aim at translating a text without significant loss of meaning. Many factors can contribute to the loss of meaning and other rhetorical effects, including syntactical features, and mood in translation. There is no denying that something is always lost in translation in the transnational circulation of cultural knowledge and products.

If immediate translatability is not on the horizon, the translator explores the possibility of translation, and the primary task is to avoid or reduce the loss of meaning. Often, the struggle to transform what is untranslatable into what is translatable shows the strenuous efforts to overcome translation difficulties. A notable example involves the translatability of metaphoric expressions and puns that are intertextually oriented and connected to the cultural sources of the original. Attempts to translate intertextual allusions demonstrate paradigmatically what is functionally translatable. As long as what is roughly translatable or not exactly translatable is acceptable, translatability becomes a realistic possibility. In the words of Kristie Lyn Miller, the "explanatorily equivalent" can be an ultimate "panacea" that can compensate for missing information (Miller 2007: 18). Contextual information helps increase translatability or reduce untranslatability since many culturally loaded or specific items in the original are casually inaccessible to the target reader.

Current contributions and research

As indicated earlier, translatability feeds on commonality and shared perceptions of the world but is complicated by difference as embodied in diverse perspectives on and approaches to translation. Many of the problems derive from the underlying incommensurability that divides source and target cultures and results in non-translatability. But incommensurability is only partially responsible for lack of translatability, and as long as the sameness between the source and target texts is not unrealistically presupposed, incommensurability can be addressed in a different light. But what cannot be denied is that incommensurability is conducive to loss of meaning and is usually perceived as a threat to translatability. Moreover, the difficulty of translatability lies in the supposed irreducibility. The irreducible plurality inherent in the original may defy translatability, but if difference, depending on its exact nature, is not considered to be strictly irreducible, there is a chance for translatability to emerge.

Translatability is predicated upon allowing for flexibility and adjustability of the available linguistic and cultural resources. The problem is that apart from semantic accuracy and relative completeness, the essentially irreducible strangeness inherent in the source text poses a serious challenge to translatability. The irreducibility is at the core of many cases of untranslatability. But irreducibility is not absolute either, metaphors, for instance, are not irreducible in practical terms, and at least they are substitutable and can indeed be simplified to a certain extent.

In general, the irreducibility of underlying difference needs to be reasserted from time to time. And the immediate task for the translator is to balance between singularity and generality, in view of the fact that they are not necessarily mutually exclusive. The limits of translatability are further tested by not only cultural codes in different languages but also, more broadly, different systems of social and cultural signification.

The necessity of translating the untranslatable urges efforts to increase translatability. To loosen the otherwise rigid demarcation between translatability and untranslatability is part of the quotidian reality: a necessity for the translator. A simple and practical way to deal with untranslatability is to translate meaning on the grounds that if something is interpretable, it is translatable. But inevitably, it is also a simplified way, and as a result, not always entirely acceptable. A semantic approach to translation simplifies the problem of untranslatability: just to translate meaning based on interpretation made by the translator with total disregard of the form and other cultural or aesthetic features of the original is not considered to be adequate, particularly in terms of cross-cultural communication. Translating meaning only seems to indicate a propensity to eschew cultural difference manifest in formal features. Many such features are culture-bound, thereby making the task of preserving them arduously difficult. Additionally, it can be said that even if something is interpretable, it may remain untranslatable, particularly with regard to cultural forms and performances.

Given that untranslatability is not absolute or final, it can be converted or transformed into translatability. On the other hand, since translatability is not absolute either, what appears to be translatable at first glance may turn out to be not exactly translatable or even close to untranslatable. In view of this, Antoine Berman may be a bit too optimistic about linguistic translatability:

> Languages are translatable, even though the space of translatability is loaded with the untranslatable. Linguistic untranslatability lies in the fact that all languages are different from each other, linguistic translatability in the fact that they are all language. From which it follows that, in this domain, translatability and untranslatability remain relative notions.
>
> (Berman 1992: 126)

He then hastens to point out that "literary translatability," which can be understood as being akin to cultural translatability, is much more difficult to achieve. Since the cultural turn in Translation Studies in the 1980s, cultural untranslatability as posited by Catford has come to the fore once again. Evaluating cultural similarities and differences plays a crucial role in creating translatability by making transmogrifications of the original. The complex interconnections between different linguistic and cultural systems must be explored thoroughly in order to illuminate how translatability is determined by culture.

The absence of cultural translatability brings about cultural concealment. To overcome barriers to translation and improve the chance for the target reader to understand as much of the source content as possible, it is another way to make what seems to be untranslatable into the indirectly translatable. The fact that the absence of cultural translatability is heeded indicates that a certain amount of attention is drawn to the source text. This does not have to be a consequence of source-orientedness but out of the impulse to avoid jeopardizing the credibility of translation. The reproduction of idiomaticity and word-play in translation relies on substitution since a literal rendition normally does not work. But the use of substitution reveals culturally vulnerable moments at which cultural references, allusions, connotation, and significance are often no longer the same because cultural contexts and unspecified values are different. Thus, the question is whether substitution is functionally effective. Substitution encompasses lexical creation, omission, addition, and, invariably, transformation, all of which are conducive to but may at the same time also compromise translatability. Nevertheless, if equivalence cannot be established, the use of substitutable resources in the target language becomes critically important. Many varieties and different degrees of substitutability allow for the possibility of dynamic translatability.

Dynamic translatability is deeply entrenched in the interplay between meaning and expression. In relative terms, meaning is more translatable than expression. It is the latter, namely the reproduction of the stylistic features of the source text, which adds another distinct dimension to translatability. However, substitution seems to problematize the attempts to translate more than just meaning. Lin Yutang once said: "The most important thing about translating literary texts is to achieve a balance between the style and content of the original. Not only should attention be directed to what is said, but also to how it is said" (Lin 1985: 31). How is it possible to reproduce in translation how "it is said" in the original? Domestication commonly disregards how "it is said" in the original and, instead, produces a version that represents what it is supposed to be said in the target language. In contrast, foreignization stays close to the original way of articulation, but at the risk of cross-linguistic or cross-cultural unintelligibility, not to mention a low degree of readability.

From a cross-cultural perspective, it is generally not considered to be a good practice to substitute the strange with the familiar without going through the process of negotiation and mediation. This does not mean, however, that substitution should be avoided altogether. The crucial point is how substitution is to be performed. The function of cultural substitution is described as "to enable the target audience to encounter the cultural aspects in the ST in a meaningful manner" (Young 2009: 131). In other words, substitution is not designed to create an interactional asymmetry to deprive the target reader of enjoying the advantages of cross-cultural experience. And translatability is only meaningful if cross-cultural communication challenges are met. The relationship between form and content in the original may be changed or strained in translation, thus raising doubts on translatability, and for the actualized translation to capture the distinctive stylistic traits of the original, the translator must explore the mediating practices of underpinning the manifestations of otherness in translation.

Limits of translatability

Translatability may be understood to refer to the possibility of representing in the target text what is meant to be conveyed in the source text. Simply put, this aligns translatability with transferability. In the cases of meaning being transferrable, translation involves, if the translator chooses to do so, minimal intervention or manipulation. Thus, translation becomes a relatively straightforward task. But in reality, the transfer of meaning is fraught with pitfalls and problems. Because the correlations between meaning and expression exist, the transfer of form is a matter of serious concern. To transfer both meaning and form bears directly upon the very limits of translatability. The non-reproduction of the stylistic features of the source text gives rise to limited translatability or untranslatability, the result of which is no more than partial or incomplete translation. It is axiomatic that despite the inherent untranslatability of many great literary texts, successful and less successful efforts have been made to translate the untranslatable.

Interactional asymmetry indicates different degrees of interest in social relations across different communicative settings. For grandparents (grandfather and grandmother), in Chinese there are more specific words. Paternal grandfather is 爺爺 or 祖父 and paternal grandmother 奶奶 or 祖母. There is a separate word for maternal grandfather 老爺 or 外祖父, and maternal grandmother 姥姥 or 外祖母. All depend on lineage, not including some regional variations. In English, for family siblings, there is no way to tell whether a brother or sister is older or younger without a modifier, namely older or younger: 哥哥 or 弟弟 and 姐姐 or 妹妹. Apart from age difference which is not indicated in English, cousin and nephew are two terms more general in English than in Chinese. By definition, a nephew or a niece is a son or daughter of one's brother or sister. But it is not clear in English whether he or she is one's brother's or sister's son or daughter. They are termed differently in Chinese: 侄子 (女) and 外甥 (女). "Cousin" is even more complicated in Chinese because age difference is also specified. According to Yuen Ren Chao, "[a] cousin in Chinese has to be not only either male or female but also either on the father's side or on the mother's side, either older or younger than oneself" (Chao 1976: 158). In Chinese there are differentiating linguistic varieties for expressing male cousin of your uncle: 堂哥 or 堂弟, depending on whether he is older or younger than you. For female cousin on your uncle's side, it should either be 堂姐 or 堂妹. And for both male and female cousin on your aunt's side, it either be 表哥 or 表弟 and 表姐 or 表妹. Such cases are not exhaustive, and in Chinese there are different terms for older and younger uncle and older aunt and younger aunt.

All the aforementioned terms, complicated as they happen to be, are still reasonably translatable, which, however, involves explanation, and which also means expanded space. Obviously, it is not always necessary to fill such lexical gaps unless relevant situational cultural information is required. The translator uses all available linguistic resources concerning certain vocabulary, but if such resources sometimes turn out to be limited, they are compelled to create translatability through compensation, paraphrase, explanation, and so forth. In truth, translation is more than a matter of translating meaning as claimed by Eugene Nida (1985) in an article that is epigrammatically entitled "Translating Means Translating Meaning." A representative example of this is the translation of puns, showing how inadequate it would be to translate only the semantic meaning involved. A Chinese translation of one pun is wide of the mark.

> Why are the Middle Ages called the Dark Ages?
> Because there were so many knights there.

Unlike nights, knights were not supposed to be responsible for darkness. But this is precisely the impression created by the following Chinese translation version:

> － 為什麼中世紀被稱為黑暗時代?
> － 因為那時武士多得不得了。

The two English homophones: nights (implied) and knights cannot be reproduced in the Chinese translation. This is a clear case of untranslatability, and there is no way for the target reader to make the connection between the two sentences because the Chinese word "黑暗" (pronounced as *hei'an*) and "武士" (pronounced as *wushi*) do not sound alike at tall. This draws attention to the inevitable limit of translatability. Peter Alan Low asserts that "If a joke is not translated as a joke, the translation is bad" (Low 2011: 59). The example cited earlier is indicative of what, according to Low, would amount to a bad translation. Likewise, a joke can be misunderstood or ruined without explanation in translation, which requires an extra space. There is no doubt that what appropriate translational behavior for the translator to abide by is a question here.

Whether they are good or bad, puns are a nightmare for translators, especially the good ones that deserve serious attention. *Alice's Adventures in Wonderland* by Lewis Carroll contains a large number of puns, which present challenges to translation. One of the puns consists of two homophones: "Mine is a long and a sad tale!" said the Mouse, turning to Alice and sighing. "It is a long tail, certainly," said Alice, looking down with wonder at the Mouse's tail, "but why do you call it sad?" One Chinese version makes no attempt to bring out the playfulness of the pun:

> "我的是一個長長的令人悲痛的故事!" 老鼠說, 並轉向愛麗絲歎息一聲。
> "是一條長尾巴, 當然了," 愛麗斯說, 驚奇地看著老鼠的尾巴, "可你怎麼說尾巴是令人悲痛的?"

Unfortunately, as can be imagined, it turns out to be the tail rather than the tale that is sad since there is no connection between tail and tale in translation. The playful use of the words is lost in translation. Another version sets out to reproduce the pun in Chinese by working on the pun by substituting them with two

Chinese homophones. Yet in order to do so, the translator has to use two different words instead of the original tail and tale.

老鼠對著愛麗絲歎了口氣道: "唉, 說來話長! 真叫我委屈!"
"尾曲?!" 愛麗絲聽了, 瞧著老鼠那光滑的尾巴問: "你這尾巴明明有長又
直, 為什麼說它曲呢?"

Its back translation goes like this: "It is a long story! It really makes me sad!"
The focus is on "sad," which is pronounced as "委屈." It is misheard by Alice as
"twisted tail," which in Chinese sounds like "sad." And then Alice asks to look at
the smooth tail: "Your tail is long and straight. Why did you say it was twisted?"
The Chinese rendition of "twisted tail" sounds very artificial. In order to make
"twisted tail" work in translation, the translator has to add "smooth" to tail
and also "long and straight." It represents a commendable attempt to combat
untranslatability, although in this particular case, it does not work very well. Due
largely to cultural specificities, resourcefulness is required to explore possibilities.
Peter Newmark describes translation as "a dynamic process that requires infinite
sensibility and resourcefulness" (Newmark 1998: 129). Unfortunately again,
however, resourcefulness does not seem to be always infinite.

Yet it is both formidable and exciting to seek to challenge the limits of translatability as shown in the case of translating the seemingly untranslatable literary works. In 1990, when a publisher in China decided to publish the Chinese
translation of *Ulysses*, its chairman tried in vain to invite practically all the eminent
translators in China to take on the translation task. He then approached Qian
Zhongshu, an eminent Chinese scholar and translator, but the latter replied: "As
a frail old man at the age of eighty, I cannot translate this book, because it would
be no different from killing myself in a phenomenal way" (Li 2008). Back then,
another 80-year-old man, Xiao Qian and his wife who was 63, decided to take
up the job. They divided their labor: his wife produced the first draft, Xiao Qian
revised and polished it. They did not seem to suffer unduly from the apprehension of untranslatability. Somewhat surprisingly, the translation of the first draft
went smoothly (Li 2008). The two Chinese translations of *Ulysses* were lauded as
a miracle at the time and celebrated as a significant cross-cultural event.

The polyglot text of *Finnegans Wake* would be the ultimate test of translatability.
According to Patrick O'Neill, by 2012, the complete translations existed in French,
German, Japanese, Dutch, Korean, and Portuguese (O'Neill 2013: 22). O'Neill's
list fails to include its Chinese translation. In September 2012, the first volume of
its Chinese translation was published by Shanghai renmin chubanshe, and in the
following year, the second volume came out. Without a doubt, James Joyce did not
intend for this novel to be understood, not to mention to be translated. Its Chinese
translator produced roughly the same amount of words as the original with half of
each page crammed with footnotes. This is hardly surprising, for the novel requires
massive annotations and commentary for the source text readers. The interesting
question is how on earth such a notoriously untranslatable text gets translated.

When being interviewed by a reporter of《兰州晨报》(*Lanzhou morning post*), the translator of *Finnegans Wake*, Dai Congrong, admitted her initial doubt about the translatability of the novel. What really concerned her was how large a portion of the work could be translated. If the novel was to be translated in its entirety, "it would be very difficult to the extent of being untranslatable" (Zhang 2012). This was attributed to the coinage of words and multiple meanings of just one word. It would be impossible to match the original word by word with all the meanings contained at different levels of each word in translation. Other transla-tors of the novel have renounced quite a bit of content. She made it clear that "[f]rom a perfectionist standpoint, it is impossible to translate *Finnegans Wake*, just as it is impossible to translate poetry." However, the consolation was that although translation could never match the original. "It could still give enlight-enment and pleasure to the reader" (Zhang 2012). The translator indicated that it was the logical meaning of the novel that was the most difficult problem for her to solve, and she had to decode it before it was possible to start translating. Remarkably, she displayed an equilibrium deriving from the recognition of the impossibility of translating this novel. Yet, at the same time, it was the translat-ability potential that gave her confidence to embark on this tortuous project that would challenge the mental and physical limits of the translator in challeng-ing the limits of translatability. Struggling with the impossible task of translating *Finnegans Wake*, the translator needs to bring into play a considerable amount of spatialization of rewriting, showing the exigent necessity of translational creativ-ity, whose typical feature is described as "hav[ing] to be novel and depart from conventional translation behavior" (Rojo 2017: 353). In many situations, con-ventional translation strategies prove to be hamstrung and, as the case may be, incapable of solving what appear to be untranslatable problems. Unconventional translation approaches, by carving spaces of engagement, can enhance the effect of empowerment.

Indeed, it is the potentiality of translatability that suggests a tantalizing pros-pect of experimenting with potential translatability. Significantly, Benjamin emphasizes such potentiality concerning the interplay between translation and the original. What first appears to be untranslatable may be deceptive. Despite his claim of "untranslatable translation" (Derrida 1998: 66), Derrida affirms that "nothing is untranslatable; but in another sense everything is untranslat-able" (Derrida 1998: 56–57). In terms of thinking about the necessity of trans-lation, the statement that "nothing is untranslatable" has great practical value. In a relative sense, translatability can be indefinite, although untranslatability is not absolute either. This patently points to both the fragility of translatability and the provisionality of the untranslatable, which must be emphasized in the process of finding a solution deriving from a multiplicity of possibilities. This is due to the fact that the impossibility of translation is predicated on the possibil-ity of translating the untranslatable, and the possibility of doing the impossible has to be extensively explored in order to tackle the long-standing problem of untranslatability.

Challenges and prospects

It is no exaggeration to say that where there is translation, there is the challenge of translatability. Even though there should not be an absolute binary between translatability and untranslatability, how meaningful it is to think about translatability or untranslatability in such relative terms remains a lingering question. Relative translatability results from the supposed untranslatable because the necessity of translation invariably prompts the translator to translate the untranslatable, no matter how completely impossible it may seem at first. They are compelled to transcend the limits of translatability. The famous Derridean dictum that translation is both necessary and impossible pinpoints the relative nature of translatability. Derrida has presented an axiomatic conception by posing the following rhetorical question: "How can one dare say that nothing is translatable and, by the same token, that nothing is untranslatable?" (Derrida 2001: 178). In the final analysis, it is not a question of being either translatable or untranslatable but rather both translatable and untranslatable. Strictly speaking, everything is no more than partially translatable and partially untranslatable. The practice of translation is inherently and necessarily marked by varying degrees of translatability or untranslatability, and varying degrees of intervention and adjustment are also needed to address the paramount concern of accessibility regarding untranslatability. How to make the limits of translatability expandable remains a perennial problem for translators.

First of all, we must not lose the relevance of the concept of translatability, even if it seems to be somewhat antiquated. The Descriptive Translation Studies may have shifted its focus of attention towards target-orientedness. Fundamentally, "adequacy" and "acceptability" posited by Toury as an irreconcilable dichotomy (Toury 1980: 55) are the two mainstays underpinning translatability, both of which should be taken both into account to achieve an appropriate balance. Also, with the rapid development of globalization and English becoming the second language of many people (and this is certainly the case in China), the validity of adhering to a purely target-oriented approach is becoming rather questionable. The target-oriented approach seems to patronize the target reader and seems to presuppose that the absence of the source text makes it irrelevant. Many Chinese readers, particularly those with diasporic experiences, who are well versed in the source language, would sometimes go to the source text to check the reliability, and the more they like the text concerned, the more likely they will do so, thus keeping translatability under the limelight.

It is of course not true to claim that everything is translatable. As Susan Bassnett observes: "It has always been obvious that not everything is translatable," and she specifies "idioms, proverbs, puns and other wordplay" as untranslatable instances (Bassnett 2013: 147). However, since there is no absolute translatability or untranslatability, it makes more sense to foreground the relative nature of translatability. Despite cases of undeniable untranslatability, it is widely agreed that a certain degree of translatability can be presupposed, seen as constitutive of partial translatability with admitted loss of meaning. The acceptance of partial translatability confirms an equilibrium deriving from the impossibility of complete translation on certain occasions. To translate the essential meaning or the essential part of the meaning to be conveyed is an effective way of making untranslatability manageable. Partial translatability may well be the outcome of painstaking negotiation and mediation through appropriation and recontextualization, resulting in something somewhat different to be identified as a form of transformation. Measuring translatability is analogous to a feasibility study. Translatability is the judgment of whether what is translated or to be translated can be accessible to the target reader. If something is only partially accessible, it is partially translatable. And also, what is theoretically translatable may turn out to be what is practically untranslatable or vice versa. Something may be untranslatable for less able translators but are actually translatable for more talented or qualified translators. For instance, a poet is better able to translate poetry, and a theorist a better translator of theoretical works.

But the incompleteness of partial translation may after all be unacceptable. There has been a resurgent interest in "thick translation" in recent years. To start with, the absence of contextual information concerning the source text can prove to be a hindrance to a proper understanding of the translated text. Thus, the main task of thick translation is to provide such information. "Contextualization is the key to achieving thick translation" (Cheung and Lin 2014: 3). Untranslatability may well be attributable to the lack of contextual information, which can be closely related to cultural intertexts, and thus thick translation is designed primarily to overcome untranslatability by rendering cultural authenticity with a high degree of accuracy and fullness. Sometimes to help the target reader recognize the intertexts is necessary and also contingent. In such cases, any real access to the source culture must rest on the fullness of the articulation in a form of nonreductive translation. Thick translation typically takes the form of paratexts that supply a frame of reference to help the target reader understand the relatively unfamiliar material in the main text. Footnotes, or endnotes or more conveniently "side notes" – the paratextual writing is printed alongside the main body of the translated text for easy reference. Thick translation relies heavily on paratextuality, but a paratextually heavy translation with the aim of enabling the target reader to recognize the contextual and intertextual dimensions under given constraining conditions.

Regarding viable strategies concerning pun translation, Huang (2001) notes that

> in translating a pun, the first consideration should be to try to come up with something like an equivalent to the original in sound and meaning. The second priority is creative transposition, and the last is to footnote which at least is better than a complete omission, but of little value in translating puns.
> (Huang 2001: 919)

How thick can or should thick translation be? There is no doubt, in most cases, that the target reader prefers non-thick translation – and for good reason. When translating a pun or wordplay, an explanatory strategy can only kill it in a bid to make sense of its meaning consequent upon, for instance, homonymy or polysemy. Understandably, the textually vulnerable translator prefers an integrative to reductive approach to translation. Needless to say, in doing so, they can barely manage to reproduce formally corresponding features. Because thick translation can sometimes be counterproductive, the translator under normal circumstances uses this technique rather sparingly and regards it as the last resort to get around untranslatability.

The complexity of cultural context reflects the limits and possibilities of cultural translatability. In recent years, as a result of steadily increased cross-cultural awareness, the focal point of concern has been shifted from linguistic untranslatability to cultural untranslatability. The primacy of cultural form highlights the compelling need for cross-cultural communication. However, the absence of the target language culture of "a relevant situational feature" in the source text has always been a source of anxiety (Catford 1965: 99). And if a relevant situational context is not available, cultural re-contextualization is in order so that more space can be opened to expand cultural translatability. The modern Chinese obsessive preoccupation with translational authenticity has been historically and culturally constructed and defined. The need to transmit cultural meaning demonstrates the centrality to preserving cultural authenticity. Cultural meaning may be intratextually determined but has to be cross-culturally represented. The authenticity of cross-cultural experience signifies that the target reader is confronted with difference, and to this end, the translator seeks to resonate with them in concentrating on increasing rather than decreasing cross-cultural interaction. Translation is not a simple act of eradicating differences. But to what extent they can be represented in translation is a test of the flexibility of translatability. To establish linguistic and cultural correspondences between the source and target languages requires strenuous efforts. This would prove to be the ultimate challenge to cultural translatability. The assumption of culture gainsays its essential translatability, which is reduced and debilitated, among other factors, by local resistance to foreign otherness. In translating culture, regarding the relation between sense and reference, it remains essential to move beyond simple referentiality and pursue approximate translatability. In a different way, through negotiating and adjusting interpretations of cultural meaning, the interactional dimension of reading can be brought into play to enhance cross-cultural readability.

It is decidedly unhelpful to examine the concept of translatability in terms of source-orientedness versus target-orientedness. After all, the most important thing to consider is how to enhance the efficacy of cross-cultural communication. In a cross-cultural sense, translatability needs to recognize the linguistic and cultural constraints that can create various kinds of translation problems. As a rule, translation is possible only through compromises, and it is sometimes possible and sometimes impossible, at least seemingly so. Therefore, we have to reckon with the contingency and plasticity of translation. The sheer necessity of translation leads, from time to time, to translating the untranslatable, which means that we must recognize the limits of translatability and, at the same time, accept that the incompleteness of translation is a normality in view of the complex and fugitive nature of translatability. To expand the limits of translatability, it is necessary to demystify untranslatability and investigate how untranslatability can be transformed and improved. It is clear that the limits of translatability are subject to change and include a large degree of fluidity, entailing relentless mediation and negotiation of both linguistic and cultural differences. Given the multifaceted and multifarious nature of translatability, many translation attempts may well be experimental in exploring and understanding a range of formal variables available. Significant advances are still yet to be made in the understanding of the dynamics of translation and translatability so as to make translation not only operationally manageable but also to enable a maximum likelihood of translatability.

Conclusion

It can be safely said that something may well be translatable at the semantic level but is only partially translatable at the cultural level and becomes much less translatable at the aesthetic level. In view of this consideration, the flexible use of interpretative space is crucial for translation, and more importantly for enabling the translator to acquire corresponding spaces to tackle untranslatability. Indirect translation is common in overcoming the limits of translatability, and alternative strategies tend to arise from indirect translation. The unavailability of readily available equivalent necessitates the creation of spaces for a solution to be found. While the transfer of meaning is often out of the question, the transfer of situation is perfectly feasible, which leads to alternative resources that are otherwise hidden, thus allowing the translated text to function in a reasonably acceptable manner. While untranslatability suggests impossibility, which is relatively rare, and what is partially possible refers to the degree of translatability. Since what is regarded as translation or good translation remains a continuing challenge for translation, more flexibility and resourcefulness will clearly be needed, with more spatial dimensions explored to reduce the symptoms of the incompetence of translation.

References

Bassnett, Susan (2013) *Translation*, London and New York: Routledge.

Benjamin, Walter (ed. and intro. by Hannah Arendt; trans. by Harry Zohn) (1969) *Illuminations: Essays and Reflections*, New York: Schocken Books.

Berman, Antoine (trans. by S. Heyvaert) (1992) *The Experience of the Foreign: Culture and Translation in Romantic Germany*, Albany: State University of New York Press.

Cao, Shunqing (2014) *The Variation Theory of Comparative Literature*, New York: Springer.

Catford, J. C. (1965) *A Linguistic Theory of Translation: An Essay in Applied Linguistics*, London: Oxford University Press.

Chao, Yuen Ren (1976) *Aspects of Chinese Sociolinguistics: Essays*, Stanford, CA: Stanford University Press.

Cheung, Martha Pui Yiu, and Lin Wusun (eds.) (2014) *An Anthology of Chinese Discourse on Translation (Version 1): From Earliest Times to the Buddhist*, London and New York: Routledge.

Darwish, Ali (2010) *Elements of Translation: A Practical Guide for Translator*, Melbourne: Writescope Publishers.

Derrida, Jacques (1998) *Monolingualism of the Other, Or, the Prosthesis of Origin*, Stanford, CA: Stanford University Press.

Derrida, Jacques (trans. by Lawrence Venuti) (2001) "What Is a 'Relevant' Translation?" *Critical Inquiry* 27(2): 174–200.

Gramsci, Antonio (ed. and trans. by Derek Boothman) (1995) *Further Selections from the Prison Notebooks*, London: Lawrence and Wishart.

Huang, I-min (2001) "Puns," in Chan Sin-wai and David E. Pollard (eds.) *An Encyclopedia of Translation: Chinese-English, English-Chinese*, Hong Kong: Chinese University Press, 918–923.

Lefevere, André (1977) *Translating Literature: The German Tradition from Luther to Rosenzweig*, Amsterdam and New York: Rodopi.

Li, Jingduan (2008) "我与《尤利西斯》中译本" (Chinese Translation of *Ulysses* and I), 《光明日报》 (*Guangming Daily*), November 1.

Lin, Yutang (1985) "林语堂论翻译" (Lin Yutang on Translation), in China Translation and Publishing Company (ed.) 《翻译理论与翻译技巧论文集》 (*Selected Papers on Translation Theories and Skills*), Beijing: China Translation and Publishing Company, 20–33.

Low, Peter Alan (2011) "Translating Jokes and Puns," *Perspectives: Studies in Translatology* 19(1): 59–70.

Miller, Kristie Lyn (2007) *Issues in Theoretical Diversity: Persistence, Composition, and Time*, Dordrecht: Springer.

Nida, Eugene (1985) "Translating Means Translating Meaning: A Sociosemiotic Approach to Translating," in Hildegund Bühler (ed.), *Xth World Congress of FIT Proceedings: Translators and Their Position in Society*, Vienna: Braumüller, 119–125.

Newmark, Peter (1998) *More Paragraphs on Translation*, Clevedon: Multilingual Matters.

O'Neill, Patrick (2013) *Impossible Joyce: Finnegans Wakes*, Toronto and Buffalo: University of Toronto Press.

Robinson, Douglas (2001) "The Limits of Translation," in Peter Franc (ed.) *The Oxford Guide to Literature in English Translation*, New York: Oxford University Press.

Rojo, Ana (2017) "The Role of Creativity," in John W. Schwieter and Aline Ferreira (eds.) *The Handbook of Translation and Cognition*, New York: John Wiley & Sons, Inc., 350–368.

Toury, Gideon (1980) *In Search of a Theory of Translation*, Tel Aviv: Porter Institute for Poetics and Semiotics, Tel Aviv University.

Wilss, Wolfram (1982) *The Science of Translation: Problems and Methods*, Tübingen: Gunter Narr.

Young, Charmaine (2009) "The Translation of Aspects of Senegalese Culture in Selected Literary Works by Ousmane Semb ne," in Judith Inggs and Libby Meintjes (eds.) *Translation Studies in Africa*, London and New York: Continuum.

Zhang, Hailong (2012) "《芬尼根的守灵夜》沉寂73年后首译成中文" (The First Chinese Translation of *Finnegans Wake*), 《兰州晨报》 (*Lanzhou Morning Post*), October 13.

6 Multicultural contextual spaces

Introduction

It can be argued that since, in general, it is inadvisable for translation to disregard the possible unintelligibility of the text, a web of significance or signification must be reproduced irrespective of seemingly insurmountable translation difficulties. Interpretation is related to the issues of cultural translation and (un) translatability in cultural terms, necessitating a clutch of interpretative modes prior to the effective formulation of appropriate translation strategies. Temporal and cultural gaps tend to create difficulties in interpretation, and cultural pluralism may lead to multiple, hence different, interpretations. Principally because of translation, we have progressed into the age of multiculturalism, and it is not just that the necessity of acculturation seems to be diminishing, but there is a real desire to spurn it.

The potential risk of unintelligibility of translation can barely be disregarded, hence the necessity to reproduce a web of significance or signification, regardless of translation difficulties. Interpretation is bound to be related to the issues of cultural translation and translatability in cultural terms, which necessitates a clutch of interpretative modes before the effective formulation of appropriate translation strategies. Temporal and cultural gaps tend to create large difficulties in interpretation, and cultural pluralism may lead to multiple, hence different, interpretations. Largely because of translation, we have progressed into the age of multiculturalism, and it is not just that the necessity of acculturation seems to be diminishing, but there is a desire to spurn it. Foreignization is a cultural political issue. Accordingly, the tensions of ideological incommensurability need to be dissipated in order to facilitate cross-cultural understanding and communication. A degree of ideological pluralism allows cultural diversity distinctively marked by tolerance of difference and discouraging an unhealthy distrust of the foreign. Multiculturalism, however, by no means denotes the demise of ideology. Despite its ostensible theoretical naiveté, intentionalism has some serious implications to the translator, who may ignore at their own peril, for instance, the complex ideological awareness that informs not only the source text but also the resulting target text. If we say that both the author and the reader are responsible for context or its construction, then the translator must play the double role of reader and author in the sense of (re)constructing the context in a different text. While we interpret with many aims, the act of interpretation is culturally and ideologically conditioned, and the ensuing complicated remapping is such that translation is always somewhat adrift.

It seems to be a simple truism to state what gets translated is meaning, but it is also a truism that meaning is not the only thing that is supposed to get translated in literary translation, particularly poetry translation. Any meaning itself is a problematic concept because often we are unable to formulate the meaning of a text, or even if meaning is deciphered, it can still be very difficult to communicate in translation for the systems of meaning are not necessarily shared. The poststructuralist skepticism about the possibility of meaning makes the task of translation extremely difficult, if not impossible. If writing is immediately perspicuous, then there is no indeterminacy of interpretation, and consequently, translation becomes relatively straightforward. For the translator, the primary thing to do is determine the object of translation, namely what to translate, and then, more importantly, how to translate, yet both of them are intertwined with meaning and the (re) production of meaning. Central to meaning is interpretation (unless it is literal or surface meaning), and the purpose of interpretation is to acquire and decipher meaning or at least to bring us closer to it. Interpretation necessarily takes place within a context, which yields and constrains interpretation at the same time. Meaning may shift from context to context and in a different cultural context caused by translation, meaning is subject to different interpretation(s). The defining role of context is particularly relevant to cross-cultural communication, and since translation provides a different cultural context, its re-defining role must not be overlooked because as a result, meaning may change, thereby resulting in an alternative understanding of the translated text. Moreover, interpretation tends to be a matter of relating what is said in one part of the text to what one finds in other parts of other related texts. And in this connection, inter-textual and inter-cultural knowledge is of crucial importance and thus must be well developed. We must acknowledge and address the inevitable cultural limitations that undermine our quest for (cross)-cultural knowledge and understanding.

Interpretation-translation formula

Interpretation is of particular relevance to translation since literal meaning is often translationally meaningless. Words can carry more than a literal meaning, and if such words are not fit to be translated literally, a certain amount of interpretation is called for particularly with regard to cultural references. To a large extent, the production of meaning is based on interpretation. If interpretation is at the core of understanding and communicating cultural meaning, we need to examine how it functions regarding translation. It is widely assumed that translation is ubiquitous in order to make sense of reading. Therefore, a basic yet inescapable formula for interpretation (not referring to oral translation, namely interpreting) and translation is proposed as follows:

To translate is to interpret →→→ To interpret is to translate.

This is deceptively simple to present but immensely complex to analyze and is both experimental and theoretical, which needs further explanation. "To translate" in the first sentence refers primarily to intralingual translation. James A. Parr observes that "translation is, in itself, a form of interpretation. Every translation offers an implicit analysis of the original" (Parr 2000: 401). In practical terms, it is more accurate to separate translation from interpretation at this stage, as Par adds, "Interpretation also offers an analytical reading, albeit a more explicit one" (Parr 2000: 401). Translation means that the reader uses his/her own language rephrasing what is in the text so as to interpret the meaning. From translation to interpretation, implicit meaning becomes explicit. It is necessary to point out that this act of interpretation is personal appropriation. "To interpret" here is to make sense of an utterance and can be called private discourse. While in the second sentence, "to interpret" is for communication, which is public discourse. If the first "to interpret" indicates to understand, the second "to interpret" signifies to be understood, and also involves cultural appropriation (acculturation). Accordingly, "to translate" in the second sentence is interlingual translation. And its nature is intrinsically different because this is cross-cultural communication. Although the purposes of the two parts of the formula are markedly different, they belong intrinsically to the process of understanding and communication. Strictly speaking, the translator cannot reproduce what they do not understand.

Interpretation is necessary and unavoidable, yet it is a potentially hazardous act. The source text is made vulnerable by the possibility of misinterpretation on the part of the translator who, as a result, will invariably mistranslate. Likewise, over-interpretation may well lead to over-translation, or even mistranslation. However, it is possible to know that a particular interpretation is not empirically sustainable, and then the translator is forced to find an alternative interpretation. It can be said that the intelligibility of a text depends on whether it is interpretable. A text consists of interpretations because "a text without interpretation is no longer a text" (Kofman 1993: 140). Interpretation is the "exposure" of meaning or the "appropriation of a system of rules" (Foucault 1977: 51), which explains certain classical texts are more accessible in translation than in the original. A text tends to yield meaning within "a specifiable frame of reference" (Hartman 1982: xxi). The usefulness of such a frame of reference "allows us to economize words or their resonances: to synthesize or disambiguate them" (Hartman 1982: xxi). But this frame of reference can be individualized in an attempt to unsettle meaning even if it is supposed to stabilize meaning. There is a collective frame of reference to be associated with a particular reading community, whose frame of reference is inevitably bounded by the experience and cultural understandings of its members. A different cultural-political frame of reference embodied in the target language system is bound to affect the decoding of meaning. Something may only be acceptable within the frame of reference of a particular culture, religion, or politics. The act of translation may challenge and subsequently alter a frame of reference, hence the subversive power of translation.

Translation and interpretation are inextricably intertwined. To interpret is to bring meaning out, to make the text somewhat clearer, and in this respect, it differs from translation. Meaning is highly complex, and translation further compounds this complexity of meaning. In the process of translation, meaning embedded in the source text becomes cultural meaning due to the change of cultural contexts as well as the expectations and conditions of reading. With the removal of a text from its original cultural context and placing it in a different cultural context, the text may acquire, by and large, a somewhat different cultural meaning. In general, what is semantically difficult is often culturally problematic. Yet if it is the outcome of interpretation that gets translated, how does interpretation affect acculturation? Cultural translation is also invariably cultural interpretation. Even foreignization is based on careful interpretation or prudent estimation of the prospect of interpretation to be attempted by the target reader. We must understand that foreignization is not the same as literal or word-for-word translation. To a large extent, the supposed adequacy of translation depends on interpretive "adequacy." Reading between the lines may not be possible in a different cultural and linguistic context, since in a different cultural context, such a space is no longer available. The relationship between the production of meaning and re-production of more or less the same meaning signifies a power transfer. In many cases it is the recreation of meaning rather than recovery of meaning that translational activity entails. And translation is no longer based on the so-called objective sameness, and instead, translation is a process of intersubjective communication, during which the construction of identity and intersubjective relating are activated internally.

If literalness in translation is impractical and unworkable, it is inevitable that differences in the grammatical structures of the source and target languages may result in some changes in the information content of the message involved during the process of translation. We may think that such a sense of natural connection between the signifier and the signified in different languages is decidedly illusory. Where does signification come from? From the reader's interpretation? The translator is, first of all, a reader as identified with the source language reader, but then he/she becomes the spokesman/woman for the original author addressing a different audience. His/her interpretative performance determines what is represented from the source text. Amid the inherent indeterminacy of meaning, the translator has to struggle to work out meaning, which is, at the same time, compounded by the fact that translation is sometimes forced to make choices among a variety of interpretations. In the final analysis, the translator is faced with the perennial conundrum about what gets translated, and even under the appearance of meaninglessness, there is something there, of which some sense must be made, even though it is not always possible to translate what is epigrammatic to be inherent in the original epigrammatically.

Lexical or grammatical ambiguity in certain parts of the text requires disambiguation through interpretation and evaluation, and the translator is obliged to offer an explication of the indeterminacy. However, the translator should be aware of the possibility of semantic changes that result from translation. As a consequence, they even need to interpret their own translations in appraising the relevant performance parameters in a real situation where translation is taking place. It is also necessary to conduct sensitivity analysis around predicted outcomes within the intrinsic constraints of the target language enmeshed in its cultural values. As Samuels and McGann rightly point out, "If editing is the paradigm of performative scholarship, translation is perhaps the same for criticism-as-interpretation" (Samuels and McGann 1999: 34). The consequences of shocking and offending should be worked out before a decision is made about the strategies of translation, since we always intersubjectively decipher signs. Allusions to sensitive issues may well disappear in translation because of censorship or self-censorship, thus radically diverting the significance of the original. Indeed, the interpretation of the translator can be seriously compromised. This is because the purpose of a given translation can be predetermined by the translator and their commissioners (patrons), which means that the act of rewriting is regulated in a way that is in line with the purpose or the supposed function of the translation. If this is the case, translation may well be at odds with the interpretation of the translator. At any rate, translation is primarily concerned with interpretation. And interpretation plays a central role before and during the process of translation and may therefore be related to the perception and acceptability of the end result of translation.

Authorial or/and translatorial intention

Translation is an intersubjective activity encompassing both authorial and translatorial intentions. Some stimulating discussion of translation dwells on the intersubjective level of the production of meaning, particularly cultural meaning. In an imagined dialogue between the author and the translator, two distinct subjectivities are somehow commingled to shape the final translation product. Some traditional views regard translation as focusing mainly on the transmission of meanings and intentions of the source text. The derivative nature of interpretation suggests that it is based on or at least related to authorial intention. But inasmuch as translation is done, on what grounds can one attribute the interpreted meaning to authorial intention or to translatorial intention for that matter? As to whether meaning is determined by authorial intention, the issue has been debated for a long time. But according to Wendell V. Harris's observation, "Fortunately, the great wall isolating a text from its author's intention appears to be collapsing – actually silently dissolving – and explicit recognition of intention is creeping into literary commentary once more" (Harris 1996: 90). And he further argues, "Hermeneutics – as I use the term – assumes that texts result from an author's intention to communicate and that the intended communication is almost always largely interpretable with reasonable accuracy" (Harris 1996: 90). Harris is distinctly positive about the interpretability and thus stability of meaning in relation to authorial intention. Similarly, E.D. Hirsch, Jr. (1967) defends authorial intention in *Validity in Interpretation*, in which he sets out to recover the authorial intention in repudiating Wimsatt and Beardsley's claim about "intentional fallacy."

It seems clear that while "New Criticism" and post-structuralism attempt to disenfranchise the author and to treat the text as an independent entity, meaning is still dependent, to some extent at least, on the author's subjectivity. In other words, there is still undeniably such a thing as authorial meaning or intended meaning. And the ontological dimension of meaning and language does exist, and it helps to clarify and demonstrate a "literal" approach to the text both in terms of interpretation and translation. Authorial intention needs to be qualified by noting that the extension or ramification of meaning may not be intended by the author. Sometimes meaning, at least part of it, can indeed be separated from authorial intention, but it is difficult to deny altogether that meaning is or can be under authorial control to varying degrees. Arabella Lyon contends, "Authorial intention, with the addition of strategic control, remains the dominant factor in communication" (Lyon 1998: 33). Even though the problem remains as to what exactly constitutes authorial intention, the "strategic control" is unquestionably exercised by the author. The underlying assumption is essentially optimistic if not reductively simplistic for the so-called strategic control may not be centrally administered. However, it is possible to observe how this control actually works. Among other things, ambiguity (not vagueness) may well be intended by the author; it is not a sign of the author relaxing or even eliminating control of meaning, but a conscious attempt to achieve a certain effect. For instance, the intended effect of terror should be reproduced by the translator who recognizes such an effect as knowingly intended by the author of the original text, and in this case, the two are inseparable. As stated earlier, authorial intention is not considered central or not even relevant to meaning in the eyes of deconstructionists and reader-response theorists. And according to Foucault, authorial intention is no longer a significant source of meaning. This may well be true, but intention is still a key issue both in communication and reading. A decision has to be made as to what meaning can or should be assigned to a given utterance.

But if meaning is attributed to authorial intention, Barthes contends that the critic's task becomes relatively easy in making a text explicable: "To give a text an Author is to impose a limit on the text, to furnish it with a final signified, to close the writing. Once the Author has been found, the text is 'explained' – victory to the critic" (Barthes 1977: 147). But this sarcastic pronouncement cannot reject or diminish the relevance of authorial intention to meaning and its production. Nevertheless, authorial intention can be vague and intangible. One way to get around it is to find out about what the text actually does, irrespective of its authorial intention, since even the declared intention may not be fully realized, or simply not genuine. Although the declared intention of the translation is sometimes indicated in the preface of a translated work, the actual translatorial intention is less readily available. Few translators would openly and explicitly state that they wish to do something radically different by blatantly disregarding the authorial intention or unmistakable textual evidence. As for translation, the issue of intention is more prominent and perhaps more contentious because it involves the moral code of the profession of translation. The source text is rarely intended for the target readership, which is unavoidably disadvantaged in terms of comprehension. As reader's response theory suggests, an interpreter brings into the text some pre-understandings that will influence the interpretation of individual texts. As a consequence, the author-centered meaning may turn out to be rather difficult to decipher by the target reader, and as a necessary protection against unbridled interpretations, the translator must also assume responsibility for the textual design by carefully marshaling textual evidence, which turns the seeming authorial irrelevance into the pragmatic translatorial relevance.

In general, the translator is supposed to aim at neutrality and interpretive objectivity with the intention of staying as close to the original text as possible, and in this sense, the author's meaning-intention must be taken into account in an empirical sense so that translation can be done properly. However, authorial intention is more like involvement than participation because the author may or may not be consulted for whatever reason, and depending on the needs and concerns of the interpretative community responsible for the production of translations, it then decides on the overall impact of the translated text on the community. It is generally assumed that part of the task of the translator is to recover the authorial intention or his or her intended effect in the source text. But is this necessarily the intention of the translator? Is the translatorial intention strictly confined to finding authorial intention? If it is the case, one may simply assume that the translatorial intention is the same as the authorial intention. After all, they are supposed to overlap. But, despite Harris's optimism, authorial intention is a problematic notion mainly because it is often not recoverable and may well be surrendered to a collaborative authorship involving the translator. However, completely doing away with authorial intention is dangerous, as it means eliminating evidence or part of evidence, about the presence and role of such an intention, which exercises a certain degree of control of the text. The endless deferral and thus undecidability of Derridean *différance* would make translation an impossible task. But the translator must start somewhere. Where and how does he/she start? Is it really possible for the translator to give up on finding authorial intention?

In reality, for the translator to find meaning is a crucial act of (re)interpretation, which admittedly may be independent of the intention of the original author. The ever – protean intentions of both the author and the translator means clearly that both the author and the translator do things in somewhat different ways in their respective texts, and often, ideologically driven and politically motivated or simply out of linguistic and cultural necessity, they may do radically different things. If the intentions of the author and the translator are quintessentially different and irreconcilable, the latter has the advantage to prevail. This is precisely why the discussion of the subjectivity of the translator continues to draw people's attention. Deeper forays into the text are required not only to reveal but also to add new meanings below the surface. But are these new meanings valid since they may not be intended by the author? In the absence of authorial intention, can we say that it is the translator's intention that is ultimately responsible for meaning as perceived by the target audience? In addition, when translating, it is critical that the original illocutionary force of an author is accurately communicated.

This may require changing syntactic form if an equivalent or comparable target language syntax does not communicate the same illocutionary force.

Language can be very shifting and deceptive but should still be graspable as something relatively stable so that translation can be made possible. Part of the complexity of the matter is the double identity of the translator, who is both a reader and a text producer: both acts are based on his/her interpretation of the source text. He/she engages in a double dialogue with the author and the target audience. Hence, the translator is a private reader and a public text (re)-producer. Such a double identity is cultural as well as linguistic. This doubleness reflects precisely the dual nature of translation, which can be regarded both as an extension of the source text and as its modes of duplication. Even if we say that meaning cannot be separated entirely from intention, to restrict the meaning of the text to authorial intention is plainly untenable. Language is prone to be transcendental beyond authorial meaning. Moreover, when authorial intention is not recoverable, textual evidence may corroborate a certain reading and provide support for an appropriate translation strategy. By the same token, how the trans-lated text is read also needs to be substantiated by textual evidence, irrespective of the claimed intention of the translator. It is barely possible to privatize words and turn them into one's own. Words are inadequate for the author and translator to express fully what is intended but, at the same time, are also excessive: they mean more than or different from what is intended. A further vexing point is that the production of the source text is very different from that of the target text with different intended audiences. In other words, intention, be it authorial or trans-latorial, bears on how a text is interpreted and understood.

Not surprisingly, re-contextualization prompted by translation is less precise and more subject to reinterpretation, which may indeed be based on the revision of the original as an act of re-writing. In this respect, translatorial intention is brought to the foreground. However, it is only fair to point out that translato-rial intention is bound to be entangled with the general concerns of the target community in terms of cultural politics. Texts that get translated are expected to be acceptable culturally and politically to the target readership, or perhaps not necessarily the readership per se, but the authorities controlling the readership or powerful patrons wishing to cultivate a readership. Ideological or cultural bias in stereotyping certain foreign cultures is also a directly relevant factor to consider. Of course, it is possible that sometimes certain political claims may belie com-mercial agendas.

The nature of the author-translator relationship is an interdependent one albeit not always a comfortable one. Occasionally the translator may decide to sever or suspend the relationship knowingly or unknowingly. If a translation is very interpretative, it probably does not fully represent textual particulars, which may turn out to be either untranslatable or deliberately suppressed or just altered. An interpretation can be arbitrary and capricious, thus making the resulting text cruder and reductive. For this reason, interpretive translation is disapproved on the grounds that it verges on paraphrase and as a result, the intrinsic qualities of directedness of reading diminish, and the semantic directedness to the external world is compromised. As an active reader, the translator has an important role to play in the interpretive process while considering what rhetorical devices are available in the target language to use and to what extent the original modes of expression can be retained or reproduced in the target text. In modern translation studies, the role of the translator is no longer viewed as marginal or passive, for in a double sense she/he functions both as a reader and as a substitute author. Thus, a translation may not necessarily be a poor version of the original; it may be better, or simply somewhat different despite the supposed necessity to present textual and stylistic similarities showing the correspondence between source and target texts. With the changed power relations between writer and reader, the position of the translator also changes. Of course, there is no way to rule out the possibility that the translator's "failure" to grasp the intended meaning is not unrelated to an unwillingness to take authorial intention seriously for various reasons, among which are a lack of sympathy or political disagreement.

Translation in cultural contexts

As noted earlier, interpretation with regard to reading is commonly of a private nature, but as soon as the translator starts to transfer meaning across linguistic and cultural boundaries, the private nature of reading changes into a public and social one because the translator is held responsible for the communicability of meaning. Communication is a social institution, and the selfhood of both author and writer is no longer private and must be inherently normative; standards against the source and target texts are judged respectively. Since norms are both public and intersubjective, the complexity of translation increases the need to pay special attention to cultural-political contexts, which are related to the production and reproduction of both literal and cultural meaning and its acceptability and reception in both cultural systems.

Due to historical and cultural factors, the intended or putatively "real" meaning of certain parts of the source text is undoubtedly not limited to their literal meaning, and then it is the responsibility of the translator to "explain" what is beyond the literal meaning. Not only does he/she run an interpretive risk largely owing to his/her cultural obligation to both the source and target cultures, but he/she may get things wrong with a particular cultural-political context, be it of the source text or the target text. Translation initiates and facilitates intercultural communication, and the translated text is transposed from one cultural context to another. In the process of translation, enough attention and respect are supposed to be given by the translator to the original cultural context in which the translated text was originally written.

If a context, be it historical, cultural, political, and textual (all of the modifiers are directly relevant to cross-cultural communication) or the combination of them all, is provided by the author, it can be reasonably assumed that at least part of his/her intention is recoverable. Even if translation leads to re-contextualization, it may still aim at restoring, at least partially so, the historical and cultural context of the source text. Of course, there are cases in the history of translation that the source text is completely de-historicized. Thus, contextualization makes reading translation less relevant to the target readership; on the other hand, re-contextualization tends to de-historicize reading – and therefore risks anachronism. Still, it is almost inconceivable to claim that the author has nothing to do with meaning. In the extreme case of intentionalism as vigorously advocated by Hirsch, textual meaning is distinctly commensurate with authorial intention, and in arguing for validating interpretation, Hirsch implicitly assumes that authorial intention can be fully recovered. It is true that in some isolated and straightforward cases, such a possibility cannot be precluded. Since such an argument does get demonstrable results, the situation becomes difficult and complicated: the author's intent, the changed cultural milieu, coupled with the translator caught in the middle, or the somewhat different mindset of the target reader, may all contribute to the destabilizing and unpredictable consequences for translation.

Among other things, the translator needs to consider whether he or she has a sympathetic, neutral, or hostile audience. Are they well-informed, ignorant, and skeptical? Like the original author, the translator is socially and politically responsible for his product(s). He or she translates what he or she understands and uses some type of interpretative rubric in order to make sense of what he/she reads and sets out to translate. Yet it requires the transcendence of cultural relativism to construct connections with other cultures. In undertaking the activities of cross-cultural exchange, vital questions about subjectivities and power relations need to be raised. Different cultural contexts signify that the author-translator relationship is never fixed in view of the ever-shifting cultural contexts. Despite the cultural-political constraints, the translator is given considerable leeway to organize alien elements from the source culture into a coherent and intelligible entity in the target text. In addition, reproduction in various cultural contexts amounts to different translated versions, as in the case where a given source text is translated into different languages. Translation is like something being taken out of context – this refers to the historical, cultural, and social context of the original text. But translation can barely be holistic in its approach to the source text, including its historical and cultural context, and it is no less difficult to bring the perspectives of other cultures into the target cultural system.

In his famous "The Task of the Translator," Benjamin likens the act of translation to destruction and transformation. What needs to be destroyed is none other than untranslatability, which is then transformed into what is considered acceptable by the target community, even though sometimes the translator may take it up as his/her responsibility to educate the target reader. However, the cultural and political acceptability of translation or the way in which a given text is translated depends, in many ways, on the cultural-political acceptability of the translated text. In this respect, it is perfectly normal for the translator to resort to cultural-political subterfuge when necessary, irrespective of translational respectability. As observed by Susan Bassnett, "[t]he idea of the origin came under scrutiny, and both Derrida and De Campos, by rereading Benjamin, formulated the concept of translation that becomes the original by virtue of its coming into existence after the source" (Bassnett 1996: 22). Benjamin famously argues that the continued life of a text depends on translation. But whether such a life is possible, or how good that life is, it is invariably related to the subjectivity of the translator, whose ability and willingness to perform his/her duty are of great importance.

As a cultural outsider, the target reader may find it difficult to make sense of perplexing historical and cultural referents and certain strange linguistic constructions as manifest in translationese. Re-contextualization, to some extent, ensures that the target reader remains an outsider, and the translated text either makes less sense or makes sense in a different (or possibly refreshing) way. Cultural alienation points to a general lack of empathy on the part of the target text reader that is required to appreciate the inherent cultural qualities of the original. Thus, cultural transformation is rendered necessary by the translator in order to achieve a level of acceptability even in a hostile environment that is politically forbidding and culturally conservative by helping the target reader to make sense of the initially what seems to be incomprehensible. This is a process of transforming the strange into the familiar, and of making necessary cultural connections between the source and target texts. Translation is a re-reading of a text with a view to transferring it to a different cultural and perhaps political setting. Cultural meaning is produced within a specific ideological and cultural context, and thus reading translation is a culturally distinct experience. If what the target reader encounters in reading translation may be something that is not desirable culturally and ideologically, they face an immediate challenge. That all human understandings are strictly culturally relative is grotesquely exaggerated if not manifestly false. It is true that certain things are "culturally specific" and not universally valid due to different cultural histories. Moreover, there may be culturally inappropriate elements embedded in translation from the viewpoint of the target readership, which encourages people to become more culturally relativistic. When source and target readers are not in tune culturally, cross-cultural communication is poor, and this no doubt hinders cross-cultural exchange.

However, critics with a psychoanalytical bent are interested in unconscious intention, and social critics, including New Historicists and Cultural Materialists, have often attributed intention to a social activity or movement, and even a form of social control or behavior. This is particularly so in terms of signification, which is more likely to be beyond authorial intention or control. As Paul de Man observes in discussing Proust's novels:

> Everything signifies something other than what it represents . . . it is always something else that is intended. It can be shown that the most adequate term to designate this "something else" is Reading. But one must at the same time "understand" that this word bars access, once and forever, to a meaning.
>
> (De Man 1979: 77)

Authorial intention is ontologically prior to the language through which meaning finds expression. What can the translator do under the circumstances? Clearly, to represent something that signifies something else as intended by the author is by no means easy for the translator, for whom translation is an epistemological and cultural act that conveys deep and sometimes even unintended messages, which would only further complicate the situation.

Decoding and re-writing

To contextualize is to localize and to delimit because meaning can only be located with certainty within a specific context. As Peter Burke notes, "Context is often regarded as local, but the idea of a 'global context' is also in circulation. It might well be asked, What is not context?" (Burke 2002: 171). Sometimes when a text provides the bare minimum of context and exposition for what is presented, the translator must think carefully about what to do in a complex cultural context. However, in a broad sense, translation inevitably provides a different cultural context for a given text when it is translated into the target language. An awareness of the changed cultural context is of particular importance to understanding how translation operates. According to Burke:

> Although it is always wise to think contextually, contextual analysis is best treated as one method rather than "the" method of cultural or intellectual history. In any case, we need to think of contexts in the plural. To do so is not only to use the word in the plural form but to remember to ask, in what other contexts might this word, action, object be placed? What looks, when one first discovers it, like "the" context for an idea, object, statement, or event generally turns out to be no more than "a" context?
>
> (Burke 2002: 174)

The defining function of context allows cultural interpretation and understanding. In other words, contextualization makes the translated text interpretable at a literal level. Moreover, translation is linked with the inevitability of cultural contextualization, and the mode(s) of contextualization inevitably affects meaning and reading, and subsequently reception.

Translation may entail an altogether different cultural context to necessitate an alternative interpretation or understanding. Therefore, the experience of reading translations may change the cultural status of the reader, though not necessarily turning them into an insider since the culturally uninformed will not change overnight.

Meanwhile, we cannot neglect the possibility that in a given context, what is otherwise acceptable may become unacceptable and vice versa. Translation requires the use of another language that is also able to employ existing cultural referents. For this reason, there is the possibility that ideas are simply misunderstood in their transmission from one cultural context to another without a proper historical and cultural context. We need a means of evaluating the processes of a realignment of priorities so that cultural interpretation can be enabled to establish relevance and coherence. Fortunately, in many places, the cultural context of the original account may bear sufficient likeness to our own to enable us to interpret what transpires without much difficulty. On the other hand, however, the target reader may not be able to interpret certain things without being helped by the translator. These activities inescapably take place within a specific cultural context, which may be a clearly defined mono-cultural situation or, more frequently, within a multicultural environment. It is thus necessary for translation to seek to re-contextualize as a means to avoid contextualizing, which would require the unrealistic supply of excessive amounts of additional historical and cultural information – an unbearable cultural burden on the target reader. Meanwhile, it is also tempting to exaggerate difference as embedded in cultural particularism, which may indicate an unwillingness to seek overlaps, and this may shift us dangerously towards viewing the others as beings who are inherently and irredeemably different from ourselves. After all, we share more with each other – culturally, socially, and even politically – than we do not share. Therefore, to radically re-contextualize leads to distortion and evasion because contextual cues can help the retrieval of associative information, which in turn enables us to catch and decode the underlying intertextual references.

To be clear, translation should be viewed as a decontextualized, semantically interpreted, and culturally negotiated act, which is conducted in a localized space, taking into account the local concerns and conditions of reception. In order to decode meaning, there is a need for creating an interpretative space in which associations are made by the translator. The primary purpose of interpretation is to seek understanding. It is necessary to state that the translator is first and foremost a reader who processes information in a private space in which subjectivity is defined and enacted.

> The translator's interpretation is always performed in and influenced by a cultural situation where values, beliefs and representations, as well as the social groups to which they are affiliated, are arrayed in a hierarchical order of power and prestige.
>
> (Venuti 2011: 237)

This localized space is made available to enable the translator to make sense of and evaluate the source text, making connection with a host of related dimensions such as the translator's evocative resonance with and emotional response to the message being processed. In deciding whether or how to align translation with the original, the role of subjectivity in reclaiming and reproducing meaning becomes prominent in bringing into shape the translated text. For the translator, there is indivisibility between reading experience and writing experiences: he translates what he reads into writing, hence the debate on authorship. Is there a creative space within this localized space? When the translator says something, what he says duplicates or is based on what someone else has already said. The different subjectivities are conducive to shaping individual understandings of the source text and production of the target text.

Viewed in this way, the translator is not so much accountable for what is said, but for how it is said. However, the translator's authorship, though fiercely defended by some translation scholars, especially Venuti (1992), is not easily attainable, despite the claim that a certain degree of creativity can be observed. For Berman, fidelity in the sense of reproducing foreignness is an ethical issue, and he argues that "to disclose the Foreign as Foreign in its own linguistic space" (Quoted by Venuti 2011: 241). This in a way justifies the claim of translation. What can be less controversially established is the status of rewriter. In contrast to the author, the translator is supposed to perform a rather different task: to re-historicize, re-contextualize, and de-alienate cultural material at least up to a point. The relationship and hierarchy between author and translator are variable in the perception of their different roles and functions and can legitimize shared authorship under certain circumstances. The interplay and tensions between the two identities are embodied in the act of rewriting and they gravitate towards overlapping in some important respects and to varying degrees. The precarious balance between private and public spaces inhabited by reader and author respectively keeps changing and they can also merge to become shared spaces. Much of the discussion of the so-called ethics of translation is related to the accountability of translation and for that matter, the translator.

Translation is the product of "an interpretative act that submits the source material to degrees of loss and gain" (Venuti 2011: 230). Whether it is loss or gain, some degree of distortion is unavoidable. However, it can well be argued that translation is more than the product of interpretation. No one would dispute the derivative nature of translation, but the resultant translated versions can deviate significantly from the original. But deviating exactly from what? Meaning, form, or effect? Sometimes maybe all of them. Navigating a culturally complex universe of the source text is a challenging task because foreignness is interpreted variously and culturally, in terms of what they believe is culturally correct and acceptable. Simply put, the role of interpretation is always contextualized, and it can be contextualized differently, thus the possibility of multiple interpretations, as a result of which different translation versions are expected.

In offering a critique of Berman's advocacy of foreignness in translation, Venuti rightly points out that differences can only by displayed indirectly (Venuti 2011: 242). He once again foregrounds the essential role of interpretation in relation to translation:

> Yet a translation can only communicate an interpretation of the source text, never that text itself or some form or meaning believed to be inherent in it. The interpretation that a translation inscribes, furthermore, is partial and contingent: partial because it is incomplete in recreating the source text and slanted towards the receiving culture; contingent because it is fixed by a set of interpretants that vary among receiving cultural constituencies, social situations and historical moments.
>
> (Venuti 2011: 246)

But to confine what a translation can communicate to interpretation is too absolute and limiting. As indicated earlier, it is precisely certain formal features and stylistic registers of the original that can be directly transferred or even relocated to the target language to be expressive of meaning. Moreover, it is not admissible to say that translation is all about translating meaning. Indeed, interpretation can only be partial since no interpretation can be exhaustive, not to mention re-articulation in the form of translation.

In the context of translation, rewriting is normally contingent and based on and governed by interpretation. However, rewriting is also precarious and con-ditional on the circumstances of a given translation task, which may well entail and justify omissions, additions, and modifications. To be sure, a translation is a rewritten text. Rewriting may permit a certain leeway and space for the transla-tor to do something different. But even if the notion of equivalence is largely discarded in contemporary Translation Studies, significant and unrestrained lexi-cal and syntactical departures are still viewed to be unacceptable. Admittedly, of course, such departures are often necessary and worthwhile. Adaptive translation, exemplified by alterations to the original, takes full consideration of and pays spe-cial attention to attain the intended function in the target text by traversing the space of the original and superimposing it with that of the target system. A more extreme form of rewriting in connection with translation is transwriting, which allows for even more spatial dimensions for reconfiguration and manipulation.

In general, the conditions of reproduction and reception vary significantly from situation to situation in different historical and contextual spaces. Does a translator translate one way rather than another because he interprets one way rather than another? Though not always necessarily so, what gets translated and the way in which it is translated is subject to some other factors, be they historical, ideological, and cultural. Rewriting takes up different forms shaped by the con-sideration of the function that is assigned to a particular translation. Translation involves, by implication, variegated forms and degrees of manipulation variously motivated and operates at different levels. Aside from obvious cases of ideological manipulation, which are universally common and account for the major reason for the source text to be rewritten in a way that seems to "legitimatize" distortion or suppression. On the other hand, however, to enhance readability, or for some other reason, the stylistic elevation of the original can be observed from time to time. A veteran Chinese translator, Xu Yuanchong, promotes the unabashed pursuit of the so-called maximum advantage of the target language (Xu 2000: 2). He rates highly Ezra Pound's translation of classical Chinese poetry, which is seen "to bring into full play the advantage of the target language. Beauty is sought at the expense of accuracy" (Xu 2000: 5). As he sees it, rewriting is the opportu-nity to improve and outshine the source text and he has no qualms about face-lifting the original because literary translation represents "rivalry between two languages and even two cultures" (Xu 2000: 2).

While interpretation can be personal, the same is true to rewriting, both of which thus become subjective so as to risk certain self-indulgence on the part of the translator in focusing steadfastly on what is construed as relevant to his moral, political, ideological or aesthetic predilections. The interpretative importance in the act of translation has been hitherto largely underestimated, since much atten-tion is still paid to accuracy and adequacy, as is shown by an abiding concern with textual resemblance or correspondence in translation. But the text that bears a secret meaning within its surface appearances and thus, in many cases, resembling the surface is not only useless but also, worse still, potentially misleading. The foreign other, as manifest in the form of the unfamiliar embedded in translation, inevitably means the occasional virtual absence of interpretative precedents. It is no doubt true that intersubjective clashes between author and translator lead to a given text being interpreted in one way but translated in quite another. Translation does not necessarily conform to interpretation. However, through the subjectively interpretive and subversive creativity of translation, meaning is subject to serious political, cultural, or poetic manipulation. Meaning can be unraveled by paying attention to the structure of signifying elements that can be replaced or re-configurated and also by interpreting from a cultural context constituted by history, culture, and politics.

Admittedly, within a relatively short span of time, there is a limit to how many foreign influences a culture can absorb before being swamped. Even when a foreign influence is deemed useful and thus initially genuinely welcomed, it may become too much to be culturally tolerable. The degrees of cultural openness to foreign texts are ideologically or politically determined. And also, cultural and political appropriation and assimilation, though generally viewed as pervasive and deleterious to cross-cultural communication, can in fact help to improve the acceptability of foreign cultures. In light of this, the cultural subjectivities of translators are necessary to negotiate cross-cultural adjustments for the sake of better reception. And to understand the different subjectivities that have shaped individual understandings of events sheds light on the indeterminate nature of cultural-political meaning. In essence, the translator does not translate a message but translates a decoded message, and to decode a message leads to the discovery of something not quite experienced by the target reader before.

Cultural politics of translation

Irrespective of the social or cultural context surrounding the original text, once it is chosen to be translated into the target language, its reading and significance may be rather different. A telling example is the translation of George Orwell's *Animal Farm* into Chinese. The translation of the novel was published in a Shanghai literary magazine in 1988. But to the great disappointment of the translator, the translation went largely unnoticed at the time and thereafter. Due to the political sensitivity of this novel in China, the translation was understandably not accompanied by a preface providing the necessary contextual interpretation. In the absence of the historical context surrounding the writing of the novel, few Chinese readers recognized it as a satirical allegory of the Russian Revolution that refers to Joseph Stalin and Leon Trotsky fighting for control of the newly formed Soviet Union after Lenin died in 1924. As far as one can tell, this translated text failed to be re-contextualized as well. Although the political, ideological, and cultural context in which each novel is produced should be at the forefront of the textual analysis in translation or literary criticism, this is not always the case, of course. Nevertheless, the real truth may be just the opposite. Perhaps the allegory was only too obvious to the target reader after the Cultural Revolution. This translation was perhaps seen as a clumsy and belated attempt to make sense of the Cultural Revolution. It was a cultural-political reflection too frightening to be faced once again since so many peoples had been involved in it! While it is perfectly reasonable to argue that the play of universals and particulars gives the translator space to manipulate reading, how to establish a meaningful working relationship between the two still poses a challenge. Nonetheless, the choice of texts for translation is politically significant, and such texts have been regarded as "cultural arms" smuggled into China. Cultural intersubjectivity and subjectivity with regard to translation are a rather intriguing issue here. Translators are cross-culturally providers, protectors, and progenitors, and as a result, the site of translation is marked by momentous political implications.

The cultural politics of translation can be intimately related to the subjectivity of the translator. The translation and publication of Orwell's *Nineteen Eighty-Four* are perfect examples of cultural politics. One earlier translated version by a Taiwan translator was published in Taiwan in 1979, followed by another translation by a mainland Chinese translator/scholar. The second version was also published in Taiwan in 1991 and then surprisingly, in 1998 it was published by Liaoning Education Press in mainland China. *Nineteen Eighty-Four* was recontextualized by the translator Dong Leshan (1924–1999) to bear upon the catastrophic Cultural Revolution and no less importantly, its traumatic aftermath. Dong's translation was first published in Taiwan in 1991, and he pointed out in his preface to the translation that it was a great deal easier to introduce Orwell to the reader in Taiwan than in mainland China, the obvious reason being that "there was much less political apprehension" in Taiwan (Dong 1991: 1). Literary writings about the Cultural Revolution are not free of official censorship but government policy is much less rigid about translations due perhaps to their indirectness. The cultural-political contextual cues do indeed have their effect by fostering the retrieval of previously suppressed information, although the target readership is somewhat culturally and politically insensitive to the political implications of certain translations. It explains why such translations are tolerated.

Of course, the reception of translations includes some cultural or political realignment or abandonment of some of the so-called harmful foreign elements, be they culturally unfashionable, politically unpopular, or commercially unprofitable. It can be argued that truth is relational; that is, relative to the social and historical location of the intersubjective action, and only emerges in relation to the cultural-political reality of the target community. Meaning exists in the process of intersubjective communication since no utterance ever is truly isolated. Regardless of what the source text actually says, it is completely up to the target reader to construct or determine the meaning of the translated text. And it is not merely a question of cross-cultural equivalencies, namely finding the appropriate counterparts within the cultural frame of reference in the target culture. In a given context in which something is uttered, the failure to grasp the intended meaning is not unrelated to an unwillingness to take authorial intention seriously. Thus, a typical translator perhaps cannot entirely avoid asking himself/herself: "What does the text try to say?" Naive as the question may be, it points to the function of words – they must have a role to play, to communicate or express something, whatever that something is. Translatorial intention is made more explicit in Dong's preface to the same translation of *Nineteen Eighty-Four* published in mainland China, the translator attempts to make direct connections with the horrific nature of the Cultural Revolution in light to the different cultural-political context by addressing the lamentable and terrifying collective unconsciousness that resulted in a collective frenzy.

The translatorial intention, inseparable from self-conscious cultural-political sensitivity, results in an imperceptible complex ownership action or ownership change. But this claim of ownership can be problematic. While the subjectivity of the translator is politicized to varying degrees, a text is subject to politically motivated interpretations and, as a result, reading is turned into a political act with noticeably less serious cultural constraints. Therefore, it can be said that impetuous interpretation has a double danger: (1) misinterpretation or under(over)-interpretation; (2) the target reader deprived of the experience of reading what is directly and distinctly articulated in the source text may miss the point altogether. While it is obviously not enough for the translator to deal with only the surface of a text, he/she needs to be careful if he/she decides to delve into it despite intertextuality. A text has its constructed realm, which means that it is not entirely open to any unbridled interpretation(s), much as such acts of interpretation may be culturally and politically desirable from the point of view of the target community. However, like reading or interpretation, translation can be easily turned into a political exercise. The surface features of a foreign text are not only immediately discoverable but sometimes actually "forced upon" the reader, particularly if the text is somewhat foreignized. Foreignization is one way of forcing the reader to accept the alien and unnatural in terms of attaining cultural value.

Foreignization is a political issue. Accordingly, the tensions of ideological incommensurability need to be dissipated in order to facilitate cross-cultural understanding and communication. A degree of ideological pluralism permits cultural diversity distinctively marked by tolerance of difference and attempts to reduce an underlying distrust of the foreign. Multiculturalism, however, by no means denotes the demise of ideology. Despite its ostensible theoretical naivety, intentionalism has some serious implications for the translator, who may ignore at his/her own peril, for instance, the complex ideological consciousness that informs not only the source text but also the resulting target text. If we say that both the author and the reader are responsible for context or its construction, then the translator must play the double role of reader and author in the sense of (re)constructing context. While we interpret with many aims, the act of interpretation is culturally and ideologically conditioned, and the ensuing complicated remapping is such that translation is always somewhat adrift.

But regardless of the chosen translation strategy in a given situation, the reader must be allowed or even enabled to penetrate the surface features to know what the text really says. Beyond the known and discoverable surface meaning, there is a deeper meaning that may or may not be captured by the reader. The surface meaning of the words may mask a contrary and hidden subtext. In theory, the translator is not supposed to let a subtext go unnoticed, although it is not uncommon to suppress a subtext that is likely to cause offense. On the other hand, as in the case of translating *Nineteen Eighty-Four*, if the subtext is not properly recognized by the target reader whose frustrating apathy diminishes the meaningfulness of translation, the translator invariably feels disenchanted with the lack of social-political impact his/her translation is potentially capable of producing. The translatorial intention is that the reading of this translation will demonstrate something deeper, a parallel suffering, a similar pain, a commensurate confusion and disorientation that echo and bring to mind what the Chinese lived through during the Cultural Revolution. A shockingly pertinent reminder is sorely needed to draw attention specifically to the sheer breadth of implications stemming from this monumental cultural catastrophe in human history.

Reading is necessarily culturally allegorized, and if the surface meaning is allegorized as something radically different from what is intended or designed, there may be problems. Cross-culturally, competing interpretations are more common as demonstrated in the entanglement of competing or conflicting cultural or political values. Moreover, it is important to bear in mind that a text is produced within a specific social and cultural milieu with its author invariably being conditioned and restricted, and the translated text is produced in a different social and cultural milieu – naturally, it is also culturally and politically conditioned. The translator needs to read transcendentally not to be moved by the source text, if so, he/she amplifies the message; otherwise, she/he treats it with apathy. One's underlying assumptions and attitudes may affect one's interpretation and translation. At any rate, it is possible to offer a given source text a sympathetic interpretation, which can make a considerable difference to the overall reading of the translated text. Simply put, it is possible that under-interpretation leads to under-translation and over-interpretation to over-translation.

Conclusion

The role of contextual factors is paramount in translation as a means of cross-cultural communication, and these factors may be considered from historical, social, cultural, political, and global perspectives because of the high degree of contextual determinacy based on textual evidence. A (re)-contextual approach to cultural political meaning creates the conditions for (re)-interpretation in the translated text. Both a contextual or/and re-contextual appreciation is necessary when the target reader needs to overcome the obliquity of both language and culture. The overarching question is how the ever-shifting cultural-political context shapes and changes meaning and, more importantly, the cultural-political signification of translated texts. A change of context that attenuates latent inhibition perpetuates the cultural complexity of translation. The underlying asymmetry in power relations between the translator and the dominant form of representation of the target culture is fully expected in cross-cultural interaction. Not unproblematically, both the breadth and depth of meaning and its (re)-presentation in translation are called into serious question when a contextual frame of reference is either unavailable or only partially available. Cross-cultural production may not necessarily be ideologically driven, but the presence or absence of cultural politics can provide important insights into various ontological predicaments of trans-cultural activity.

References

Barthes, Roland (ed. and trans. by Stephen Heath) (1977) *Image-Music-Text*, London: Fontana.

Bassnett, Susan (1996) "The Meek or the Mighty: Reappraising the Role of the Translator," in Román Álvarez and M. Carmenfrica Vidal (ed.) *Translation, Power, Subversion*, Clevedon: Multilingual Matters Ltd., 10–24.

Burke, Peter (2002) "Context in Context," *Common Knowledge* 8(1): 152–177.

De Man, Paul (1979) *Allegories of Reading: Figural Language in Rousseau, Nietzsche, Rilke, and Proust*, New Haven: Yale University Press.

Dong, Leshan (1991) "《一九八四》台湾版译序" (Translator's Preface to the Taiwan Edition of *Nineteen Eighty-Four*), in George Orwell (ed.) 《一九八四》 (*Nineteen Eighty-Four*), Taipei: Zhiwen chubanshe, 1–4.

Foucault, Michel (ed. by Donald F. Bouchard; trans. by Donald F. Bouchard and Sherry Simon) (1977) "Nietzsche, Genealogy, History," in *Language, Counter-Memory, Practice: Selected Essays and Interviews/Michel Foucault*, Ithaca, NY: Cornell University Press, 139–164.

Harris, Wendell V. (1996) *Literary Meaning: Reclaiming the Study of Literature*, London: Macmillan.

Hartman, Geoffrey H. (1982) *Saving the Text: Literature/Derrida/Philosophy*, Baltimore and London: Johns Hopkins University Press.

Hirsch, E. D., Jr. (1967) *Validity in Interpretation*, New Haven, NC: Yale University Press.

Kofman, Sarah (trans. by Duncan Large) (1993) *Nietzsche and Metaphor*, Stanford, CA: Stanford University Press.

Lyon, Arabella (1998) *Intentions: Negotiated, Contested, and Ignored*, University Park: Pennsylvania State University Press.

Parr, James A. (2000) "Don Quixote: Translation and Interpretation," *Philosophy and Literature* 24(2): 387–405.

Samuels, Lisa, and Jerome McGann (1999) "Deformance and Interpretation," *New Literary History* 30(1): 25–56.

Venuti, Lawrence (1992) "Introduction," in Lawrence Venuti (ed.) *Rethinking Translation: Discourse, Subjectivity, Ideology*, London and New York: Routledge, 1–17.

Venuti, Lawrence (2011) "The Poet's Version; or, An Ethics of Translation," *Translation Studies* 4(2): 230–247.

Xu, Yuanchong (2000) "新世纪的新译论" (New Translation Theories of the New Age), 《中国翻译》 (*Chinese Translators Journal*) 21(3): 2–6.

7 Spatial trajectories of "back" translation

Introduction

This chapter attempts to delineate the trajectory of translation and back translation by examining a few related cases in which Chinese American literature draws
on its cultural material from the "native" Chinese culture in combination with
American literary tradition, thereby generating spatial dynamics. It can be argued
that such literature is, in a broad sense, the outcome of translation – or rather,
of cultural translation. A shifting of cultural spaces signifies the uprooting and
adaptation of Chinese culture and its haunting influence on the writing practice
designed for the needs of the American reader are juxtaposed and culminate in
acculturation and assimilation as part of a creative process. The retelling of Chinese stories, therefore, involves indirect translation and direct rewriting based
on fascinating transnational experiments. In many instances, the author, either
a Chinese immigrant or descendent, can also be seen as a translator, and in this
light, the meaning and function of the ostensible primacy of the original are different as compared with conventional translation. It must be emphasized that the
seemingly non-existent source text(s) is/are not non-existent. Chinese American
literary texts transmigrate Chinese into English, often revealing linguistic and
cultural traces of the "original" in all its complexity with cultural Chineseness
being retained or reproduced in parallel with the construction of and interaction
with literary Americanness. The invisible source text(s) is/are embodied notably by a trove of cultural references, playing a central role in the functionality
of transcoding ethnicity. The travel of the Chinese culture has generated cultural translation that enriches the original host culture, which is characterized by
negotiation, reconciliation, and transformation by moving beyond or abolishing
previous cultural confinement. After Chinese raw material is thus "translated"
into English, it is integrated into American literature. Meanwhile, some Chinese
American literary texts are translated "back" into Chinese, exhibiting a peculiar
linguistic and cultural displacement, and therefore suggests the need for "cultural
restoration." Chinese American transnationalism is demonstrably exemplified in
such practices of translation and "back translation," rewriting and re-rewriting.
Translation and re-translation foreground not only defamiliarized Chinese culture but also its creative assimilation into American literature.

The travel of culture is not a singular motion, but the combination of interactions and vibrations between different cultures. Cultural transnationality features prominently in Chinese American literature, which thrives on Chinese cultural heritage. The success story of Chinese American literature has prompted rethinking of Chinese culture that has been alienated and estranged through translation as a constitutive part of the literary and creative process, in a more cultural than linguistic sense. The Chinese translation of some of the more successful Chinese American literary texts re-contextualizes and problematizes the perception and representation of Chinese culture through translations of various forms. The ubiquity of translation, especially in its broad sense, is best manifest here, and the examination of how culture is presented through translation in relation to the re-creation of the source text(s) gives rise to some challenging questions about the central role of cultural translation in Chinese American literature and its "back translation" into Chinese, relocated in a different spatial environment and back to its original cultural context. The conditions of cultural production and reception are so closely intertwined that they shed light on the ways in which translation and back translation function and on how creative writing is thus boosted in this process. Within their sociopolitical contexts of cultural production and reception, it is meaningful to investigate the dimension of cultural translation in Chinese American literature and the fascinating modes of culture traveling translationally and translationally, consisting of historical and cultural spaces in which cultural interaction and transformation take place.

Chinese American literature

It can be said that a significant part of Chinese American literature involves cultural translation in its broad sense. Some well-established Chinese writers, such as Lin Yutang and Eileen Chang, immigrated to America and translated their own works into English as well as wrote directly in English. American writers of Chinese descent, including Jade Snow Wong, Amy Tan, Maxine Hong Kingston, and Frank Chin, have inherited the oral tradition of Chinese culture and translated it into American writing with resounding success. What has been translated as raw material for their fiction writing is based on traditional folklore, myth, historical fact, and talk-story. The transnationally situated subjectivity is of central importance to Chinese American writers whose ethnic-cultural identity is fraught with the challenge of how to process such cultural material from a different spatial location. The intercultural hybridity arising out of the experiences of these writers, past and present, direct and indirect, establishes the uniqueness of Chinese American writing. Invariably, conflicts between Chinese and American value systems are often uncomfortably juxtaposed within shifting Chinese and American cultural contexts and literary practices. Transnational communication consists of interaction among transnational families whose stories are told in many of the Chinese American texts. Yet, unbridgeable chasms and irreconcilable differences in cultures appear constantly between what is Chinese and what is American as reflected in conflicts between parents whose native language is Chinese and children whose native language is English. For these mothers' children, most of whom happen to be daughters, both the Chinese language and culture become, to a certain extent, parts of otherness.

Broadly speaking, Chinese American writing can be divided into two categories according to the native language of the author, which is either English or Chinese. Lin Yutang, whose native language is Chinese, studied at Harvard and Leipzig before settling in America in 1935. He published a novel *Moment in Peking* in 1939. It is a Chinese story written in English for an American audience rather than being about the Chinese experience in America or any American events or people. Lin's primary purpose of writing for Americans was to introduce Chinese culture deriving from an external space. However, the reason for Eileen Chang writing a novel in English is less straightforward and requires some explanation. Commissioned by the US Information Service in Hong Kong to produce anti-communist literature, she wrote two novels entitled *Rice Sprout Song* and *The Naked Earth: A Novel about China* respectively. The former is her first novel in English published by Charles Scribner's Sons, following an outline prepared by the United States Information Service in Hong Kong (Wang 2015: 73–173). It is a story about China in the early 1950s during the period of land reform and the abject state of poverty in the rural area. The novel was never well received, although there has been some rekindled interest in it recently. By the same token, the native language of the well-acclaimed writer Ha Jin is also Chinese. While he writes in English, most of his stories are retrospectively set in earlier times in China. His *Waiting*, which has won the US National Book Award, is based on a story told by his Chinese wife. It is a Chinese story told in English from a Chinese perspective primarily for an American audience. Therefore, there seems to be no lack of cultural genesis in the aforementioned novels. Meanwhile, it needs to be pointed out that the diasporic conditions of these transplanted writers are significant in shaping their writings.

In contrast, however, writers of Chinese descent and whose native language is English are much more likely to draw on their American experiences. With limited direct knowledge of Chinese culture, they tend to move between old and new cultural homes and spaces. Generational and cultural connections are explored and well represented in their works. Unlike those Chinese American writers whose native language is Chinese, they make no serious effort to mediate the differences between Chinese cultural heritage and immediate American experience. The end result seems to be knowingly inaccurate as far as presenting Chinese culture is concerned and points to subversion and transformation. Kingston is chastised by Frank Chin, among others, for mistakenly representing China in her fiction, which is a "fake" China. The apathy of cultural authenticity is ascribed to the desire to cater to white American readers. Chin lampoons Kingston in his article "The Big Aiiieeeee?" for her misleading portrayal of Chinese sexism in *The Woman Warrior*, part of which is based on Chinese legends and myths. Significantly, Kingston is adamant that her identity is not Chinese. By refusing to be called a Chinese woman, Kingston does not wish to be given ethnographic authority to introduce to America an authentic Chinese culture or its tradition.

Nevertheless, the Chineseness underlying the works by the American writers of Chinese descent reflects the power of transnational capital and their dual identity resulting from linguistic and cultural accommodation and transformation. Another similar example is *Fifth Chinese Daughter* by Jade Snow Wong, and drawing on autobiographical material, it is unmistakably Chinese and about members of a Chinese family living in San Francisco. As is often the case, powerfully manifest is the combined influence of Chinese cultural heritage and American social reality. Meanwhile, it can be observed that the definition of American literature is being expanded through the study of ethnic literatures produced in the US, including Chinese American literature with its unique cultural, historical and social knowledge. This is interestingly shown in the early Chinese translation of the very term "Chinese American literature" in the People's Republic of China: it was rendered as "American Chinese literature" at the time. The deliberate change of order suggests that at least it was understood that Chinese American literature was regarded as an integral part of American literature.

Yet, the uniqueness of Chinese American literature as distinct from mainstream American literature is that it is evidently transnational. It is more than a minority literature but part of more broadly conceived American literature and has already been integrated into the latter. Martha J. Cutter points out:

> Ethnic American writers use the trope of translation, then, to speak in a double voice that finally attempts to dismantle the line between a process of translation that colonizes and a process of translation that enriches and to undermine the demarcation between the "majority" discourse and the "marginal" dialect.
>
> (Cutter 2005: 16)

The translational nature of many of the works means that Chinese American writers are confronted with cultural tension that has emerged in their creative/translational writing/ rewriting, which compounds the issue of cultural identity. Undeniably, the oscillation between centrality and peripherality is characteristic of Chinese American literature. And the resonances of these works with Chinese cultural tradition have prompted oldness to become newness with the boundaries between insiders and outsiders being crossed and even redrawn from time to time. Inevitably, Chinese American writers are somewhat personally involved in the text being created by mediating in different spaces cultural differences and practices. And their relationship to otherness becomes complicated because of its elusive nature. Consequently, the transnational identities concerning Chinese and American cultures collide and merge into an exciting domain of creative experimentation.

Transnational representation

It is plain that the transnationalization of Chinese stories in America is quintessentially related to cultural translation that is open to transformation. The uniqueness of this type of translation is the general lack of a visible or tangible source text which is then translated into English and transferred to a new cultural context. Nevertheless, it is also worth mentioning that linguistic translation, though of a secondary order of importance in our discussion, is still necessary. In "Pangs of Love" by David Wong Louie, for instance, a Chinese woman has lived in New York for 40 years without acquiring the ability to speak English. On a daily basis, she communicates to her son and others in Chinese. In some novels by Chinese American female writers, the daughter, whether she likes it or not, is imposed on the thankless and often mildly annoying task of doing translation for her mother. Although spatially contiguous, mother and daughter are culturally divided and conflict-prone: they often speak different languages, not only linguistically but also culturally. In a broad historical and cultural context, cross-cultural translation is more important than linguistic translation. As Jing-Mei Woo comments in *The Joy Luck Club*: "We translated each other's meanings and I seemed to hear less than what was said, while my mother heard more" (Tan 1989: 27). Mother and daughter have disparate ideas, representing different cultural spaces that turn out to be mutually inaccessible. There is a severe communication problem because what is at stake is the possibility of conveying cultural meaning. Chinese-speaking immigrant mothers need to be translated by their English-speaking daughters. In this sense, the original does exist to be translated into English.

In truth, traces and remnants of the "original" are everywhere. The mixed-ness of cultures as shown in Homi Bhabha's emphasis on cultural hybridity is not the same as the mixture of cultures because they are still traceable and identifiable. The Chineseness in the English text is an embodiment of the presence or traces of a source text or a cluster of source texts. *The Joy Luck Club*, for instance, strives to create the effect of bearing some semblance to authenticity by using Chinglish extensively, which is tantalizingly reminiscent of "bad" translation or literal translation from the Chinese original. At first glance, the author seems to refuse to translate or rather, to translate properly, and in effect, the awkward syntax in the colloquial form of mothers' English is painstakingly kept. In a sense, this mode of expression can be construed as an extreme form of foreignized translation. This practically unmediated linguistic translation foregrounds the alienation of otherness that gives some idea of the formidable difficulty of mutual understanding between mother and daughter by demonstrating that even filial communication between mother and daughter is constrained by different and thus inhibiting cultural codes, which are starkly juxtaposed but rarely shared.

In terms of accuracy and reliability, some basic linguistic mistakes arising from translation by some Chinese American writers have been pointed out by scholars. Amy Tan, in an amusing way, mistakenly translates "*tangjie*" (cousin) into "sugar sister." But of course the character "*tang*," though sounding the same as "sugar" in Chinese, is written as "hall." The combination of "hall" and "sister" forms the word "cousin." The two homonyms are the cause of the confusion. Tan's inadequate knowledge of Chinese is revealed here, as pointed out by Wong (Wong 1995: 27). A similar mistake has been made by Kingston, which is less forgivable, as noted by Karen Kai-Yuan Su: *tianji* (frog); it literally means field chicken but is mistakenly rendered as heavenly chicken. To be sure, in Chinese tian as field and tian as heaven are not strictly homonyms because their tones are markedly different (noted by Su 1998: 43). Kingston simply elides the distinction between the two totally different characters forming the word. Such a distinction, though not necessarily of great importance, cannot be dismissed as an anomaly. If this is the real cause for concern about the reliability of her Chinese, authenticity becomes a liability, even though it can be argued that, in terms of cultural sources in general, such a concern is probably superfluous or irrelevant. Compared with some other Chinese American literary texts, Kingston's work "only rarely includes Chinese words and their English translations, but it is nonetheless preoccupied with a series of translation dilemmas written into the English language of the text" (Cutter 2005: 4). Toming Jun Liu argues that instead of being a translator in its conventional sense, "Kingston is trying to describe the 'stories' her Chinese-speaking mother tells" (Liu 1996). This narrative method is free from word-for-word translation, not confined by any requirement of literalness. Nevertheless, the "source text" is still unequivocally Chinese, despite its uncannily invisible and elusive nature.

Aside from lack of linguistic competence in Chinese, Kingston has been censured by a number of critics for her inauthentic translation of China, and for that matter, Chinese culture. Frederic Wakeman refers to her treatment of Chinese folklore as "inauthentic" (Wakeman 1980: 43). Admittedly, Kingston's knowledge of Chinese culture is superficial, and for this reason, it is like an incompetent translator not well versed in the source language. In all fairness, however, her primary concern is with the target reader with scant knowledge of Chinese and little interest to encounter the unadulterated purity of Chinese culture. She wants to tell a story and Chinese cultural elements are just ingredients of that story, plain and simple. Chinese American writers glean cultural materials through the Chinese language, and by weaving Chinese cultural references and allusions into their creative works, they embark on a translation process of a creative kind, rather like a third text different from both the original and a conventional translated text. While moving between different cultural traditions and spaces while reformulating cultural and linguistic practices, their works present a productively expansive understanding of Chinese culture and American society. Consequently, the distinction between the "source text" and the "target text" has become somewhat blurring and indeed, blending. Thus, cultural mixedness is a result of hybridization – a preferred concept for Bhabha as opposed to hybridity, which suggests an ongoing process of cultures being hybridized prompted by translation. It also seems that these writers are cultural translators as if yearning to re-create the source text by translating from a diversity of sources, most of which are oral (talk-story) told by mothers or from other sources.

As a way to confront difference, translation signifies that communication with mother and daughter is informed and conditioned by different cultural traditions, values and practices and is thus fraught with misunderstanding and tension and results in either an Americanized Chinese or Sinicized American. The daughter needs to translate constantly and effectively not only for others but also sometimes for themselves. Given the actual circumstances, however, biculturalism seems to be far more important than bilingualism. As Shan Qiang He aptly asserts: "Cultural translation and repetition blur the line between 'authenticity' and 'fakeness,' thereby opening up the space for a genealogy of 'origins' both as a source of patriarchy and as a history of subaltern insurgency" (He 1996: 45). There exist invisible or intangible but recognizable cultural source texts, from which the Chinese American writers translate and based on which they rewrite. And in this process of rewriting, the original created from fragments is de- idealized and dethroned. The observation of Jing-Mei Woo in *The Joy Luck Club* is no doubt telling and provides a glimpse of how they communicate to one another: "My mother and I spoke two different languages, which we did, . . . I talked to her in English, she answered back in Chinese" (Tan 1989: 23). This bilingual conversation belies a lack of bilingual knowledge, and both mother and daughter prefer to rely on their own languages to feel comfortable, confident and above all, competent. Linguistic competence ensures and enhances cultural and psychological security. There is a clear advantage to be gained from speaking a language that can be claimed as one's own in a psychological and practical sense. However, for the daughter, the English used by both of them on limited occasions is a "language of intimacy," which is "a different sort of English that relates to family talk, the language I grew up with" (Tan 1991: 197). This shared English is like translationese, namely bad English, non-standard English, which is almost tantamount to a third language, uncannily real for mother – daughter communication. Because it is a privately coded language, it is to a large extent exclusive and needs translation (or a certain degree of translation in order to preserve the authentic voice of her mother) so that it can be understood by others as well. No doubt, it can barely be called "translation proper," but it is an offbeat form of translation.

Cultural knowledge is the key to effective translation, and in many cases, linguistic translation is shown to be feckless if the innate cultural differences involved are not well understood and tackled appropriately. Kingston's recollection of her translation experience is telltale: she had to translate for her mother on one occasion, even though the latter did speak some sort of English:

> And my mother was standing in the back whispering loudly. "Why he don't send me check, already two weeks late. So mad he lie to me, losing me money." And then I said in perfect English, "Yes, I'm getting rather concerned. You had agreed to send the check two weeks ago, but it hasn't arrived."
>
> (Kingston 1976: 82)

As part of the strategy of cultural translation, the original message is filtered and blocked to avoid embarrassment. The realistic and graphic description of the scene entails a switch between *pidgin* English and standard English to underscore the tension arising from a cultural conflict between mother and daughter.

In *Woman Warrior*, the mother forced her daughter to translate her bargaining transaction in a department store, "word for word," to the great shame of the daughter (Kingston 1976: 82). Again, the irony is that, due to cultural incompatibilities, word-for-word translation is not the best mode of communication in this particular situation:

> The daughter is the one who must make sense of clashing cultures and learn how to "translate" effectively, who must figure out why translation is such a perplexing feat to accomplish within the context of having to negotiate cultural understandings, a feat that includes nothing short of having to construct her own Chinese American female identity.
>
> (Kingston 1976: 159)

Likewise, in *The Woman Warrior*, the mother forced her daughter to stop the curse at the drugstore and say this to the druggist: "You get reparation candy," she said. "You say, 'You have tainted my house with sick medicine and must remove the curse with sweetness.' He'll understand" (Kingston 1976: 170). The daughter is very reluctant to comply, knowing that this will not work. In an unreasonable reaction to recalcitrance by her daughter, she simply says: "You just translate" (Kingston 1976: 170). By artificially creating untranslatability to avoid embarrassment, the daughter mumbles something like "Mymotherseztagimmesomecandy" (Kingston 1976: 170). The complexities of mother – daughter relationship in a cross-cultural context are demonstrated dramatically here. This is a way of avoiding what is essentially a possible cultural confrontation.

The repossession of language has much to do with cultural control. In the case of the target language being the native language of the author, this strategy is of particular relevance and value. Mindful of the link between linguistic competence and real-life experience, Kingston speaks of her translation in the two novels depicting Chinese past:

> When I wrote *The Woman Warrior* and *China Men*, as I look back on it, I was trying to find an American language that would translate the speech of the people who are living their lives with the Chinese language. They carry on their adventures and their emotional life and everything in Chinese. I had to find a way to translate all that into a graceful American language, which is my language.
>
> (Quoted by Chen 2001: 91)

A clear sense of not belonging is registered here. What she does is to translate Chinese into what is justifiably claimed to be her own language because Chinese and English languages are closely associated with different cultural experiences and practices. A subtle revelation is given through by dint of the word "graceful," which implies what comes naturally among other things. The ownership of language lies at the root of cultural awareness and competence, and through acculturation, Kingston blends her talk-story into American cultural context and life experience.

Significant for these Chinese American writers, maternal language represents an unfamiliar yet fascinating culture that requires decoding and translation: to overcome cultural as well as generation gaps. It amounts to a different sense of translation for the purpose of real understanding:

> The traumatic translation of devalued and ambitious Chinese speaking immigrant mothers from their motherland to an unfriendly and alien country and the assimilation of their second-generation, English speaking Chinese daughters into mainstream America cause serious fractures in their relationship and communication with each other.
>
> (Ho 2001: 104)

Plainly, this act of translation as a radical form of rewriting and transformation is a painful one. The daughter is caught in the disquieting situation of clashing cultures and must mediate between cultural differences on behalf of the mother by playing an indispensable, though often reluctant, role of cultural translator. It is the cultural implications that the daughter must bear in mind in attempting cross-cultural communication. Cultural untranslatability is due to intrinsic incommensurability and fear of the perceived communication problems that are likely to lead to incomprehension.

Chinese translation of Chinese American literature

The picture is very different when "back translation" takes place. To translate translation is particularly fascinating, especially in the case of retranslation into the "original" when the latter is so insubstantial without specific identity in a cultural sense. Large-scale Chinese translations of Chinese American literary works began in the 1980s, and in recent years, there has been an increasing amount of translation of Chinese American literature and research work on this particular literary form. Chinese American literature, sandwiched between traditional Chinese culture and American mainstream white culture, has long been in search of recognition. And this literary discourse assumes the form of special cultural translation. When it comes to the Chinese translation of Chinese American literary texts, the back translation of Chinese culture presents a different challenge. If translation is based on and closely connected with the play of difference, back translation foregrounds and problematizes difference again in a different light, from a different perspective, and for a different purpose. As a form of rewriting, translation opens up possibilities of not only addressing difference but also creating it. To reiterate the earlier point, the Chinese translation of the term "Chinese American literature" is of epidemiological significance, which has given rise to two different versions. One is a deliberate reversal of the original order: "American Chinese literature" is understood to be a branch of American literature. Therefore, it should be, first of all, American literature, which is the overall identity of "Chinese American literature." Largely because scholars like Shan Dexing in Taiwan have insisted on "Chinese American literature," it seems that more scholars in mainland China have accepted Chinese American literature. However, it is fair to say that they still implicitly treat it as a separate identity from orthodox American literature.

Chinese translation of Chinese American literature dates back to the 1940s when *Moment in Peking* by Lin Yutang was translated into Chinese in 1941 and retranslated in 1977 by Zhang Zhenyu, a Taiwanese translator. Strictly speaking, such translations are not qualified for back translation because of the non-existence of a Chinese source text. However, numerous cultural allusions and references are distinctly Chinese, with palpable intertextual connections with Chinese culture. For this reason, such a translation practice can be viewed as a special kind of back translation. Due primarily to ideological reasons, the availability of this translation in mainland China was delayed until 1987. In this regard, the travel of culture is very revealing with regard to the impact of cross-cultural encounters in translation and back translation, neither of which is conducted in a conventional manner. It transpired that the initial sporadic translation activities in the 1980s erupted into an avalanche of translations in the 1990s when *The Joy Luck Club* turned out to be the most-translated novel in China. In 1992 alone, as many as three translated versions were published in Liaoning, Anhui, and Zhejiang. Amy Tan's *The Kitchen God's Wife* had two translated versions, one published in 1992 and another in 1994. The Chinese translation of *The Woman Warrior* was published in 1998, and the same year witnessed the publication of the translation of *Tripmaster Monkey*. In 2000, *Typical American* by Gish Jen and *China Men* (retranslation) came out, both published by Yilin Press in Nanjing. And in 2002, Ha Jin's novel *Waiting* was published by Hunan Wenyi Publishing House. In December 2004, Yilin Press launched a series of translations of Chinese American literary works, including such writers as Jade Snow Wong, Frank Chin, Gus Lee, David Wong Louie, and Fae Myenne Ng. In 2005, Qiu Xiaolong's three popular crime-thriller/mystery novels were published in Chinese translation by Shanghai Wenyi Publishing House. And in 2006, Amy Tan's *The Bonesetter's Daughter* and *Saving Fish from Drowning* were published in Shanghai and Beijing respectively.

Succumbing to a passion for Chinese American literature, many Chinese scholars turned their interest to this emerging field of research. Since most of them had insufficient reading knowledge of English, there was a growing demand for translation of the original. At the same time, without any doubt, there was popular demand as well, emanating from the desire to know about Chinese experience in America and curiosity to find out about how China was portrayed for the Western reader. With a vast exodus of Chinese going to America to study and work, there is a natural need to know about the circumstances under which Chinese immigrants live in that country and to comprehend and interpret Chinese immigrants in a strange foreign land. The unremitting displays of familiarity and intimacy with Chinese culture in Chinese American literature seem to be something of a reassurance that the country they are about to visit is perhaps not too dauntingly incomprehensible. Anxious about the prospect of alienation or not belonging, they are naturally eager to make sense of a different cultural and linguistic environment through reading Chinese American literature.

It has to be said that common cultural resources that can be shared make both reading and translation of Chinese American literature deceptively simple and straightforward. In effect, the extraordinary travel or exile of culture and language problematizes translation. Some translators, in order to avoid possible misconceptions of cultural images analogous to those perceived by the Chinese reader, domesticate the imagined source text rather freely and with little restraint. There is some irony in the fact that these translators choose to domesticate what is supposed to be Chinese culture found to be distorted and alienated, hence the conscious attempt at the voluntary "restoration" of the so-called cultural purity and authenticity. Similarly, stark omissions of the so-called false or misleading descriptions of Chinese culture are detected to indicate the fact that acting out of an inclination for familiarity and intimacy, these translators tend to take liberty with the original as if to suggest that they know the "real" original better.

Textual translation

Cultural and linguistic alienation is made concrete and tangible in the translation of *China Men* by Kingston, who has made it plain the separation of men from China is deliberate and reflective. Instead of the racist pejorative "Chinamen," the title of the novel consists of two separate words. However, the Chinese translation misses the point and treats it as Chinamen 中国佬 instead of 中国人 (China men) (Xiao 2000). *The Chicken-coop Chinaman* by Frank Chin is translated as 鸡舍的中国佬, which is perfectly acceptable. But the translation of the title of Kingston's novel is no doubt problematic. Furthermore, the translation of Cantonese in the original also gives rise to problems. In *The Woman Warrior*, the daughter is called by her mother as "Ho Chi Kuei," which is the transliteration in Cantonese. As a non-native speaker of Chinese, the daughter is bewildered and then determined to find out about its precise meaning. Yet her frenzied search in books for a plausible answer is completely off the mark. The amassed long list includes centipede, grub, bastard carp, chirping insect, jujube tree, pied wagtail, grain sieve, casket sacrifice, water lily, good frying, non-eater, duspan-and-broom. She then tries a different spelling Hao Chi Kuei, which literally means "Good Foundation Ghost" (Kingston 1976: 204). However, in view of the context, none of the translations makes any sense at all. Ken-fang Lee's interpretation makes better sense: "ghost-like" (Rice 2007: 207). In reality, it should be devil-like because the standard translation is foreign devil, a derogatory term for foreigners dating to the sixteenth century. In the eyes of Chinese immigrants, the next generation of Chinese is no longer Chinese but rather like Americans, and for this reason, they are also perceived as devil-like.

Similarly, in *The Joy Luck Club*, there is also a problem with the translation concerning the transliteration of "*shou*": "My auntie, who had a very bad temper with children, told him he had no *shou*, no respect for ancestors or family, just like our mother" (Tan 1989: 35; my italics). One translation version simply ignores the word "*shou*" and translates only its meaning but verges on over-translation (with the translator's interpretation added); "*Shou*" should be filial piety. But

Tan's transliteration is based on Cantonese rather than on Mandarin or Putonghua. The second version, by inferring from the context, renders it as 孝 ("filial piety"). In the third version, "*shou*" is understood to mean 羞 ("shame"), but this is not contextually appropriate. As it stands, "no respect for ancestors or family" is none other than an explanation for "*shou*." To capture 孝 in back translation is important for the target reader, considering that it intensifies cultural resonance in the reproduction of a familiar cultural concept. Thus, something that may have appeared to be insignificant in terms of the function of translation becomes an important detail in back-translation.

It is also interesting to examine the different ways to treat "This is the best marriage combination" in *The Joy Luck Club* (Tan 1989: 44), and once again, this sentence is culturally loaded, with three available Chinese translation versions focusing on different degrees of "cultural restoration." Version A brings out the customary association between marriage and family backgrounds: 门当户对. Both families are similar in terms of social status concerning not only the couple but also their family backgrounds that are nicely matched. Although this is not necessarily uniquely Chinese, it is generally regarded as part of Chinese cultural tradition. Version B is 天生的一对. You two are cut out for each other. It emphasizes the great suitability for each other by birth. Version C stays close to the original: 婚姻的绝配. This is a perfect match in marriage. And this version deviates little from the original. Different degrees of cultural familiarity and intimacy are displayed in these versions through the application of different translation strategies for cultural re-adaptation. A similar example can be found in *Moment in Peking*: "long rice noodles for long life" whose literal back translation is 长米粉象征长寿 as shown in one translated version. Another version, however, adds something familiar from Chinese culture: 长长的米线象征着长命百岁. Long rice noodles symbolize a long life of 100 years. According to Chinese tradition, longevity is specified as 100 years for ordinary mortals whereas 10,000 years are reserved for emperors. This elaborate translation reflects a heightened awareness of cultural difference by reinforcing the epitomized Chinese cultural tradition.

Moreover, back translation provides the translator with opportunities to employ Chinese proverbs and sayings, with which the target reader is familiar. Translations of images are of particular relevance as in *Moment in Peking*: "Even we are girls and sooner or later must leave this family, still it is our own home, and I will not allow a Siamese fighting fish to upset a glass of bowl of goldfish!" (Lin 2005). Any attempt at literal back translation can still make sense but is bound to appear awkward at the same time. The images of "Siamese fighting fish" and "gold fish" are dropped in translation. Instead, we have 横行霸道 run amuck and 窝里斗: good at infighting. More familiar images are chosen for the Chinese reader. These efforts at cultural restoration are meant to re-create what is supposed to be like in Chinese. The previously cited examples signify a return of culture to its original habitat and offer an empowering resource for the translator who is impassioned to restore Chinese cultural practice on behalf of the target reader. The translator acts as a self-appointed cultural representative drawing attention to an alleged cultural populist tendency in back-translation. The liberating provision for the needs of the target reader to re-decode culture that has traveled extensively and is now treated as a homeward journey.

Suffice to say, the return of Chinese culture in Chinese translation is culturally significant. However, the popularity of Chinese American literature in China has become a cause for concern with its blatant impurity of Chinese culture yet adding a substantial dimension to its revival based on the comforting thought that American readers are interested in Chinese culture. The acclaim of Chinese American literature in the West is seen as a source of national pride. To meet the needs and cultural expectations of the target reader, the Chinese translators give themselves free rein to re-appropriate the familiar that is strangely reminiscent of exoticism. It is in light of this understanding that any possible foreign otherness is expressly reduced and is consequently enabled to result in better readability. If the supposedly familiar that has been de-familiarized in the source text is allowed to remain strange in translation, it seems rather absurd and makes little cultural sense to the Chinese reader. The translator is thus uncannily tempted to re-familiarize Chinese elements inherent in the original. Yet, there is a danger of hackneyed clichés being restored since strangeness is often synonymous with freshness and evocativeness. On the other hand, some stereotypical depictions of China in the source text, if anything, are made worse in translation. Still, one of the delights of unexpected twists is cultural hybridity that emerges from a dialogical understanding of Chinese culture seen in the cultural, historical, and ideological context of the target reader in the West.

Cultural re-adaptation

The issue of authorship is of particular interest in connection with the Chinese translation of *Saving Fish from Drowning* by Amy Tan. Its rewriting and cultural adaptation not only brings the foreignized (Americanized) Chinese culture home but also serves as a cultural filter to make sure that the translated text is well received. For ideological reasons, the American perspective is brought under control or effectively blocked on some occasions. Reception was the major consideration when the publisher planned to get the novel translated into Chinese. To minimize the problems caused by the original language, the translation strategy was based on the successful model of late Qing translator, Lin Shu, who had no knowledge of any of the source languages from which he translated: he had helpers who told him the basic meaning of the original. The first draft of the translation of *Saving Fish from Drowning* was more or less faithfully done by several students without too much attention paid to readability. Accuracy was given the top priority, and not a single word was left out at this initial stage of translation. Then a Chinese writer whose name is Cai Jun rewrote the whole draft in fluent, idiomatic Chinese without altering the basic plot of the source text but adapted to the common reading habit of most Chinese readers. According to Cai, if formal features of the original style happen to inhibit reading, they are normally removed so that more readers can access the quintessence of the novel (Cai 2006: 6). So the translation is called *yixie*, meaning literally transwrite (translate and write at the same time).

This practice, however, is viewed as questionable and the identity of Cai Jun as the translator has been called into question. He acts more like a co-author to form a team of cross-cultural reproduction. An anonymous person of the publishing industry questions the very act of transwriting, which is "analogous to infringement of copyright," and obviously suggestive of "deceiving the reader" (Shu 2007). This represents a typically traditional way of looking at translation.

Any formal prolixity, as is called by Cai, is expunged, and his aesthetic concerns play out in his word choice. He firmly believes that Chinese remains in many ways "an aesthetically more powerful literary language than many other languages" (Cai 2006: 6). According to Cai, in addition to linguistic rewriting, he has taken the liberty of deleting certain parts, particularly the ponderous ones (Cai 2006: 7). But what really happens is less innocent than Cai claims: some of the supposedly ponderous parts conveniently happen to be culturally or politically sensitive. For instance, the parts about a gay character are deleted. Similarly, when Miss Rong, the tour guide faces dismissal, some of the American tourists start a conversation: "But we do pity her," Vera said. "God knows they don't give people unemployment benefits in China when they've been fired." "If she gets fired, why don't we sign a petition of protest?" Wendy said. Dwight sniffed. "Come on, this isn't Berkeley. Besides, she really is a pretty *bad* tour guide" (Tan 2006: 92–93; my italics) Perhaps not entirely surprisingly, the italicized parts are not translated into Chinese or kept in the transwritten version. They are sensitive parts of a discussion about one aspect of Chinese reality.

Another unflattering description of the experience of a group of American tourists in China is similarly treated by the translator. The sanitary state of toilets in China used to be notorious and disgraceful. In the source text, some of the following details in italics are removed:

> with an open trough through which a constant paltry stream of water constantly ran, failing, however, to wash away the deposits . . . The other women crouched and buried their faces in their sleeves, *trying not to retch*.
>
> (Tan 2006: 80)

> 里边有个小槽, 有不间断的水流冲洗。 . . . 其他人蹲在那用袖子蒙住脸。
>
> (Cai 2006: 57)

The original is altered to such an extent that the passage has lost its coherence. Chinese-language readers may wonder why these women "buried their faces in their sleeves." Apparently, this is the result of (self)-censorship. However, the claim of transwriting seems to make this kind of omissions convenient and justified.

In addition, some detailed descriptions are thought to be putrid and thus deemed unnecessary for the target reader to know:

You were too big to come out between her legs, so the midwives had to slice her nearly in two and pull you out like a fatty tapeworm. You weighed over ten pounds, and you had bloody hair down to your shoulders.

(Tan 2006: 25)

你太大了，没法从她两腿间出来，接生婆几乎把她切成两半才像搜肥绦虫一样把你弄出来。你体重超过十磅，沾满血的头发披在肩膀上。

("Faithful" back-translation)

The passage is simplified by Cai as "你出生时太大了，难产，接生婆好不容易把你出来，满身是血": "You were too big at birth and it was difficult labor. The midwives had great trouble in getting you out. You were covered with blood" (Cai 2006: 21). Of course, it can be said that the translator has failed to deal adequately with the graphic description of the process of childbirth, but he finds it apt to expunge it from the translated text for the sake of his Chinese readers, or more to the point, his censor(s), potential or actual.

Somewhere else, also taking the role of author, the translator decides to step in and contribute to the writing as the text is being (re)produced. In Burma, when the tourists go to the edge of a lake with its beautiful landscape, the narrator comments: "There is a famous Chinese sentiment about finding the outer edges of beauty. My father once recited it to me: 'Go to the edges of the lake and watch the mist rise'" (Tan 2006: 228). But there is no such poem in reality, and even if there is, its source is by no means traceable. In its place, Cai Jun provides a whole poem by Li Bai about the landscape of a lake. Thus, a different "source" text is provided.

As a famous writer of horror fiction, Cai Jun seemed to be a good candidate for the job, and he set out to minimize translationese in his translation. Mindful of the fact that her earlier novels were not so well translated into Chinese, Tan was asked by the Chinese publisher to agree to a different approach. And she agreed. She admitted that she did not know a better way to get her work translated and to improve reception since she could not control translation (Zhang 2006). The end product is a different kind of cultural translation in which cultural meanings are open to negotiation so as to make the end product better from the point of view of the Chinese translator as very often Chinese American writers have been accused by some critics and scholars of making the text worse in their cultural translation. Exclusion and misrepresentation are always associated with translation, thus provoking strong responses from critics and readers alike. The cultural trauma in the experience of translating Chinese elements into literary creation and their back translation in Chinese provides the most salient evidence of cultural translation shaping our understanding of culture and intercultural communication.

Conclusion

The production and re-production of Chinese American literature is a remarkable literary phenomenon. It is not unusual that the second or third generation of Chinese immigrants speak little or do not even speak the ethnic tongue. In this case, not only is there no source text but also no source language. And it is certainly not an issue of transcribing Chinese into English. Yet translation is essential to Chinese American literature. It is a very special kind of translation because the original is none other than oral culture. On the subject of creative translation, accuracy is given precedence to narrative engagements. It is Chinese culture that represents cultural otherness, which in turn empowers the narration and effectiveness of storytelling. The spatial interaction of two cultures and, to a lesser degree, two languages makes it possible for Chinese American writers to explore a multitude of exciting ways of writing. Irrespective of their linguistic and cultural inadequacy, the authors' Chinese cultural heritage has turned out to be extremely powerful and versatile in engendering a stark juxtaposition between misunderstanding and insight to create a poignantly dramatic significance.

It is important to consider Chinese American literature interculturally and translationally, and to appreciate the particularly important and pivotal role played by cultural translation in the creative process of these literary texts because sheer linguistic translation is not efficacious. Acculturation is intimately related to adaptation as a major writing strategy. Through acculturation, talk-story is seamlessly blended into American cultural context and life experience. Complex cultural negotiations are necessitated by heightened tension of mother and daughter on the one hand and the construction of a cross-cultural dialogue between two worlds of tradition and experience on the other. Although on the surface, manifest disregard of the accuracy of cultural source material seems to downplay the relevance of translation, it provides, in a fundamental way, the driving force that makes it possible for the narrative to be compelling and animated. Cultural authenticity is apparently not prioritized because it may lead to cultural confrontation, thereby undermining the function of the translated text. Consequently, it is diluted or undermined by cultural hybridity, or rather, cultural hybridization. Notwithstanding, as in the typical case of *Saving Fish from Drowning*, the simplification and distortion of the aboriginal culture are rectified in Chinese translation, which functions as a kind of back translation so that a somewhat different intertextual interplay is allowed to take place within the narrative discourse. The fascinating corollary is that because of and despite translation, a transformed literary text has come into being. In a nutshell, a different cultural text resulting from cultural translation assumes a different cultural form that is responsible for creating different cultural meanings.

References

Cai, Jun (2006) "序言" (Preface), in Tan Enmei (Amy Tan) (ed.) 《沉没之鱼》 (*Saving Fish from Drowning*), Beijing: Beijing Press, 1–7.

Chen, Victoria (2001) "Chinese American Women, Language, and Moving Subjectivity," in Harold Bloom (ed.) *Amy Tan*, Philadelphia, PA: Chelsea House, 83–92.

Cutter, Martha J. (2005) *Lost and Found in Translation: Contemporary Ethnic American Writing and the Politics of Language Diversity*, Chapel Hill: University of North Carolina Press.

He, Shan Qiang (1996) "Chinese-American Literature," in Alpana Sharma Knippling (ed.) *New Immigrant Literatures in the United States: A Sourcebook to Our Multi-cultural Literary Heritage*, Westport, CT: Greenwood Press, 43–66.

Ho, Wendy (2001) "Swan-Feather Mothers and Coca-Cola Daughters: Teaching Amy Tan's *The Joy Luck Club*," in Harold Bloom (ed.) *Amy Tan*, Philadelphia, PA: Chelsea House, 99–113.

Kingston, Maxine Hong (1976) *The Woman Warrior: Memoirs of a Girlhood among Ghosts*, Harmondsworth: Penguin Books.

Lin, Yutang (2005) *Moment in Peking*, Beijing: Foreign Languages Teaching and Research Press.

Liu, Toming Jun (1996) "The Problematics of Kingston's 'Cultural Translation': A Chinese Diasporic View of *The Woman Warrior*," *Journal of American Studies of Turkey* 4: www.asat-jast.org/images/JAST-ISSUES/JAST-04/03_Liu.pdf.

Rice, Maria J. (2007) "Migrations of Memory: Postmemory in Twentieth Century Ethnic American Women's Literature," PhD diss., State University of New Jersey, New Brunswick.

Shu, Jinyu (2007) "谭恩美新作译写模式招质疑" (The Transwriting Mode of Amy Tan's New Work Attracted Questioning), 《侨报》 (*China Press*), September 29.

Su, Karen Kai-Yuan (1998) "'Just Translating': The Politics of Translation and Eth-nography in Chinese American Women's Writing," PhD diss., University of California, Berkeley.

Tan, Amy (1989) *The Joy Luck Club*, New York: Ivy Books.

Tan, Amy (1991) "Mother Tongue," in Joyce Carol Oates (ed.) *The Best American Essays*, New York: Ticknor and Fields, 196–202.

Tan, Amy (2006) *Saving Fish from Drowning*, London: HarperCollins.

Wakeman, Frederic, Jr. (1980) "'Chinese Ghost Story' Review of *China Men*," *New York Review of Books* 43: 42–44.

Wang, Mei-Hsiang (2015) "Eileen Chang: The Unknown Story: *The Rice-Sprout Song* and *The Naked Earth* under the USIS Book Translation Program," *EurAmerica* 45(1): 73–173.

Wong, Sau-ling Cynthia (1995) "'Sugar Sisterhood': Situating the Amy Tan Phenomenon," in David Palumbo-Liu (ed.) *The Ethnic Canon: Histories, Institutions, and Interventions*, Minneapolis: University of Minnesota Press, 174–210.

Xiao, Suozhang (2000) *China Men* (Chinese Translation), Nanjing: Yilin Press.

Zhang, Ying (2006) "谭恩美: 为母亲而写作" (Amy Tan: Writing for My Mother), 《南方周末》 (*Southern Weekend*), November 3.

8 Deconstruction and translation research

Introduction

Deconstruction with its alleged emphasis on indeterminacy and seemingly nihilistic free play of interpretive possibilities is decidedly unsettling in that it destabilizes the otherwise comfortably assumed understanding of the nature of translation. What is also controversial is that it may make translation impossible, considering that it explicitly acknowledges the impossibility of translation. Yet Derrida emphasizes the necessity of translation as well, thus foregrounding the need to negotiate with the non-negotiable, and for this reason, to translate the untranslatable. Deconstruction captures and elucidates the complexity of translation in relation to the variability and complexity of its nature and practice. In spite of the disconcerting observation of his devastating relativist overtone and open-endedness, Derrida does not uphold complete free play, as is repeatedly pointed out by himself and other scholars. This chapter argues that the context of translation plays a regulating role and intends to unravel what he calls translation as both possible and impossible, both respectful and abusive. Inspired by Derrida's profound contention that translation is in a way more about "what is not there" than "what is there," this chapter will map some of the multiple implications of meaning and various modes of representation in translation, in which different meanings can be played with so as to give rise to spaces for exploring and expanding the range of translation strategies and methods. The profound impact of deconstruction on the Chinese traditional concept of fidelity in translation will also be discussed.

The indications of the usefulness of deconstruction that informs translation are manifested in challenging the assumption about surface reading and literal meaning by questioning the primacy of the signifier. If literal meaning already articulates the possibility or space of interpreting the figurative, the concept of *différance*, while playing with the idea of literal meaning, further problematizes the roles of intention and representation. Since translation also involves cross-cultural spaces, which invariably interact with one another, a more energized experience of engaging in translation research can be possible in view of the powerfully insightful and inspirational results deriving from deconstructive thinking.

Deconstruction and theory of translation

In "Doubts about Deconstruction as a General Theory of Translation," Anthony Pym writes scathingly: "Philosophers have no time for the rubbish that most of us have to improve when we translate" (Pym 1995a: 16). And by this he means that deconstruction as a philosophical discourse has little to offer to the real world of translation practice. Earlier in the same article, he asks rhetorically: "So what can deconstruction say that most practicing translators don't know already? And what can it say to actual users of translation?" (Pym 1995a: 15). Strongly emphasizing "the reception situation," he gives precedence to the target-oriented approach by pointing out that the target reader "does not know the source anyway (Pym 1995a: 17). This is very much in line with the basic tenet of "Skopos Theory," which would advocate the end justifies the means. Nevertheless, the target reader can be given the false impression that the translated text is basically what the original is really like. The linguistic ignorance of the target reader is the most significant factor responsible for their uncritical acceptance of what is presented to them as translation.

Chinese translation scholars have voiced similar doubts and concerns. An article summarizing some of the views of the translation community states that deconstruction is typically seen as semantic nihilism, and translators "can translate in whatever way they please" (Han 2008: 73). An earlier article published, however, is not so dismissive. It states that "people are showing a considerable interest in deconstruction" (Liu 2005: 16). At the same time, the author points out that the response to it is sharply polarized. He believes that new vitality has been brought to translation research, "or at least research horizons have become broader" (Liu 2005: 16). But he also observes that the opponents of deconstruction in China urge to jettison it altogether (Liu 2005: 16). In a similar vein, the article entitled "Investigating Deconstructive Translation Studies" published in 1995, widely regarded as the first comprehensive article to introduce deconstructive translation to China, concludes rather hastily: while acknowledging that the theory as bringing something new to the discipline of Translation Studies is inspiring, he identifies its negative impact as "providing justification for all kinds of ingenious interpretation devoid of any criteria" (Jiang 1995: 66).

Nevertheless, most of the articles published in Chinese respond positively to the relevance of deconstruction to translation as is indicated in the assertion: "There is an intrinsic inevitability about the fact that deconstruction theory is related to and wields influence on translation studies" (Zhang 2006: 55). This is not illusory because the deconstructive perception of language and meaning-making has provided a powerful tool for analyzing translation in a new light:

> The charm of deconstruction lies in its new perspective and thinking, as well as its insight and examination to challenge old conventions and hackneyed ways of thinking theories and also to clarify ·or subvert some of the basic concepts and methods in traditional translation theories.
>
> (Zhang 2006: 55)

Despite doubts about the relevance of deconstruction to translation in many quarters, it is plain that many Chinese translation scholars believe firmly that it can help unravel a host of related issues bearing on the theory and practice of translation. It provides a fascinating insight for translation scholars who are interested in exploring translation from a fresh perspective.

The opposition between sameness and difference is dismantled (deconstructed). In other words, the translated text cannot be the same as the original: it is different, but it is not that different – if it is too different, it ceases to be a translation but something else. Although complete free play is never intended by Derrida, deconstruction has created some cognitive confusion with regard to the nature of translation. As observed by Pym, translators "have to make choices between available alternatives, many of which involve potentially beneficial reductions of plurality" (Pym 1995a: 17). Yet specific questions such as beneficial to whom and in what way need to be asked. It is no doubt true that in reality, translators have to make choices. But it is precisely choice making that can cause problems regarding meaning transfer. Pym certainly has a point here. He cites four translation versions of one sentence by Derrida. They are all very different and do not seem to make the same sense (Pym 1995a: 13). Pym offers a critique of the translation by Rosemary Arrojo, a pioneer of deconstruction in Translation Studies, who produces a version that "eclipses the passage from Greek to Greek. Her translation seems peculiarly unworried by any return to original languages or anterior contexts" (Pym 1995a: 13). This raises doubts about meaning transfer, which is problematized, as it can be presupposed (Pym 1995a: 14). In response to these doubts, Arrojo has published a robust rebuttal, championing deconstruction as a powerful means of viewing translation (Arrojo 1996: 9–20).

Notably, despite his earlier skeptical views about the pertinence of deconstruction to translation, Pym invited Kathleen Davis (2001) to write a volume entitled *Deconstruction and Translation* for the "Translation Theories Explained" series published by St. Jerome Publishing. The slim volume came out in 2001 and has proved to be influential and widely cited in translation research.[1] It has also shown that despite its esoteric nature, deconstruction seems to have significant implications to translation research and is thus by no means negligible but potentially profound and far-reaching. Many scholarly articles on translation, even if not directly addressing deconstruction, are informed by deconstructive insights and methods. Its influence is lasting and pervasive.

It cannot be denied that deconstruction is unsettling in terms of destabilizing the comfortably assumed understanding of the nature of translation. To start with, semantic security does not exist anymore and has become more than a one-dimensional problem. After the supposed security is lost, endless possibilities are gained. But are these possibilities coveted? Are they of any use to real translation? One argument, however, must not be overlooked. If endless possibilities are created, translation is offered spaces in which meanings can be played so as to adequately articulate the plurality in the original. It is true that while open-endedness problematizes the whole practice of translation associated with the comfortable illusion that translation should definitely be manageable and straightforward, it opens up and explores possibilities to enable the translator to overcome what is essentially untranslatable. Rather than create translation problems, deconstruction empowers the translator to explore related approaches to translation problems. Deconstruction has fundamentally overturned the traditional concept of faithfulness. In view of the pluralistic nature of meaning, exactly to what translation is faithful is seriously and ultimately challenged. The intimation that meaning is not to be overdetermined is both insightful and thought-provoking. Furthermore, by acknowledging the impossible nature of translation and yet by addressing it in terms of recognizing its necessity, deconstruction provides theoretical and cognitive resources to make translation possible despite the prevalent nature of untranslatability in its absolute sense.

Deconstruction can yield a deeper and more accurate understanding of the differences between languages and the specific expressions of each language by interrogating, dismantling and also transcending binary oppositions, which has profound implications to translation as the latter is characterized by dichotomies such as literal translation versus free translation, foreignization versus domestication, truth versus mimesis, adequacy versus acceptability, inside versus outside, insider versus outsider, signifier versus signified, presence versus absence, self-versus other, center versus margin, writing versus speech, and so on. Moreover, Derrida emphasizes understanding the play of and interaction between the concrete and the conceptual in both temporal and spatial terms, which is conducive to *différance*, thus dynamizing and moving our thinking about the nature of translation. Translation is seen as possible and impossible and a text as translatable and untranslatable at the same time. How this seemingly irreconcilable paradox plays out is a fascinating part of deconstructive thinking and can lead to insightful views about how translation functions.

One of the "negative" attributes of writing is described as: "It appears derivative, lifeless and artificial, in contrast to 'living' speech with its seeming proximity to presence as thought, consciousness or intention" (Burman and Maclure 2005: 285). If this description is accurate, then rewriting that features translation, if anything, is more "derivative, lifeless and artificial" and perhaps even doubly so. This perception seems to overtly reinforce the secondary or less than secondary status of translation. In this regard, deconstructive thinking can provide a means of demystifying and reconceptualizing originality and reconstructing ways to discern resemblances and analogies and also to articulate different forms of movement. There are many deconstructions as need be. But what cannot be denied is that deconstructive thinking opens up the multiplicity of possibilities that comprise ways of thinking and talking about translation. Slippages, silences, spaces of indeterminacy are brought to prominence, revealing a series of interlocked contradictions and inconsistencies inherent in texts while foregrounding irreducible alterity and incommensurability. Thus, in absolute terms, there is no such thing as a correct translation, and all translations are mistranslations. Self-referential and intertextual practices contribute to plurality as contained in Derrida's *différance*, which undermines the hierarchical relation between original and translation. As Koskinen puts it, "The endless intertextuality and the plurality of meanings give no preference or primary to the first-comer" (Koskinen 1994: 449). They challenge the primacy of the original, compounding the complexity of translation, which is always done in an intertextual space.

Translation equivalence

In the view of Venuti, the history of translation theory has been concerned with, among other things, the two dichotomized concepts of equivalence and function (Venuti 2000: 5). As mentioned earlier, Translation Studies is fraught with a long list of analogous dichotomies, including here, in close connection with equivalence, word versus sense, and form versus content, which often appear to be almost mutually exclusive, and it seems that translation cannot attend to one without attending to the other. Since the 1980s, equivalence as an established concept of translation has been viewed with increasing suspicion and even derision, if not totally abandoned. Nevertheless, it would be difficult to imagine altogether eliminating it from Translation Studies. It can be observed that some variable terms associated with equivalence remain part of the active vocabulary of translation research and criticism, such as accuracy, adequacy, correctness, correspondence, and above all, faithfulness or fidelity. Rather piquantly, Derrida has also asserted that "the translation must be quantitatively equivalent to the original, apart from any paraphrase, explication, analysis, and the like" (Derrida 2013b: 356). This seems to refer to the required adequacy of translation. It is noteworthy that although deconstruction is supposed to challenge the conventional notion of equivalence, Derrida still uses the term. Why is "quantitatively equivalent" used here instead of "qualitatively equivalent" or "essentially equivalent"? Patently, the latter would be an antithesis to the very nature of deconstruction. To be "quantitatively equivalent to the original" seems to aim at allegedly attempting to be isomorphically equivalent. Moreover, to be quantitatively equivalent to the original (after all there is an original) would, by implication, allow for substitutions (without which translation does not exist), as if to avoid reduction or simplification, which would not be considered to be qualitatively equivalent to the original. As a result, a series of spaces needs to be introduced for the initiation and operation of these activities.

Although in the strict sense equivalence does not exist, it serves as a necessary functional illusion (Pym 1995b: 167). This non-existent illusion is useful in a practical sense because it makes translation operationally achievable so that it can make a start and move towards finding effective and feasible solutions to whatever problems that may render the task of translation difficult or impossible. What troubles meaning transfer is the conventional concept of equivalence, and Derrida still obliquely questions its validity, is shown in his loose and generic definition of "relevant translation":

> Well, whatever feels right, whatever seems pertinent, apropos, welcome, appropriate, opportune, justified, well-suited or adjusted, coming right at the moment when you expect it – or corresponding as is necessary to the

object to which the so-called relevant action relates: the relevant discourse, the relevant proposition, the relevant decision, the relevant translation.

(Derrida 2001: 177)

Then he concludes that a relevant translation is "a good translation" . . . which is "the most *relevant* equivalent for an original" (Derrida 2001: 177). Apparently, the words quoted earlier are Venuti's translated words. But they are essentially indicative of Derrida's concern, although what this contains may be in a similar way to a circular argument. Particularly mindful of the limits of signifiers, he has tautologically used a list of synonymous words, denoting what seems to be ineffable and implying a perceptible lack of reliability, but he obviously has a point: to capture what he means by "relevant," and equivalence is meaningful only if it is relevant.

The fact that Derrida brings in such dizzying circumlocutions does not mean any attempt to hide anything on his part, but on the contrary, it unequivocally shows that he is determined to hit his target. Instead of firing one shot, which may fail to hit the target, a barrage of bullets is released. Derrida's exhaustive search for the most suitable word is demonstrably related to undecidability rather than indeterminacy inasmuch as there is often a chance of finding a better word. This serves as a perfect illustration of undecidability in action, and undecidables are found to permeate throughout his work. His unwillingness to accept reducibility is duly manifested. This undecidability has prompted a spatial experimental mapping in the hope of getting closer to a more suitable solution. Yet on the other hand, since none of the words appears to stand out as the best choice, the problem of incompleteness in relation to translation is shown not to be evaded, which in turn gives rise to undecidability. The postulate of the repetitiveness is an unequivocal indication of his anxiety about the precision of meaning. This act of exploration exemplifies that the translator needs to reach out to activate a series of spaces to search so that relevant translation can be achieved. This shows the near impossibility of articulating in translation denotations, connotations, and assumed cultural values associated with the original. Much of the unreproducibility of multiplicity of shades of meaning can be ascribed to Derrida's notion of difference.

As Venuti sees it, "poststructuralist textuality redefines the notion of equivalence in translation by assuming from the outset that the differential plurality in every text precludes a simple correspondence of meaning" (Venuti 1992: 7). The awareness of plurality in meaning indicates a sophisticated understanding of the nature of meaning from the point of view of deconstruction. For it is known that a superficial correspondence would be reductive and simplistic and can barely do justice to the depth and richness of the source text. Derrida categorically denies ever speaking of indeterminacy (Derrida 1988: 148). Importantly, for him "différance is not indeterminacy" (Derrida 1988: 149). Moreover, undecidability is not the outgrowth of indeterminacy either. And the former is in part an implicit recognition of the rich plurality inherent in the original since heterogeneity in language is manifest in the free play of meaning. In this regard, both gaps and traces are suggestive of and conducive to plurality. In a nutshell, deconstruction denotes infinitely plural meanings and the play of infinite plurality.

The potential loss of and damage to plurality raise concerns about the lack of adequacy of translation and simultaneously defines the limits of translatability. The optimization of the performativity of translation is an interactive process and can help overcome what seems to be insurmountable. Derrida states:

> This is why, whenever several words occur in one or the same acoustic or graphic form, whenever a homophonic or homonymic effect occurs, translation in the strict, traditional, and dominant sense of the terms encounters an insurmountable limit – and the beginning of its end, the figure of its ruin. . . . A homonym or homophone is never translatable word-to-word. It is necessary either to resign oneself to losing the effect, the economy, the strategy (and this loss can be enormous) or to add a gloss. . . . Wherever the unity of the word is threatened or put into question, it is not only the operation of translation that finds itself compromised; it is also the concept, the definition, and the very axiomatics, the idea of translation that must be reconsidered.
>
> (Derrida 2001: 181)

The necessity to reconsider what exactly happens to translation by breaking away from the traditional perception of translation needs to be highlighted and properly recognized. Derrida propounds that translation is much more complicated than direct transfer. There is a repeated emphasis on the observation that translation is more than the semantic transfer of the basic information.

Derrida is caught in the perennial either-or dilemma of translation when it comes to untranslatability. However, as he has made it very clear, untranslatability is only relative. By and large, the fear of actual or potential loss of plurality causes concern about untranslatability. In a sense, undecidability is a reflection of exactly what to do about untranslatability. It can also be construed as uncertainty or indecisiveness concerning how to avoid or reduce the loss of plurality in translation. For this reason, concentrating exclusively on signifiers is not commendable. Most importantly, undecidability raises questions about the traditional concept of faithfulness. For instance, when something has both a literal meaning and a figurative one, and there is an apparent disparity between them, to which is the translator supposed to be faithful? If the translator is faithful to what is there yet cannot be faithful to what is not there – we need to bear in mind that what is signified may not be necessarily what is there – faithfulness is not of much practical importance, and worse still, can be seriously misleading. The Chinese translation of the title of *Thirteen Days*, an American historical political film about the Cuban Missile Crisis in 1962 is 《惊爆十三天》. The literal back translation is *Volatile Thirteen Days* with the modifier "volatile" added. In relative terms, for the Western audience, there is an immediate sense of historical relevance. For the Chinese audience, however, due to geopolitical distance and limited familiarity with the event, the need to remind them is underscored by spelling out the nature of what happened. More to the point, "volatile" is inadequate. The two Chinese characters "惊爆" can be more accurately rendered as "shocking" and "explosive" respectively, which encompass the denotation and connotation of the original word.

Often, translation needs to find a signifier that is not superficially "equivalent" to what is there in the original. It is important to point out that the concept of *différance* plays with the idea of literal meaning as found in surface meaning. To translate superficially with matching signifiers carefully put together can be problematic, one of the reasons being that the etymological chain in the source language can barely be followed or reproduced in the target language. Etymology is crucial to a functional and contextual meaning, yet it tends to be overlooked in translation research because it is reproducibility is relatively low.

It is well-known that, in Chinese-English translation, a word in the original is translated differently in different contexts (situations, spaces), and the underlying spatial movement ultimately undermines the stability of equivalence. Take the word "认识" (know) for example:

> 我认识他。
> I **know** him.
> 我算是认识他了。
> Now I have **seen** him **through**.
> 认识自己的错误。
> **see** one's mistake; **realize** one's mistake;
> 我们一个共同的朋友介绍我们认识了。
> We were **introduced** by a mutual friend. (no need to mention 认识 in translation to avoid redundancy because it is implied: so we know each other after being introduced).
> 我们认识到了这种可能性，并且采取了一些预防措施。
> We **recognized** the possibility and took steps to prevent it from happening.
> 他们被劝服，认识到了和平的好处。
> They have been **persuaded of** the merits of peace.
> 他认识到自己错了，答应改过自新。
> He **realized** he was in the wrong and promised to turn over a new leaf.
> 我认识乔治已经是一年多前的事了。
> I met George well over a year ago.
> 女性目前已经认识到了自己的权利，随时准备和她们的雇主抗争。
> Women are now **aware** of their rights and are prepared to stand up to their employers.
> 人们对食物经常会有不正确的认识。
> People often have incorrect **information** about food.
> 人类对自然界的认识在不断发展，永远不会停留在一个水平上。
> Man's **understanding** of nature is developing all the time, it never remains at the same level.
> 关键任务是让学生们自己认识到成功和努力之间的关系。
> A key task is to get pupils to **perceive** for themselves the relationship between success and effort.
> 兴高采烈的情绪不见了，取而代之的是对局面更为清醒的认识。

The euphoria is giving way to a more sober **assessment** of the situation.
他们认识到了复苏经济的紧迫性。
They **recognize** the urgency of righting the economy.
在与别人一起工作的过程中，你会进一步认识你自己。
In working with others, you **find out** more about yourself.
我对当时发生的事情曾有一种错误的认识。
I had a mistaken **view** of what was happening.

Translation is meant to reject the static fixedness of meaning. It is precisely the dynamic and pluralistic nature of meaning that confirms the need for translation. Pertinaciously seeking equivalence may well jeopardize the chance to produce a successful translation. The truth is that the relationship between signifier and signified is never stable or fixed, although admittedly, it can be arbitrary.

Meanwhile, it can be observed that undecidability concerning multiple meanings that stem from multivalent meanings is substantively about possibility, or as Derrida puts it, "the condition of possibility of acting and deciding" (Derrida 1997: 137). To be sure, it is undecidability that "gives us something to decide" (Derrida 1997: 137). In other words, without undecidability, there is nothing to decide. Moreover, undecidability calls for opening up: for other identifiable (hence determinable) referents to be included to act upon. As a result, it has become possible to turn undecidability into decidability, but only under certain conditions. The emergence of these conditions rests with sufficient space(s). Translation is known to be a decision-making process, yet it is predicated on, in a way, what is undecidable, which then amounts to what is untranslatable: the undecidable allows us to gain endless possibilities, thereby enabling and empowering translation. If more space is made possible, the translator is in a better position to avoid translating superficially. It is thus untenable to argue that two different sets of signifiers belonging to the source and target texts respectively can directly correspond to or precisely match one another. Given the fact that these signifiers derive from etymologically different roots, all-inclusive equivalence would be too elusive and illusory to be attainable. Sometimes a special effect depends on polysemy and homonymy, particularly if the original is a distinctively allusive text.

Meaning and transformation

Translation works on the basis of some degree of reciprocity and mutual transformation. A symbiosis can thus be achieved, which, as Derrida sees it, is vital to the survival of the "original," echoing Benjamin's concept of afterlife. For Derrida, it is the transformation of the original that ensures its survival. Equally, the survival of translation itself is inseparable from the afterlife of the original. There is therefore a compelling reason to explore the shared ground between source and target texts and the associated spaces in which different elements interact and are entwined with one another. Signifier and signified are reciprocally linked, and it is impossible to change one without affecting the other (Koskinen

1994: 448). Therefore, nothing is stable or fixed with regard to the relation between source and target texts. In this light, for Derrida, translation is none other than transformation, albeit a regulated one because equivalence is virtually impossible. Indeed, translation is "a notion of transformation of one language by another, of one text by another" (Derrida 1981b: 21).

Taken as a whole, translation is not or cannot be a passive transfer of meaning but a transformation of something potential. The transfer of ontological presence is not what translation purports to deliver. In view of the transforming nature of translation, Derrida further argues:

> Translation augments and modifies the original, which, insofar as it is living on, never ceases to be transformed and to grow. It modifies the original even as it also modifies the translating language. This process – transforming the original as well as the translation – is the translation contract between the original and the translating text.
>
> (Derrida 1985: 122)

The constant modification is an exercise of revision, which constitutes not only the transformation of the original but also the growth of the target language. This is a constituent part of continual rewriting, the essence of which is also transformation. Translation entails another signifying chain which is, among other things, culturally complex and variegated. For this reason, the structure of the signifying chain is often different, and thus everything exists in different dimensions, referring primarily to different time and space.

Thus, it has to be emphasized that it is the signified that is most likely to cause problems. And it is often no good to reproduce the signifier as pointed out by Venuti:

> Yet the fact is that any translating replaces the signifiers constituting the foreign text with another signifying chain, trying to fix a signified that can be no more than an interpretation according to the intelligibilities and interests of the receiving language and culture.
>
> (Venuti 2003: 252)

When the original signifying chain is replaced in translation, the "etymological resonances" in the source text are also invariably lost (Gentzler 1993: 160). This in part explains Derrida's quantitatively equivalent concept. Due mainly to different etymological roots and derivations, translation relies heavily on interpretation instead of attempting, often in vain or thanklessly, to preserve the formal features of the original. Without confining itself to basic semantic information in order to ensure intelligibility, translation focuses on the function of interpretation, whose purpose is to address and examine a whole gamut of related dimensions, historical, social, political, cultural, and aesthetic.

The skopos theory has been in line with deconstruction for it renders the concept of equivalence almost irrelevant or at least marginalizes it – the once central concern in translation. However, whether one likes it or not, equivalence cannot be thrown away. In an important sense, translation can be made to be strategically equivalent to the source text so as to allow different spaces to function within a given setting and for a particular purpose. Moreover, the concept of equivalence is constitutive of the very identity of translation. As the term is restrictive and rather inaccurate, it can perhaps be replaced by less committed words such as "matching" or "correspondence." Among the synonyms that may be candidates, Benjamin has used the word "echo," which seems to be a "distanced" version of equivalence. We can give different names to it. Nonetheless, translation is still derivatively related to its original, and this can barely be denied.

Furthermore, deconstruction takes into account the irreducibility and incomparability of what translation can offer. According to Derrida, a fundamental problem for translation is "the redoubtable, irreducible difficulty of translation" (Derrida 1981a: 72). Derrida's notion of difference is a key feature of deconstructive thinking and can be seen as essentially about the irreducibility of meaning and, for that matter, difference. This is because that if meaning is univocal, it is straightforwardly translatable. But in reality it is often not univocal, and then it becomes untranslatable or less translatable. Polysemy is much less controllable or masterable. Thus, it can be said that the ultimate challenge to translation is irreducibility of meaning. Irreducibility is rooted in multiplicity, which can be profoundly unruly, disorderly, and unsettling. Moreover, in the process of reconfiguring the target system in response to the demands of translation in a given situation, ideologically and aesthetically motivated preferences lead to rejection and suppression, thus impairing multiplicity and consequently undermining irreducibility. Hence, some form and degree of transformation can be expected, and the multiple variants of a source text as a result of translation can be seen as an unquestionable testimony to what happens in this process.

Another major destabilizing effect is cross-cultural intertextuality, indicating traces of other texts and transformation of them. It cannot be denied that intertextuality plays a central role in any meaning-making activity, presenting multivariant versions. The intertextual weaving of both source and target texts is predicated on other texts related to the production of meaning. Derrida asserts that any act of translation is a transformation. He describes translation as "a regulated transformation of one language by another, of one text by another" (Derrida 1981b: 26). Translation creates an intertextual space that opens up to a variety of texts produced in different cultural locations and from different cultural perspectives. The resultant intertextual and linguistic heterogeneity invariably engenders hybridization, culminating in transformation. Translation requires incessant recontextualizations that are intertextually linked, recursively generating intertextual references while at the same time identifying and solving translation problems caused by intertextual gaps.

Such references, be they overt or covert, direct the translator to the related spaces for ways of mapping and navigation. To varying extents, these references are absorbed and hybridized. Complicated cross-referencing web resources are explored to search for effective and relevant solutions to translation problems, and in this process, the inevitability of hybridization and transformation represents a key aspect of intertextuality. If translation carries the traditional implication of transportation of meanings, as stated by Derrida, it should be replaced by transformation, which is suggestive of change and difference. To unravel the interactive nature of intertextuality, which means that a text is spatially connected with other texts, it should be understood that a text, in the process of being reproduced, traverses different spaces. In other words, if a text is left open to a multitude of readings and interpretations, more spaces are created and intersect with one another.

Connectivity and signifieds

Translation functions by means of signifieds deriving from a chain of related signifiers, which are signs activated and appropriated through reading interpretation and translation. Such a process necessarily entails transformation. Furthermore, given that translation produces signifiers of signifiers, when signs are appropriated, differences are introduced. Signs containing differences produce meaning, which, however, is also endlessly deferred to avoid the annihilation of difference. The way in which signs are connected to a changed context and with one another in translation during which different sets of codes are put together is responsible for signifieds. Lack of coherence, which is typically associated with translation, can to some extent at least impede the control and performance of referents and signifieds, which is compounded by an evident tendency towards explicitness in translation detrimental to irreducibility. It remains an arduous challenge to connect and organize signs in translation to ensure that signifiers and signifieds in the target text are correspondingly related to those in the source text and mutually interacting in a similar way. Signifieds are rarely transferable. Translation entails a corresponding yet different set of signifiers referring to other signifiers within the target language.

Translation entails a movement from signs of signs, signifiers of signifiers, and traces of traces, but ultimately from signifier to signified. How can the latter part be controlled? What is intrinsically untranslatable is concerned with the shift from signifier to signifier. Signs refer to other signs forming a chain of substitutions inevitably characterized by differences, which contribute to delays. All the denotations and connotations inherent in the source text are never fixed, and through a dynamic spatial approach, translation is enabled to respond to representing these denotations and connotations. Meaning is not only historically determined but also culturally determined – filtered or altered through interpretation. This link from signifier to signified is based on cross-cultural knowledge and adjustment, as well as a positive and open attitude towards irreducible difference.

Deconstruction engages a ceaseless movement, thus making it possible to expand the space to discover traces and alterity. Further, wordplay also strongly suggests movement, involving traces, which in turn generates space(s). While strict adherence to denotation risks glossing over connotation in translation, denoting that to match signifiers is one thing, but to match signifiers with signifieds is quite another.

The referential and allusive complexity signals that surface or superficial translation is rarely adequate or satisfactory. Concentrating only on the surface meaning is decidedly dangerous, and what can be ignored or repressed, consciously or otherwise in translation, requires serious consideration. All this points towards a necessarily explicit emphasis on the crucial relevance of context in relation to translation. Derrida underscores the determining role of context, which contributes to regulating transformation, and translation entails and is mediated and appropriated by a series of contexts that are conditioned by or linked to social, political, cultural, and historical factors. It can be observed that meaning to be conveyed emerges from a dynamic and intricate interplay between a distant context that is general (without details) and a local context that is specific (with details).

To argue that translation must go beyond the limits of semantic interpretation underscores the necessity of a holistic approach. Translation can be burdened and troubled by references or allusions. But it is always difficult to attend to everything at the same time, hence undecidability with regard to inclusion or exclusion defined by a continuum of decision-making uncertainties. On the one hand, undecidable oscillation between at least two perspectives and significations is agonizingly complex; on the other, and in a positive light, undecidability itself calls for opening up: for other identifiable (hence determinable) referents to be included and to act upon. It is possible to change undecidability into decidability under certain conditions. The creation of these conditions depends on sufficient space(s), which will subsequently generate possibilities. As for which possibility is more appropriate or relevant, contextual factors are particularly important in this regard.

Contextual factors are of great significance particularly in relation to cultural difference involved in translation. Signifiers are loaded with cultural meanings. It is not just signifiers that are to be translated but also, more importantly, signifieds. How can signifieds be translated? Gentzler refers to the symbiotic relationship between the original and its translation as "mutually supplementing each other, defining and redefining a phantasm of sameness, which has never existed nor will exist as something fixed, graspable, known, or understood" (Gentzler 1993: 146–147). Gentzler states that *différance* refers "not to what is there (language), but what is not there, and thus calls into question any ontological approach that attempts to determine a notion of Being based on presence" (Gentzler 1993: 158–159). Meaning must be distinguishable and indeed separable from words. Moreover, words in the source language are to be substituted by words in the target language to rearticulate meaning. In this sense, meaning is like a kernel whereas words its shells. Words are meaningful because of other words and their traces. Words are combined syntactically, but can syntax be imitated as suggested by Benjamin?

In his characteristically encrypted way, Benjamin writes about the relationship between the original and its translation:

> Just as a tangent touches a circle lightly [flüchtig] and at but one point, with this touch rather than with the point setting the law according to which it is to continue on its straight path to infinity, a translation touches the original

lightly and only at the infinitely small point of sense, thereupon pursuing its own course according to the laws of fidelity in the freedom of linguistic flux.

(Benjamin 1969: 80)

A translation need not necessarily intersect with the original, for if too closely entangled with it, translation is deprived of freedom, without which its performance can barely be delivered. On the other hand, however, it must not deviate too much from its original, which would endanger its identity as translation.

Derrida questions the practicality of looking at the infinitely small point of sense: "What can an infinitely small point of meaning be? What is the measure available to evaluate it?" (Derrida 2013a: 122). Maybe it is not meant to be evaluated. A small point of meaning is analogous to broken fragments, a metaphor used by Benjamin. The task of the translator is to glue them together. While Benjamin suggests restitution, what Derrida contends is related to what is at work in translation:

> It does not reproduce, does not restitute, does not represent; as to the essential, it does not render the meaning of the original except at that point of contact or caress, the infinitely small of meaning.
>
> (Derrida 2013a: 122)

This on-and-off touch or contact with the original accounts for what happens in the process of translation. Derrida does not expand on the echo metaphor used by Benjamin, which suggests a non-touch approach. Instead, he uses the trope of trace as a point of departure and contact. Evidently, echo suggests some distance without any touch whereas trace point of contact.

A set of points, on the other hand, however small they may be, is in a way indicative of traces but can be more visible. Points are linked together in an invariable manner, and they are determined by a context condition. The connectivity of points is of crucial importance, and to link these points, which may appear to be isolated, the translator is required to acquire context-specific task-related knowledge, which makes cross-space mapping possible to link the points in space where they are detectable in movement. The assemblage of points, as opposed to the gluing together of fragments, can be perceived as less coherent but more fertile and inclusive so as to enable patterns to emerge after connections are completed. Moreover, as pointed out by Derrida, "Whenever the immediate and full presence of the signified is concealed, the signifier will be of an indicative nature" (Derrida 1973: 40). Signifiers are founded upon small points and traces and function to provide the translator with clues to what is to be translated. In this connection, parallel corpora can make parallel resources easily available to researchers and practitioners. And these resources also give rise to much-needed spaces.

Spaces and appropriation

Translation activity is restrained by limited resources, which results in limited translatability, hence the need to enter into multiple spaces to canvas and enhance possibilities and experimentation by relating to the points of sense in the original and identifying the corresponding points in the target language. These points in both source and target texts are seen as reciprocal and interconnected in a dialogic relationship on which to build further upon the network of possibilities. It should be noted that translation can be imprisoned within a given space, and if this happens, it must move to another related space. The distancing effects of space for reflection and meaning-making are exemplified in showing its usefulness only as an interpretive act but, more importantly, as a translation act where it becomes possible to gain a different perspective on the nature of the challenge. Our perception of space(s) allows us to make better use of the referential power of language.

In Derrida's article "Freud and the Scene of Writing," writing is defined in relation to spacing (Derrida 1972: 99). He also refers to "[t]emporality as spacing" and "the temporality of writing" (Derrida 1972: 111, 113). Rewriting, which involves intertextual interpretation and articulation, is even more so. The operation of signifying substitution in translation is a complex issue. Deconstruction aims at showing how meaning is deferred. But translation entails the practice of rewriting. André Lefevere has reconceptualized translation as a practice of rewriting, necessitated by the consideration of the referential dimension, including its interpretation and reproduction. Yet significantly, translation is not all about interpretation or paraphrasing based on interpretation. To keep or represent the formal features of the source language is of paramount importance according to foreignization translation strategy, which seems to pose less demand on spatial need. However, unmediated reading experience of translation is rarely possible. Domesticating translation is typically marked by overt appropriation, including alteration and adaptation. But this could lead to superficial over-determination to which translation is notoriously prone, and this approach requires more spaces.

Dai Congrong has once discussed her strategy concerning the dichotomy between foreignization and domestication in translating *Finnegans Wake* into Chinese. In a seemingly surprising revelation, she chooses foreignization as her translation strategy, for as she points out that in translating *Finnegans Wake*, if domestication is adopted, it may well be based on one's own understanding and explication of the numerous multi-semantic sentences. Polysemes in the original are in competition or confrontation with one another, which are designed as such by Joyce, whose outrageous language is meant to dash everything (Dai 2015: 273). In this case, even thick translation, which is heavily used with massive annotations, very often does not really work. How is rewriting possible as in this translation? It is out of untranslatability that the translator has managed to work out translatability in the main body of the text, although in the eve of the publication of the first volume, she still doubted the translatability of the novel (Dai 2011: 222).

According to Dai, before starting to translate *Wake*, she tried to explore all possible associated meanings, and the process took two whole years. There were innumerable obstacles beset by polysemous pitfalls, and every turn could be a dead-end in a labyrinth, "practically precluding a conventional approach to translating it" (Cao 2013). By creating a profusion of portmanteau words, James Joyce poses the ultimate challenge to translation. In Dai's translation, the primary meaning appears in normal print size whereas other associated meanings are in smaller print in the form of footnotes in the hope that this strategy "can approximate the attempt of Joyce's indefinite deferral" in acknowledgment of indeterminacy of signification (Cao 2013). The translation is heavily annotated without countenancing complete free play, and through strenuous effort and experiment, the translator seems to aim at representing a full spectrum of possible meanings by exploring and confronting the complex consequences of translating more than surface meaning. In a way, translation has no choice but to explicitly articulate what implicitly encoded as in the understanding of the original that registers the absence of what is intended and implied. Given the postulate that neither presence nor stability can be expected, deconstruction discloses and emphasizes the instability of meaning, which is concerned with iterability but also enables texts, both source and target.

Finnegans Wake has profoundly influenced Derrida's thinking. The production of meaning is closely linked with the transformation of meaning, which is inevitable, especially in translating texts like *Finnegans Wake*. Derrida does not trust appearance as inherent in logocentrism. Undecidability seems to be a consequence of the availability of pluralistic and what is multiple and unfixable. In Derrida's view, meaning results from the transformation of meaning. And it has been argued that "all meaning depends on a future rewriting of past writings as rewritten in the present writing which confronts the interpreter" (Rosenfeld 1998: 18). Rewriting is based on interpretation that is governed by context, and as an act of rewriting, translation is invariably contextualized and connected with a specific task. A transformed writing is yielded as a result of ineluctable appropriation and a certain degree of adaptation. Derrida defines the notion of transformation as "a regulated transformation of one language by another, of one text by another" (Derrida 1981b: 20). It is transformation that makes the seemingly impossible task of translation possible whereby an otherwise untranslatable word, phrase, or sentence is transformed into something translatable. It can thus be claimed that the fundamental need for transformation epitomizes the essence of translation. Rewriting is a dynamic that shows a multiplicity of interconnected spaces, intersecting and aligning with one another, in order to achieve plurality, which brings out connotative range and interpretative variation.

Différance is also spacing, indicating absence, difference, and deferral. Given that translation inevitably entails the substitution of signifiers, transformation to retain the same signified in the original is induced and sustained. The change of spacing regarding the signified whose signifier(s) is/are substituted by (an)other signifier(s). The Derridian model of multiple interpretive spaces suggests that primordial spatiality of the original that should not be reduced to simple dichotomies that feature so heavily in translation. The absence of the author is supplanted by the presence of the translator who emerges from a different space with variables and dimensions. After the hierarchy of original/copy is overturned, it is meaningful to investigate the essence/appearance and presence/absence distinction that is concerned with what is there and what is not there. Sometimes what is not there matters more since it is related to the irreducible heterogeneity and difference. Translation manipulates direct and indirect discourses through the spatialization of representation, generating substantial shifts between various spaces, which are brought together by the exigency to address irreducibility and also to enable translation to function in a certain way.

Deconstruction upsets the way in which meaning is understood and rejects the static spaces of traditional criticism. Deconstructive translation praxis suggests a more open-minded and tentative form of rewriting that is subject to reinterpretation and transformation. As a result, meaning in translation is in perpetual displacement, continually shifting, and constantly renegotiated in multi-leveled spaces. Insomuch as translation functions, the precariousness of meaning is exemplified in resemblance and movement. Meanings cannot be translated exhaustively as they are always delayed and not completely present. The indeterminacy and open-endedness of meaning mean that *différance* and spacing are interrelated, suggesting strong spatial correlations reading and interpreting, writing and rewriting, reproduction and transformation. As a result, translation constantly renegotiates different limits and boundaries. It is clear that mediation is achieved through appropriation, yet without spaces, appropriation cannot be achieved. Many translation scholars are at once attracted and repelled by deconstruction, but what is undeniable is that with deconstructive thinking, translation can be examined more productively and meaningfully.

Conclusion

Although deconstruction may not be regarded as a general theory of translation, its actual and potential significance should not be underestimated. It makes a positive contribution to understanding and exploring the very nature of translation, which can be seen to be primarily about opening up spaces for the free play of signifiers and meaning so as to not only promote a better understanding of how translation functions but also empower it in actual practice. Further, the operation of translation reveals the act of decentering and the way in which it is performed in and through translation. Consequently, conventional notions associated with translation, such as equivalence and faithfulness, are not only subject to questioning but can be undermined to varying degrees. Due to the multidimensional nature of translation, it is essential to perceive it as operating at different levels and in different spaces. It is important to conduct further analysis of the concepts of trace and context that regulate translation and also ensure what is translated can be rightfully claimed to be translation. Translation Studies requires a higher level of conceptual sophistication. The fecundity of deconstruction is best encapsulated in the observation that it has provided a powerful theoretical framework for understanding of how translation works.

Note

1 It was republished by Shanghai Foreign Language Education Press in 2004 and reissued by Routledge in 2014.

References

Arrojo, Rosemary (1996) "On Perverse Readings, Deconstruction, and Translation Theory: A Few Comments on Anthony Pym's Doubts," *TradTerm* (São Paulo) 3: 9–20.

Benjamin, Walter (trans. by Harry Zohn) (1969) *Illuminations*, New York: Schocken Books.

Burman, Erica, and Maggie Maclure (2005) "Deconstruction as a Method of Research," in Bridget Somekh and Cathy Lewin (eds.) *Research Methods in the Social Sciences*, London: SAGE, 286–294.

Cao, Lingjuan (2013) "翻开'天书'给你看" (Opening a "Heaven Book" for You),《人民日报》(*People's Daily*), May 28.

Dai, Congrong (2011) "《芬尼根的守灵》的中文翻译" (The Chinese Translation of *Finnegans Wake*),《外国文学评论》(*Review of Foreign Literature*) 25(4): 216–222.

Dai, Congrong (2015) "翻译的灵感与技艺" (The Inspiration and Craftsmanship of Translation),《世界文学》(*World Literature*) 44(4): 265–275.

Davis, Kathleen (2001) *Deconstruction and Translation*, Manchester, UK and Northampton, MA: St. Jerome Publishing.

Derrida, Jacques (trans. by David B. Allison) (1973) *Speech and Phenomena, and Other Essays on Husserl's Theory of Signs*, Evanston, IL: Northwestern University Press.

Derrida, Jacques (trans. by Barbara Johnson) (1981a) *Dissemination*, Chicago: University of Chicago Press.

Derrida, Jacques (trans. and annot. by Alan Bass) (1981b) *Positions*, Chicago: University of Chicago Press.

Derrida, Jacques (trans. by Peggy Kamuf and Avital Ronell; ed. by Christie McDonald) (1985) *The Ear of the Other: Otobiography, Transference, Translation*, Lincoln and London: University of Nebraska Press.

Derrida, Jacques (trans. by Jeffrey Mehlman and Samuel Weber) (1988) "Afterword: Toward an Ethic of Discussion," in Jacque Derrida (ed.) *Limited Inc*, Evanston, IL: Northwestern University Press, 111–160.

Derrida, Jacques (ed. by John D. Caputo) (1997) *Deconstruction in a Nutshell: A Conversation with Jacques Derrida*, New York: Fordham University Press.

Derrida, Jacques (2013a) *Acts of Religion*, London and New York: Routledge.

Derrida, Jacques (2013b) *Signature Derrida*, Chicago: University of Chicago Press.

Derrida, Jacques, and Jeffrey Mehlman (1972) "Freud and the Scene of Writing," *Yale French Studies* 48: 74–117.

Derrida, Jacques (trans. by Lawrence Venuti) (2001) "What Is a 'Relevant' Translation?" *Critical Inquiry* 27(2): 174–200.

Gentzler, Edwin (1993) *Contemporary Translation Theories*, London and New York: Routledge.

Han, Ziman (2008) "解构主义翻译理论与解构主义理论的翻译: 以本雅明《译者的任务》中译为例" (Translation Theory and Deconstruction with Reference of the Chinese Translation of Benjamin's "The Task of the Translator"),《外语研究》(*Foreign Languages Research*) 25(1): 73–77.

Jiang, Xiaohua (1995) "解构主义翻译观探析" (Investigating Deconstructive Translation Studies),《外语教学与研究》(*Foreign Language Teaching and Research*) 28(4): 64–67.

Koskinen, Kaisa (1994) "(Mis)translating the Untranslatable: The Impact of Deconstruction and Post-Structuralism on Translation Theory," *Meta* 39(3): 446–452.

Liu, Quanfu (2005) "当'信'与'化境'被消解时: 解构主义翻译观质疑" (Interrogating Deconstructive Interpretation of "Fidelity" and "Transmigration"),《中国翻译》(*Chinese Translators Journal*) 26(4): 16–20.

Pym, Anthony (1995a) "Doubts about Deconstruction as a General Theory of Translation," *TradTerm* (São Paulo) 2: 11–18.

Pym, Anthony (1995b) "European Translation Studies, Une science qui dérange, and Why Equivalence Needn't Be a Dirty Word," *Orientations européennes en traductologie* 8(1): 153–176.

Rosenfeld, Michel (1998) *Just Interpretations: Law between Ethics and Politics*, Berkeley, Los Angeles, and London: University of California Press.

Venuti, Lawrence (1992) *Rethinking Translation: Discourse, Subjectivity, Ideology*, London and New York: Routledge.

Venuti, Lawrence (ed.) (2000) *The Translation Studies Reader*, London and New York: Routledge.

Venuti, Lawrence (2003) "Translating Derrida on Translation: Relevance and Disciplinary Resistance," *Yale Journal of Criticism* 16(2): 237–262.

Zhang, Yongxi (2006) "解构主义翻译观之再思" (Rethinking the Deconstructionist Approach to Translation Studies),《外语研究》(*Foreign Languages Research*) 23(6): 55–58.

9 Empowering translation

Introduction

Given the disempowered status of translation as is shown in the fact that it is typically regarded or treated as secondary, derivative, and thus inferior, it is necessary to further explore ways to empower translation. Only by viewing translation as a primary activity can it acquire the capacity to function as fully as possible. How this derivative text can be invested with enough power to make good reading hinges on the resourceful use of translational spaces. Since translation is conditioned, constrained, and motivated by multiple and disparate factors and forces, it is exposed to and affected by conflicts, tensions, and uncertainties, and for this reason, easily compromised. Translation is weakened and devitalized by the possibility of its impossibility. Moreover, it is variously compromised by ideology and poetics, patronage and power relations, gender and reception, functionality, and inadequacy. In the practice of Chinese-English translation, it can be observed that some translations are more possible than others but can still be poor or weak, as they may focus on one overriding concern at the expense of other functions or dimensions. Thus, the translator needs to carve out a space or a series of related spaces to empower translation in an attempt to penetrate the surface meaning into the interior of linguistic structure and cultural complexity. The spatial nature of writing and rewriting has the potential to energize translation in experimenting with the rhetoricity of language. It has become increasingly meaningful to move away from the confinement of descriptive translation studies by reconsidering the nature of translation and the role of subjectivity in terms of how systemic interaction generates spaces to empower translation through the fullest possible array of resources available or made available. The potentially liberating nature of creativity is brought out in a series of spaces in which related possibilities can be explored to develop more effective translation strategies.

The impossibility of translation is a well-accepted view in the modern age, although the "pathos" that often is invoked is attributed to the anachronistic view of equivalence (Beals 2014: 284). But the ubiquitousness of translation is glaringly apparent. While, as claimed by Derrida, translation is impossible but necessary, translation is fundamentally impossible. It is the necessity to communicate what has turned the otherwise impossible task of translation into what seems to be possible. However, the question remains: How is it possible for translation to take place when untranslatability is seen to be insurmountable? Paul de Man puts forth a prankish but serious question: "if you have a text which says it is impossible to translate, it is very nice to see what happens when that text gets translated" (De Man 1986: 74). In a related vein, a typical descriptive statement of translation is neatly encapsulated in the definition given by Toury: it is what is "presented or regarded" as translation (Toury 1982: 27). To put it differently, if something is called translation and no one challenges its claim or identity as translation, then it is accepted as translation. Useful as it may be in a practical sense, it is ill-defined and notoriously nebulous. As an all-encompassing term, it conveniently circumvents the "what happens" question. His definition only concerns what happens to translation after it is completed.

Perhaps due to the virtual impossibility of translation as posited by Derrida, there is apparently no shortage of "bad" translations, or substandard ones, which however are more possible than others since the task of translation is much less challenging. A bad translation is typically reductive and lacking in nuance in the sense that it merely conveys the basic information of the original, which is deemed "inessential" by Walter Benjamin (1969: 69). He refutes the unreflective traditional view of faithfulness, which is implicitly attributed to bad translation. Moreover, in view of this, we should move on to a more relevant question concerning what makes good translation possible. The real problem is how it is possible to produce a good translation, in the sense intended by Benjamin. This can be further complicated by the probable scenario that a bad translation may not be regarded as bad at all. Ironically, sometimes a good translation may well be regarded as bad. Who is there to judge? One way of making a judgment is that a good translation is to consider endurance, which is related to the afterlife of translation whereas everything being equal, a bad translation is less likely to possess enduring attributes. Due to a multitude of situational constraints or considerations, to avoid "bad" translation may appear to be an impossible task.

The impossibility of translation

What is impossible for translation, according to Benjamin, is that if "it strove for likeness to the original" (Benjamin 1969: 73). To be exactly like the original is not only impossible but also would lead to, even if it is possible, inferior translation. To bemoan the impossibility of translation underlines implicit assumption or explicit expectation that translation must match its original in every detail, and refusal to accept the unavoidable fact that any rewriting is bound to be different from the original. But unless difference is accepted as the precondition of translation, its impossibility is existential. For Benjamin, just to translate information, which is considered to be inessential, is also poor translation. However, in a paradoxical way, the value of bad translation cannot be denied. Moreover, if a bad translation is not regarded as bad and functions well, it stands a chance to survive and even succeed. Or they may incite retranslation(s), which can be good translation(s). However, if striving on the part of the translator "for likeness to the original" is a distinctive feature of bad translation, Benjamin's illustrious metaphor of gluing fragments together may at first glance seem contradictory. He maintains that such fragments "must match one another in the smallest details, although they need not be like one another" (1969: 78). These fragments are broken parts of a vessel. It is about mending a vessel, but the restored vessel is something else – a greater language, namely pure language. This mystified perception of translation demonstrably indicates the pronounced inclination to match closely even the details the original.

Significantly, what this famous statement suggests is that translation is a violent act – out of necessity of course: the vessel must be broken in the first place. And then it represents a delicate process: the fragments have to be glued together "lovingly" and "in the smallest details." The application of Benjamin's metaphor of reassembling fragments by Derek Walcott can shed light on what happens in the process of translation:

> Break a vase, and the love that reassembles the fragments is stronger than that love which took its symmetry for granted when it was whole. The glue that fits the pieces is the sealing of its original shape. It is such a love that reassembles our African and Asiatic fragments, the cracked heirlooms whose restoration shows its white scars. This gathering of broken pieces is the care and pain of the Antilles, and if the pieces are disparate, ill-fitting, they contain more pain than their original sculpture, those icons and sacred vessels taken for granted in their ancestral places. Antillean art is this restoration of our shattered histories, our shards of vocabulary, our archipelago becoming a synonym for pieces broken off from the original continent.
>
> (Walcott 2004: 3)

Despite not suggesting the restoration of the original shape, Benjamin emphasizes that minute attention must be paid to the act of reassembling the fragments, and the translator, in trying to piece together the broken pieces, needs to give the best possible care and attention to details. Walcott's statement pinpoints the more challenging nature of translation: the pieces can easily be both "disparate" and "ill-fitting." In this sense, translation can be more difficult than the original. Moreover, the mention of a scar is also significant. Scars are distinct marks of damage, indicating that translation results from acts of violence, hence the need for care in the process of putting together a compelling translation. The fragility of translation highlights the precarious position of the translator, who is typically held responsible for piecing together the "ill-fitting" fragments into a coherent and operational form.

However, undue domestication is not the answer. Berman's understanding of bad translation is that anything that conceals the foreign in the original. For this reason, an echo of the original's strangeness is what characterizes good translation. As stated by Benjamin, "[a] real translation is transparent; it does not cover the original, does not block its light, but allows the pure language, as though reinforced by its own medium, to shine upon the original all the more fully"

(Benjamin 1969: 79). Clearly, "a real translation" here is also meant to be a good translation whose transparency denotes that it has to be seen through. What about the role of interpretation in relation to translation? One of the reasons for Benjamin's profound influence is his open space for interpretation. Therefore, other scholars, including Derrida, find "The Task of the Translator" fascinating. However, there could be a problem here: the translator's interpretation can block the light of the original and is consequently at odds with the transparency precept. Moreover, an undue emphasis on transparency is a rather restrictive way of defining "good translation" because it limits the potential spaces for a certain degree of creativity, which is generally considered to be indispensable to functional translation, good or bad. This intrinsically source-oriented approach may be good for the source text in a narrow sense, but not necessarily so for reception. Benjamin has made it clear from the beginning in "The Task of the Translator": "In the appreciation of a work of art or an art form, consideration of the receiver never proves fruitful" (Benjamin 1969: 69). He dismisses the entire notion of reception in order to enable the translator to gain freedom in deciding how to translate as if to suggest that any consideration of the target reader imposes a restriction on the translator. The denial of the role of the target reader does increase the space for the translator, who is thus much less inhibited. The outcome of translation is not his concern. For Benjamin, it is the aesthetics inherent in the original representing its "essential quality" that is worth capturing.

In contrast to what is argued in "The Task of the Translator," the functionalist approach to translation reverses the central focus. The nature of the task is very different. Interestingly enough, this approach has opened up a space to gain freedom of a different kind by removing constraints on the practice of translation as in staying close to the original. The priority is given to specific communicative purposes, and reception is of primary concern. As a result, a considerable distance between the source and target texts is allowed and probably also consequently inevitable. Such a broader definition of translation is to ensure a positive reception of translation. From this point of view, what constitutes good translation is not confined to the "essential quality" posited by Benjamin. Specifically, for translation to serve a particular purpose claims the paramount importance of function. In order to overcome the constraints of the source text together with its culture, it is necessary to create translation spaces. However, it can be problematic if any contact with strangeness or foreign otherness is circumvented to a disproportionate extent. The potential lack of correspondence with the original would certainly lead to bad translation in the view of Benjamin, even though he disproves striving for likeness. Meanwhile, it has to be pointed out that the function of the original may well be changed because the purpose of translation can be significantly different from that of the original. It can be said that functionalist approach assertively recontextualizes the text for translation by establishing a different contextual space to make the translated text function in a certain way, regardless of the originally intended function, although some functionalists, for instance, Katherina Reiss has made claims about preserving the predominant function of the original. This is an exemplary case of translation turning into a product of transformation. Given the fact that the source and target languages do not always share a contextual space, they tend to function differently in different contextual spaces. Thus, translation needs to explore a shared space for communication by exploring at least some degree of commonality. And in this sense, the task of translator is defined by its purpose, which may well be aligned with the needs of their patrons. And in order to satisfy or fulfill such needs, the translator must be provided with a certain amount of freedom. The potentially liberating nature of freedom is brought out in a series of spaces in which related possibilities can be explored.

Depending on the nature of the task of the translator to be performed, different strategies are developed to counter the alleged impossibility of translation. Even the German title of "The Task of the Translator," which is "Die Aufgabe des Übersetzers," leaves the space for interpretation. For it can be "The Surrender of the Translator." Despite Benjamin's repeated references to translatability, the essay is essentially about untranslatability, and his primary concern is the ineluctable inadequacy of translation. Ironically, this essay is also an introduction of his own translation of Baudelaire's *Tableaux Prisiens*, which was severely criticized by Stefan Zweig as "icy, unsensual and dead German way" of translating Baudelaire (Quoted in Dudek n.d.). Is it a good translation? The undesirable result of translation may be caused by Benjamin's categorical assertion that translation should imitate even the syntax of the source language. Meaning must be distinguishable and indeed separable from words. Words in the source language are to be substituted by words in the target language to rearticulate meaning. In this sense, meaning is like a kernel whereas words its shells. Words are meaningful because of other words and their traces. Words are combined syntactically, but a serious doubt can be cast on whether it is practicable to imitate syntax, which patently contradicts his claim for the freedom of the translator. Imitation is a somewhat polemic concept in modern translation studies, but surely translation is still in many cases a form of imitative practice. To reproduce something implies a certain degree of imitation. Perhaps it can be said that many translations, consciously or otherwise, produce at least partial interlingual imitation. However, imitation is restrictive in nature and poses multiple constraints on the translator. Among other things, it would be extremely difficult to imitate indeterminacy embedded in the original, which without any doubt presents a perpetual impediment to translation.

The age-old concept of equivalence has been problematized in recent years given its constraining effect on the space of translation. Translation is not utterly impossible, yet the fact that it is constantly subject to severe restrictions inevitably disempowers its performativity. Thus, the pathos of impossibility is linked to culturally encoded spatial restrictions. Translation is boxed into a confining identity with its true function seriously compromised. The prevalence of preoccupation with equivalence contributes to the elusiveness and unattainableness of translatability. Inadequacy in translation can rarely be avoided and often engenders feelings of anxiety and guilt. Equivalence accountability that leads to deadlock is related to a general sense of frustration and powerlessness on the part of the translator, who works within the constraints of the limited space immediately available. The polyvalence of significations to be reproduced can invalidate any attempts at so-called faithful translation, which tends to verge on impossibility.

Translation and transformation

Despite different views on equivalence, translation entails appropriation and subsequently, transformation. Ambiguity and vagueness open up spaces for interpretation, hence transformation. Words or phrases in the source text can well be polysemous, occupying a semantic field that is not shared by the target system. Moreover, that field cannot be transferred to the target system without some unexpected consequences. Since the scope of the field is limited to or determined by a specific context, the translator is unable to make use of the existing semantic field in the original. Should this be the case, strong interpretation with its aim to mitigate vagueness and ambiguity is not uncommon in translation. A space reduction exercise is unavoidable but can be identified as one of the contributory causes of the inadequacy of translation. The general tendency for explicitness in translation is due primarily to the consideration of reception and result from linguistic and cultural differences. If the distance between the signifier and the signified cannot be crossed, the target reader's space for interpretation and creative response is reduced if not eliminated. In effect, this treatment of the original is tantamount to altering its form, in which case, the broken fragments are not glued together to match the original but are altered or reassembled, and ultimately, transformed.

In poetry translation, the reproduction of forms often ends up in abandonment. The impossibility of poetry translation has long been "a topos of translation criticism" (Coldiron 1993: 119). To be sure, poetic adaptation features prominently in translating poetry. It is an act of recreating both meaning and form through adaptation, which is in essence symptomatic of transformation. Since there is no such thing as conversion formulae in translation, how to translate the poetic remains a perennial problem. To rearticulate the poetic phraseology, it is necessary for the translator to explore a wide range of possibilities to empower her/his creativity and so as to enable the translated text to function aesthetically. To this end, translation has to travel through possible spaces of interpretation that are connected with intertextual spaces of allusion, adaptation, and rewriting. Very often, it is meaning rather than form that gets translated. In this sense, translation is inevitably an interpretative activity. The metaphor of fruit and skin is invoked by Benjamin to refer to "content and language" is patently true (Benjamin 1969: 75). The congeniality between them in the original does not exist or barely exists in translation where the inevitably changed relationship signifies that what is natural in the original writing is turned into something unnatural in the process of rewriting. This is what happens in the act of using a different language for the same content. The inherently artificial nature of translation, defined as such, is understood to restrict the scope of reproduction (but not interpretation), which explains that very often than not, it is meaning rather than form that gets translated. Translation is thus called an interpretative activity.

In reference to translatability, Benjamin is not so much concerned about the problem of the correlation of form and content but indicates that it transcends them. So the translator must move beyond and outside where translatability can be established. There is also the need to establish a complex interweaving web of intertextuality and its negotiation. Traditional translation fidelity that concentrates on producing linguistic alikeness to the original never leads to good translations. Therefore, real and metaphorical spaces between untranslatability and translatability, or between bad translation and good translation, can be constructed to open possibilities and perspectives, multiplicity to extend the limits of translatability.

Translation is quintessentially viewed as "a process of difference working through difference" (Lacayo 2014: 224). To address difference properly requires different spaces in which to work out appropriate strategies for a translation task. A mix of spaces is required and generated to allow and facilitate unimpeded access to the inner structure of meaning. Moreover, if for some reason a field for translation is not fertile, a new space or spaces can be carved and explored. In other words, given the primary function of spaces designed for the purpose of appropriation, if one specific space turns out to be dysfunctional or less than satisfactory, another space may be considered as can be illustrated by the following example. Reading the different translation versions of a very unconventional lyric entitled "Slow Voice" by a female Chinese poet during the Song dynasty is quite a revealing experience. The poem begins with "寻寻觅觅, 冷冷清清, 凄凄惨惨戚戚." It sounds like this: *xunxunmimi, lenglengqingqing, qiqicancanqiqi*. In a series of parallelisms, strong feelings of sadness and despondency are conveyed.

One version by Kenneth Rexroth exhibits the shortest possible spatial distance as:

> Search. Search. Seek. Seek.
> Cold. Cold. Clear. Clear.
> Sorrow. Sorrow. Pain. Pain.
> (Rexroth 2008: 34)

This is a direct literal translation. However, at least the line "Cold. Cold. Clear. Clear" is not exactly comprehensible. "冷冷清清" derives from "冷清" as a reduplication, which should not be separated because it is a serious distortion. The word does not mean "cold," which is what the character 冷 literally means. Instead, depending on the context, it means desolate, deserted, or subdued.

A similar strategy is as follows:

> So dim, so dark,
> So dense, so dull,
> So damp, so dank,
> So dead!

The translation is also restricted by an equivalent space. The rhetorical structure of the reduplicated words in the original is destroyed.

The following translation represents a different strategy, markedly different from the previous two versions:

> I've a sense of something missing I must seek.
> Everything about me looks dismal and bleak.
> Nothing that gives me pleasure, I can find.

It seems that a somewhat different semantic space is implemented here. This translation version is based on paraphrases, and thus tinged with pathos and arbitrariness. While moving into an interpretative space, the translator reduces and, to some extent, deprives the target reader of their interpretative spaces. In other words, insufficient justice is done to the interpretative space between the target reader and the translated text.

A notably less interpretative translation, which purports to address the formal features of the original, is cited here as yet another example:

> I look for what I miss
> I know not what it is
> I feel so sad and drear
> So lonely, without cheer.

The translation situation is located in another different space. However, the sense of urgent desperation and despair as manifested in the progressive repetition and parallelism fail to be captured. However, the rhyming pattern is carefully reproduced. Although none of the previously quoted versions is truly satisfactory, what is revealed is the fact that if different spaces are involved, better possibilities can emerge. If a retranslation is attempted, yet another space can be explored by referring to the traversed spaces. At any rate, poetic subjectivities determine the extent to which spatial selection and alignment occur in response to the formal interplay between source and target languages and cultures.

A translator is first and foremost a reader. How the translator reads the source text determines the way in which it is translated, at least to a large extent. Almost equally, however, the way in which he/she conveys what has been read determines the end-result of translation. There can well be a distance between the translator/reader and the translator/writer. However, it can be observed that a bad reader cannot be a good translator, although there is no guarantee that a good reader will make a good translator. In addition, the attitude of the translator is also a relevant factor. For instance, an emotionally engaged reader is more likely to generate an emotionally engaging translation. Derrida's statement that translation is essentially an impossible but necessary practice reveals the paradoxical and uncertain nature of translation. But necessity does not necessarily solve the problem of impossibility. What makes translation possible is worthy of further investigation. Supposedly, if translation is possible, what happens to the process of translation is what interests Derrida, who regards translation as "a constantly transformed and transformative activity" (Derrida 1988: 98). This is inspired by Benjamin's view. Significantly, it is transformation that makes the seemingly impossible task of translation possible.

One important contribution of deconstruction to Translation Studies is that the assumption about surface reading and literal meaning has been powerfully challenged and by questioning the primacy of the signifier, there is no reason to believe the underpinning of word-for-word translation, which has traditionally been regarded as a necessary precaution to ensure the faithfulness of translation. This type of literal approach translation mitigates the vitality and performative energy of the translated text. No matter how faithful a translation appears to be, if it is characterized by flatness as rooted in literal or surface meaning and devoid of depth and dimension, it is unavoidably lackluster. Unfortunately, for fear of faithlessness, many translations are susceptible to such a simplistic and irresponsible lack of appropriate mediation for the sake of the target reader. Because of its passive involvement, flat translation, as it were, can barely do justice to the original. Unless the latter is perspicuously and appropriately represented, it is not entirely groundless to blame the translator if the original fails to function properly through translation. Thus, the translator needs to carve out a space or a series of related spaces to empower translation in seeking to penetrate the surface meaning into the interior of linguistic structure and cultural complexity. By turning passive translation into active translation, it becomes possible to move beyond the one-dimensional transfer of surface meaning to unfold a fuller presentation of the original in translation.

Transcultural practice

Cultures are historically conditioned and constructed. Correspondingly, translation is a transcultural practice involving a dominant language as opposed to a disempowered one, and cultural politics can easily come into translation and its reception. On 4 August 2017, *BBC News* published an article online entitled "*Wolf Warrior 2*: The nationalist action film storming China." It is about a Chinese soldier who saves Chinese and local lives in the hands of Western mercenaries. It is reported that one line in the film said by its protagonist is "犯我中华者，虽远必诛。" And it is translated rather irresponsibly as "Anyone who offends China will be killed no matter how far the target is" (Beijing Bureau 2017). It is not clear what this line was translated by the reporter or his/her translator. It is not found to be taken from the subtitle of the film, which means that it can be an interpretation of the film or understood as the message conveyed by it. One blogger, who is probably British, does not like this line: "I am not sure someone deserves to die for being offensive. . . . I think they meant to say "attacks" (Wendao 2017). Clearly, the translation is problematic, the reason being that it is taken out of context. It has been translated literally in a way, hence also superficially. Whose fault is it? If "犯" here merely means "offend" as in making China unhappy or upset, a death penalty would be outrageously out of proportion. It is translated out of context and can be easily misread. Even if the immediate context can be established, the verb 犯 is essentially mistranslated with serious repercussions.

In view of the profoundly misleading representation, what is meant in the film has been crudely distorted. An impudent disregard of the etymology of 犯 engenders this disempowered translation version. A referential space is necessary to clarify the meaning: in his written statement submitted to the emperor, Western Han general Chen Tang wrote: "明犯强汉者, 虽远必诛" (Those who have invaded the strong Han Empire will be destroyed no matter how far they escape). "Those" refer to the Huns (*Xiongnu*), a large nomadic group from northern Asia, who invaded China during the Han dynasty. They were not disciplined soldiers and carried out burning, killing, and looting, which certainly constituted a war crime that was a grave criminal offense. The basic message is: "If you kill any of us, we will kill you wherever we find you." This shows that even if something is not mistranslated linguistically on the surface, it can be mistranslated in its essence. The tone, rhetoric, and sentiment are all conducive to making the right sense. This line is meant to be a warning rather than a threat. So it is perhaps not quite appropriate to render it as "If you mess with China, you will be a dead man, no matter where you are on the planet." On the other hand, if the translator tries to avoid creating the impression of nationalism, the translation can be something like: If you mess with China, you won't get away with it. However, this may seem to be too mild; after all, the line is not meant to be friendly advice either. A more powerful translation of the line could be: "If you harm any of these people (Chinese), we will hunt you down and kill you." A range of possibilities can be explored and experimented with, and it is no doubt essential to avoid the problem of translating superficially and misleadingly.

It is only fair to point out that etymological translation can be fallacious. Sometimes historical past is of no or little relevance, as is evidenced in numerous clichés, the use of which may well be involuntary. As for how to translate a cliché, Brian Leonard Mott has this advice for the translator:

> If you have to translate a cliché, then it is necessary to find an equivalent stereotyped expression in the target language. Remember that a cliché is a word or expression whose meaning has become attenuated through overuse, so we must make sure that the expression we use to translate a cliché is likely to have the same impact in the target language or, as we are talking about clichés, perhaps we should say the same lack of impact.
>
> (Mott 2011: 59)

This may seem to be good advice but is not exactly workable. To match a cliché with an equivalent one in the target language is indeed necessary. But the problem is that such equivalent clichés can easily be unavailable in the target language. In general, equivalents are in short supply in translation, let alone equivalent clichés. By the same token, producing the same impact in translation is reminiscent of dynamic equivalence in the terminology of Eugene Nida, which again raises doubt about feasibility.

This underscores the difficulty in reproducing the associated meaning of the original. A simple transfer of what is meant to be metaphorical use of language can be problematic and even dangerous, which shows the sterility of placing indiscriminate emphasis on the faithful translation of surface meaning. On the one hand, it is perfectly justifiable to opt for hackneyed translation for clichés in political writing, for which the reproduction of the trite and the banal is necessary. On the other, if clichés are not reproduced as stereotypes in translation, they may well appear to be rather refreshing or just exotic in the target language. Does or can or should the translator resist the temptation to do so? A "recalcitrant" translation may decide to bring out the foreignness of the original as manifest in clichés and stereotypes. To insist on searching for equivalence, even though proving successful, can amount to domestication of some kind, which is not always a preferred way of translation. In terms of functional equivalence, a cliché in the source text can be superseded by a non-cliché in the target language. Metaphorical clichés are often cultural ones, and thus transcultural contextualization is practiced in various ways to enable transcultural communication. On account of transcultural aesthetics that can be both transformative and transformed, it is sometimes necessary to avoid what could be perceived as aesthetically unacceptable and functionally debilitating from a transcultural perspective, even if foreignization is thought to be cross-culturally desirable and operationally viable.

A Dream of Red Mansion, a famous eighteenth-century Chinese novel, was translated into English by Yang Xian-yi and his British wife Gladys Yang. The same novel was also translated by David Hawkes, whose approach is markedly different, as is exemplified by the comparison between the two versions of the poem about crabs. The different spatial perspectives rooted in the cultural backgrounds of the translators have yielded some interesting results. While eating crabs, some of the characters are composing poems, and the one by Xue Baochai is lauded as a masterpiece.

桂霭桐阴坐举觞，
长安涎口盼重阳。
眼前道路无经纬，
皮里春秋空黑黄。
酒未敌腥还用菊，
性防积冷定须姜。
于今落釜成何益？
月浦空余禾黍香。

Yang's translation is a more "faithful one, which can almost function as "back translation," retaining and reproducing some specific details in the original, whereas Hawkes's version is characterized by a more spatial distance.

Version 1

We sit, cups raised, in the shade of Osmanthus and Wu-tung;
Mouths watering, for the Double Ninth we pine;

It crawls sidewise because the ways of the world are crooked,
And, white and yellow, harbours a dark design.
Wine won't purge the smell without chrysanthemums,
And ginger is needed dyspepsia to prevent;
What can it do now, fallen into the cauldron?
On the moonlit bank all that remains is the millet's scent.

> (Trans. by Yang Xianyi and Gladys Yang)
> (Cao and Gao 1999: 565)

Version 2

With winecups in hand, as the autumn day ends,
And with watering mouths, we wait for our small friends.
A straightforward breed you are certainly not,
And the goodness inside you has all gone to pot . . .
For your cold humors, ginger, to cut out your smell
We've got wine and chrysanthemum petals as well.
As you hiss in your pot, crabs, d'ye look back with pain
On that calm moonlit cove and the fields of that grain?

> (Trans. by David Hawkes)
> (Cao 1977: 257)

In the first line of Version 1, "Wu-tung" is the transliteration of Chinese para-sols, which sounds exotic to the Anglophone reader, but it is incomprehensible. Fortunately, it is not difficult to infer its reference to a tree. In the second line, there is a culture-specific item, the Double Ninth, which is ninth day of the ninth lunar month and celebrated as a festival especially for climbing mountains. Rather than interested in mountain climbing, the characters involved cannot wait to eat crabs at the festival. However, Version 2 dispenses with such details. There is no mention of "the shade of Osmanthus and Wu-tung" nor the "the Double Ninth" festival. Whether they are strictly dispensable or not is open to debate. There is a humorous twist with "our small friends," referring to crabs. But they are nowhere to be found in the original. Yet this "insertion" serves a specific purpose, namely to rhyme with "ends" in the previous line. And it also spells out "crabs" in line 7, whereas in Version 1, as in the original, there is no indication of "crab" at all. While in the third line "the ways of the world are crooked" can be construed as an explanation for "crawls sidewise," this trenchant tone is softened in "A straightforward breed you are certainly not."

Additionally, in Version 2, we have "As you hiss in your pot, crabs" as mani-fest in the subjectivity of the translation, and it is no doubt more graphic than "fallen into the cauldron" in Version 1. Varying spatial distance and zooming range are observed in Version 2, bringing more coherence to the translated text, which is good for readability, thus rendering the translation more powerful. Yet despite the overt overall superiority of Version 2, a couple of key points are miss-ing in Version 2. A cultural connotation associated with crabs is that they crawl "sidewise," which by extension, alludes to "bullies," thereby insinuating that they do not care about obstructing others. Thus, when "the ways of the world are crooked" are expected to be linked with crabs, this crucial linkage is not provided in Version 2, which also contains two mistranslations: "the goodness inside you has all gone to pot" lacks textual support in the original. Likewise, "d'ye look back with pain/On that calm moonlit cove and the fields of that grain?" The question mark is misplaced. The last line "On the moonlit bank all that remains is the millet's scent" is meant to be a paradigmatic contrast, and it is not part of "looking back." On the surface, Version 2 is a more readable translation, invigorated by some creative intervention. However, in this cross-cultural space, the symbolic image of crabs is not captured. As noted earlier, in Chinese culture, the innocent-looking crabs, because of the way they crawl, have acquired an odious connotation, thus conjuring up negative associations. In Hawkes's translation, certain subtextual meanings fail to be delivered, resulting in a weakened translation in a somewhat different way and with a crucial point missing, which can be found in Version 1: while "all that remains is the millet's scent," there is no sign of crabs anymore, no matter how berserk they used to be.

Recasting and recreation

It may perhaps be a truism to say that translation theory is dichotomized. Lawrence Venuti encapsulates one of the central dichotomies: the two concepts of equivalence and function (Venuti 2012: 5). Schleiermacher's famous either/or approach to translation presents a dilemma for the translator: either to bring the author back home or to send the reader abroad. In Gideon Toury's words, the polarity or binary opposition is between adequacy and acceptability (Toury 1980: 50). Of course, the opposing pair can also be identified as accuracy and readability. Many practical issues in translation reflect and reinforce these dichotomies. The exponential development of Translation Studies has been testified in efforts to address inherent tensions and conflicting forces that contribute to revealing its nature and ramifications. However, the discursive variety and substantive complexity concerning translation are still a major consideration. Since there is no such thing as replication in translation, and the umbilical connection to the source text needs to be affirmed from time to time, rewriting is not a runaway exercise. In a paradoxical sense, the original can be regarded as a source of stability. Even though the general target reader has no or little knowledge of the source text as pointed out by some translation scholars, the role of translation criticism is not always passive or marginal. At any rate, the source text, in a way, stabilizes the practice of rewriting. Thus, translation can be viewed as a regulatory process of rewriting, which does not mean the total erasure of the author by systematically blocking his/her stylistic signature, among other things.

Translational rewriting and adaptation are related yet separate realms and by no means mutually exclusive, since it contains a certain amount of adaptation. As John Minford put it, the process of translation is one of "transformation" or "transmutation," and he contends that "[r]ecasting is the best and most practical single English word to describe this process" (Minford 1997: 19). And he proceeds to elaborate: "It is a process in which the translator actually lets go of the original, but without betraying it" (Minford 1997: 19). Recasting is a form of rewriting, more on the technical side, however. Syntactical reconfiguration yet rewriting is suggestive of a more spatial and relational perspective and coverage.

Translation is made possible often through adaptation. But adaptation can barely supersede translation because at least simply calling an adaptation based on a source text a translation is likely to be controversial. There is a restrictive principle at play here, as adaptation may undermine the legitimacy of translation (Bastin 2008: 3). Arguably, adaptation is a more radical form of appropriation, involving spatial expansion, whereas appropriation is localized adaptation. Although appropriation can occur regularly or routinely, it is generally found in more isolated cases rather than in general circumstances, unlike adaptation. Whatever way of defining or distinguishing the two terms, linguistic and cultural transformation is sure to ensue when translation takes place.

In the context of translation, whether it is rewriting or recreation, the space involved is normally limited because "gluing together," in Benjamin's words, connotes a form of imitation in a restorative sense, which already carries the implication that this action is different from transfer. This is because cultural products are often untransferable. As discussed earlier, imitation in translation is only possible under certain conditions or circumstances. If it is recreation, translation cannot be completely devoid of some elements of imitation. To start with, among other things, indeterminacy can barely be the object of imitation because it will lead to incomprehension. Strictly speaking, interlingual imitation denies the translator the space to be creative, unless the translator can be, in a paradoxical way, creatively imitative. It must be admitted that creative imitation leaves a limited space. Admittedly, creativity in translation is a sensitive topic. As noted by Brigid Maher, "Creativity in translation does not, of course, equate to unfettered freedom" (Maher 2011: 161). Maher gives the reason for this emphasis on the limited scope of creativity: "What distinguishes translation from other kinds of creative writing is its close relationship with and obligation to its source text, as well as to readers" (Maher 2011: 161). Though blatantly obvious, this serves as a timely reminder. Nonetheless, creativity is something essential in translation, although it is within boundaries. Simply put, a translation can never be as creative as its original. It cannot be denied that, however, creativity in translation is of a very different kind.

Furthermore, Peter Newmark points out: "Creativity in translation starts where imitation stops" (Newmark 1991: 9). In other words, when imitation reaches its limit, creativity or at least a certain degree of creativity is necessitated. More often than not, direct translation, which is identified with imitative translation, constricts the space for creativity. It is important to note that creativity in translation characterized by indirectness is based on and derives from interpretation. Sometimes interpretation itself is a creative act because it entails making sense of the source text or certain parts of it in an imaginative way. Both creativity and imagination are needed to make this possible. The need for textual interpretation induces spatial heterogeneities, which allows the translator to explore alternative modes of signification in translation. Apart from the fact that translation itself is necessarily interpretation or a more explicit, committed form of interpretation, reading translation also requires and indeed generates interpretation. Furthermore, indirect translation creates space for strong interpretation. In general, the more indirect the translation is, the stronger interpretation is called for. It needs to be pointed out that while strong interpretation gives more space to the translator, it reduces the space for the target reader's interpretation. A most distinctive feature of strong interpretation is the raised level of explicitness in translation as compared with the original.

It can be observed that adaptation requires recasting which is often tantamount to creative rewriting and the translator's interpretation is inherent in the act of rewriting, which brings about difference and is inextricably linked with subjectivity and intersubjectivity. To make rewriting possible, different possibilities are explored and evaluated. To some extent, rewriting in terms of translation is akin to recreating, and because it is simultaneously derivative and creative, it is also writing of its own right but necessarily predicated on mediation and negotiation. Meanwhile, translational rewriting generates spatial configurations of possibilities that can become potential sources of heterogeneity. Once motivated by possibilities, translation is afforded various opportunities to rewrite the source text in some "creative" way. The enabling and constraining dimensions of rewriting are equally salient and highly charged. Certain degrees and kinds of deviation from the original in its distinctive manifestations are exhibited and incorporated into translation. To be sure, meaning itself is interpreted and prioritized according to the needs of the target system. Translation or at least successful translation is not about searching for an exact one-to-one match between words in the source and target texts but about moving words from one system of meaning to another.

It is undoubtedly true that some rewritings are inspired by ideological motivations or standpoints, but it is untrue to say that all rewritings belong to this category, which would oversimplify and misrepresent the complex interrelations between writing and rewriting and indeed also, re-rewriting. Andre Lefevere's seminal book *Translation, Rewriting, and the Manipulation of Literary Fame* (1992) has been closely associated with ideological rewriting, even though it addresses the poetic dimension of rewriting as well. However, for some reason, this dimension seems to be overlooked by many translation scholars, especially in China. It is time to look afresh at translational poetics through rewriting. Invariably, translation necessitates rewriting. And admittedly, rewriting implies change, hence difference, part of the reason being that it is contextualized and also possibly politicized. In other words, the forces at work behind rewriting can be complex and varied, thus defying a uniform characterization or explanation. In a nutshell, translation is not authorized to be creative in an unrestrained way, and thus tantalizingly analogous to, albeit still somewhat different from, adaptation which is significantly more creative than imitative.

There are unmistakable elements of creation and invention in translation. Chloë Starr has mentioned with regard to the Chinese classic *Hongloumeng* the three reading experiences of the source text, the target text separately, and also the two texts side by side, which suggests three spatial relationships: "to read *The Story of the Stone* in English (translation) was an entirely different experience to reading *Hongloumeng* in Chinese . . . to read the two texts in parallel creates a third, different reading experience" (Starr 2012: 116). Despite being the case of bilingual knowledge, which is relatively rare for readers of translation, it indicates the way in which translation is shaped is directly related to how it is read, and it can be read very differently depending on situational variables and individual circumstances. Commenting on David Hawkes's translation of the what may well be the author's preface of *The Story of the Stone*, John Minford discusses the process of "transformation" or "transmutation":

> If one reads this as a piece of English, it has none of the telltale signs of a translation. It is authentic English. And yet compare it carefully with the Chinese, and you will find that everything is there – every idea, every image, transformed and recast. And the feelings, the tender, passionate, wry feeling are all there. It speaks from the heart. It is Cao Xueqin speaking. It is David Hawkes speaking it. It is Cao Xueqin sitting in a Welsh shepherd's house, sipping a hot Whisky toddy after a long rainy walk across the hills; it Hawkes sitting Cao's cottage in the Western Hills outside Peking, sipping congee after a night of hard drinking and writing poems. It is both, and it is neither.
>
> (Minford 1997: 21)

Mutual transformation or transmutation arises out of a spatial illusion evoked by juxtaposing the past experiences of the translator, who brings into translation his perceptions of the source text in connection with how to rewrite it in a dialogic mode and under the influences of different historical and cultural settings. The subsequent creativity performance is a reflection of mixing or hybridization across times and locations, marked by interpenetration of past and present induced by spatial variability and interaction.

Translational poetics

As previously noted, translational rewriting entails poetics and language intersecting with one another in diverse ways to influence linguistic signification and aesthetic experience. To what extent the translator enters into authorship is difficult to establish, and putting the spotlight on poetics or aesthetics has been part of the compulsion on the part of the translator. This determines the complexion of translational rewriting. The fact that the remnants of the umbilical connection to the original are not as many as the translator would like makes the task of translation difficult but also gives the translator spaces to be "creative." It is worth pointing out that tensions inherent in the two different linguistic and cultural systems can energize translation. How can a network of linguistic and cultural connections embedded in the source and target texts respectively be found and expanded? The connections may sometimes be close or not so close. The possibility to transform the original may even justify the claim to novelty, which can be experienced by the target reader through a spectrum of different new things that have been introduced through translation.

Yet in reality, translation is prone to be weakened by a host of constraining factors. Extratextual connections and dimensions with different references correlate appreciably with intratextual features in the source text, particularly in the notable absence of contextual clues. A typical example of this kind can be found in the English translation of "我们没有窃笑, 默对弥留的病床" ("In utter seriousness, without a snigger, we watched silently by the deathbed"). A more literal (or faithful) rendition would be: "We did not snigger and faced the deathbed in silence." As an interpretive comment, "in utter seriousness" is added, presumably to make things clearer. But this interpretation is patently subjective. Although it can be argued that all interpretations are subjective to varying degrees, some are palpably more subjective than others. To juxtapose "seriousness" with "snigger" is bizarre and defies common sense unless a special effect is intended. What is more, the Chinese character "对" denotes a sense of direction, meaning "toward." But there is no verb in the original! The translator has chosen a relatively weak verb: watched. The overt explicitness displays a heavy-handed insistence on the control of meaning, and does not constitute a subtle form of manipulation, which, however, does happen from time to time in translation. Admittedly, the original Chinese is not a wonderfully constructed sentence, yet the English translation makes it even weaker.

The immediate causal upshot of untranslatability is weak or passive translation, with the latter attributable to lackadaisical attempts to overcome it. What often happens is that after much struggle or simply due to lack of effort or less than adequate competence, translation becomes lifeless, devoid of vitality, hence losing readability. How can translation be empowered? Passive transfer, though overtly faithful because it dwells too much on surface meaning, is unable to do justice to the original, particularly in reference to readability. Readability does not necessarily mean easy to read in the sense of improving accessibility but refers to, more importantly, the quality of reading experience. In 2018, the first volume of Jin Yong's *Legends of the Condor Heroes 1 – A Hero Born* was published by MacLehose Press. In translating literature, directness in conveying information is not an appropriate approach, especially regarding martial arts fiction known for its entertaining yet powerful storylines. The translator, Anna Holmwood, apart from offering reasonably accurate information, sets herself a goal to create a fun reading experience for the target reader by creating an exotic space. The principle of her translation is as follows:

> I have really tried to emphasize fluency in English. I thought about how Jin Yong would speak to English readers. For me, translation is not just about making sure that it is accurate or correct word for word. If it's a fast and fun read in Chinese, it should be fast and fun read in English.
>
> (Zhang 2018)

Not only is the balance between accuracy and readability difficult to attain, but also there is the question of invoking cultural resonances in translation. However, how on earth fluency can be achieved in translating the fighting skills such as降龙十八掌, "the eighteen palm attacks to defeat dragons," and九阴白骨爪, "nine *yin* skeleton claw," is open to imagination and interpretation.

It is noteworthy that there are early "academic translations," including *The Deer and the Cauldron* translated by John Minford (Thorpe 2017). Perhaps because of the "academic" consideration, this translation does not appear to be sufficiently dynamic. It may be as well to quote one passage from the novel:

> 韦小宝见茅十八神情前倨后恭, 甚觉诧异, 问道: "这小子是什么来头? 瞧你吓得这个样子。茅十八道: "什么小子不小子的? 你嘴里放干净些。" 眼见饭店中的老板与店伴探头探脑, 店堂中一塌糊涂, 满地鲜血, 说道: "走罢!"
>
> Trinket was extremely puzzled by this sudden transformation on Whiskers' part, from anger to abject awe.
>
> "Who is this man?" he asked. "He seemed to put you in a dreadful funk all of a sudden."
>
> "Mind your language!" retorted Whiskers. He looked around, and saw the innkeeper and waiters peering into the room, surveying the scene of destruction and bloodstains on the floor.
>
> "Let's go!" he said.
>
> (Minford 1993: 87)

Perhaps it is necessary to introduce more spatial dimensions into the translation in preparation of instilling more vigor and energy into the narrative. "Mind your language" is meant to be a retort but sounds out of place since it does not support the angry response. "小子" can of course be legitimately translated as "man," but in this context, to call a stranger "小子" is more than disrespectful. Further, the translation reads a bit disjointed. However, because there is no direct equivalent word in English, if we can "manipulate" the translation, it can be something like: Trinket asked: "Who the hell is this guy? You look scared out of your wits." The translation "Mind your language!" sounds slightly weak. "Watch your tongue!" is stronger. The translation of "满地鲜血," literally meaning "fresh blood everywhere," is "bloodstains on the floor." An alternative could be the floor was literarily awash with blood. Thus, the smell and visual image of blood are better captured. It is these seemingly unimportant details that make a difference, which shows that better readability can be yielded not necessarily at the expense of accuracy. Even "Let's go!" can be replaced with "Let's get out of here!" so as to bring out the intended effect in relation to contextual demands.

Moreover, contextual variables, such as attitude, emotion, feelings, and even moods which may compete with other concerns and factors, exerting a significant influence on the process and outcome of translation, come into an analytical view. Needless to say, not everything about translation is related to ideology, and translational poetics can be a prime locus for rewriting and manipulation as well. In terms of translational poetics, the word manipulation may not register a negative connotation. It can be neutral or even positive if the intension is to realign and reconfigure certain aspects of the original for the purpose of enhancing cross-cultural communication. By means of arduously manipulating a series of signifiers in the original, the translator addresses one of the central concerns of translation: to accommodate different and competing traditions of poetics that often operate differently at the intersection of poetics and politics. It is understandable that cultural politics governs the evolution of aesthetic preferences and also necessitates different poetic strategies in translation. Therefore, translational poetics can be easily differentiated from authorial poetics. It is sometimes more meaningful and significant to look at the transformed poetics than the reconstructed poetics represented by the source text.

For whatever reason, some form of cultural filtering can be observed as manifest in translation, and this is necessary and justifiable from time to time as a means of adaptation or localization. One version of Chinese translation of the two lines in Shakespeare's *Romeo and Juliet* is a case in point: "He made you for a highway to my bed;/But I, a maid, die a maiden-widowed." It is rendered as "他要借你做牵引相思的桥梁, /可是我却要做一个独守空闺的怨女而死去." The back translation of these two lines reads as: "He wanted to borrow you as a bridge to evoke lovesickness,/but I would die as a lonely, distressed girl." To avoid the sexual reference, something new must be invented to move the scene to a different cultural space where the conditions for reception are different. As discussed earlier, the three reading experiences for bilingual readers are markedly different as a new contextual space has emerged to dominate the consideration of what is thought to be an appropriate translation strategy.

Indeed, cross-cultural contextualization establishes an essential connecting space conducive to generating interpretation, which is subsequently open to manipulation and leads to recreating the text in somewhat different and quite often new ways. Interpretative diversity and possible aesthetic incompatibility prompt translation to vacillate between fidelity and freedom, and between reconstructed poetics and transformed poetics, although there is not a sharp dividing line between the latter two. As a form of rewriting, translation provides a framework for cross-cultural intertextuality, hence the inevitability of some degree of ramifications. Cross-cultural intertextuality is embedded in the literary tradition and aesthetics of the target system. Both the semantic and cultural polysemy encoded in the source and target languages can breed manifold forms of difference to be mediated and balanced. In a literary system associated with the target culture, the readability issue must be addressed properly. To a considerable extent, whatever the lexical markers may be, the translated text needs to be culturally acceptable. It can barely be denied that cross-cultural poetics initiated by translation is directly related to readability, which correlates with the match and alignment between the target text and its readers. Poor readability can be a true reflection of weak translation, and the translator finds it necessary to calculate the risk in pushing the limits of readability. With particular reference to literary translation, how to make it possible for a translated text to travel well remains a major part of the task of the translator. It is therefore necessary to deploy all possible resources, linguistic and cultural, to empower the act of translation.

Conclusion

The immanent plurality and multiplicity of the original can be seriously compromised after translation. The fundamental question of what happens to translation requires, by virtue of its essential function and design, an imaginative grasp of what is or can be involved in making translation not only possible but also efficacious. What happens to translation entails a negotiated system of meaning. To be able to negotiate, spaces are of critical importance in avoiding dysfunction. Numerous interrelated predicaments threaten translatability and are predisposed to debilitate translation. How to overcome many of the perilous predicaments is a constant challenge. Because of the inherent incomparability and incommensurability between the two systems involved in translation, the modes of signification are or can be different, thus leading to the possibility or even inevitability of manipulation. Once the fusion of content and form in the original is broken in translation, transformation naturally ensues. Benjamin's fragmentary metaphor implies the separation of content and form, and the resultant attempts at re-contextualization and reconfiguration play a decisive role in shaping the final product of translation. To glue fragments together lovingly is an incremental process and requires microscopic reading, so as to enable translation to be more compelling and powerful. To empower translation, greater ease of navigation has to be represented in translation, thereby enhancing readability in relation to functionality and aesthetics. Meanwhile, we also need to remind ourselves that translation is subject to constraints of language and culture, among other things. The widely held assumption that the target reader only passively consumes the translated product due to their lack of knowledge of the original has proved to be somewhat questionable and outmoded in some instances. The scope of the implied freedom for the translator is of course limited. If a translation lacks cross-cultural resonance, it is probably due to insufficient attention to translational poetics. Translation must and can be empowered, and to avoid weak translation, the translator needs to be prepared to engage with complexity and search for better alternatives by relentlessly probing the network of possibilities.

References

Bastin, Georges L. (2008) "Adaptation," in Mona Baker and Gabriela Saldanha (eds.) *Routledge Encyclopedia of Translation Studies*, London and New York: Routledge, 3–6.

Beals, Kurt (2014) "Alternatives to Impossibility: Translation as Dialogue in the Works of Paul Celan," *Translation Studies* 7(3): 284–299.

Beijing Bureau (2017) "*Wolf Warrior 2*: The Nationalist Action Film Storming China," *BBC News*, August 4: www.bbc.com/news/blogs-china-blog-40811952.

Benjamin, Walter (trans. by Harry Zohn) (1969) *Illuminations*, New York: Schocken Books.

Cao, Xueqin (trans. by David Hawkes) (1977) *The Story of the Stone, Volume II*, London: Penguin.

Cao, Xueqin, and E. Gao (trans. Yang Xianyi and Gladys Yang) (1999) *A Dream of Red Mansions*, Beijing: Foreign Languages Press.

Coldiron, A. E. B. (1993) "Rossetti on Villon, Dowson on Verlaine: 'Impossibility' and Appropriation in Translation," *The Comparatist* 17: 119–140.

De Man, Paul (1986) *The Resistance to Theory*, Manchester: Manchester University Press.

Derrida, Jacques (1988) "Roundtable on Translation," in Claude Levesque and Christie McDonald (eds.) *The Ear of the Other: Otobiography, Transference, Translation: Texts and Discussion with Jacques Derrida*, New York: Schocken Books, 91–162.

Dudek, Sarah (n.d.) "Walter Benjamin and the Religion of Translation," *Cipher Journal*: www.cipherjournal.com/html/dudek_benjamin.html.

Lacayo, A. A. (2014) "Queer and Embodied Translation: Ethics of Difference and Erotics of Distance," *Comparative Literature Studies* 51(2): 215–230.

Lefevere, Andre (1992) *Translation, Rewriting, and the Manipulation of Literary Fame*, London: Routledge.

Maher, Brigid (2011) *Recreation and Style: Translating Humorous Literature in Italian and English*, Amsterdam and Philadelphia: John Benjamins Publishing.

Minford, John (1993) "The Deer and the Cauldron: Two Chapters from a Novel by Louis Cha," *East Asian History* 5: 1–100.

Minford, John (1997) "Kungfu in Translation, Translation as Kungfu," in Liu Ching-chih (ed.) *The Question of Reception: Martial Arts Fiction in English Translation*, Hong Kong: Centre for Literature and Translation, Lingnan College, 1–40.

Mott, Brian Leonard (2011) *Semantics and Translation for Spanish Learners of English*, Barcelona: Edicions Universitat Barcelona.

Newmark, Peter (1991) *About Translation*, Clevedon: Multilingual Matters.

Rexroth, Kenneth (2008) "Autumn Love by Li Qingzhao," in Jean Elizabeth Ward (ed.) *Li Qingzhao: An Homage to*, N.p.: Lulu, 34.

Starr, Chloë (2012) "Mind the Gap: The Hawkes-Minford Transition in *The Story of the Stone*," in Tao Liu, Laurence K. P. Wong, and Chan Sin-wai (eds.) *Style, Wit and Word-Play: Essays in Translation Studies in Memory of David Hawkes*, Newcastle: Cambridge Scholars, 115–138.

Thorpe, Vanessa (2017) "A Hero Reborn: 'China's Tolkien' Aims to Conquer Western Readers," *Guardian*, November 26: https://bit.ly/2XV9L7n.

Toury, Gideon (1980) *In Search of a Theory of Translation*, Tel Aviv: Porter Institute.

Toury, Gideon (1982) "A Rationale for Descriptive Translation Studies," *Dispositio* 7: 22–39.

Venuti, Lawrence (2012) "Introduction," in Lawrence Venuti (ed.) *The Translation Studies Reader*, London and New York: Routledge.

Walcott, Derek (2004) "The Antilles: Fragments of Epic Memory," in Malena Kuss (ed.) *Music in Latin America and the Caribbean: An Encyclopedic History*, Austin: University of Texas Press.

Wendao (2017) "BBC这样翻译'犯我中华者，虽远必诛,'对吗？" (BCC's Translated "犯我中华者，虽远必诛" as Such. Is It Correct?),《外宣微记》(Small notes on international publicity), August 5: https://bit.ly/3ixrARL.

Zhang, Dailei (2018) "Feature: Jin Yong's Chinese Martial Arts Novel Published in English for First Time," *Xinhua News*, August 12: www.xinhuanet.com/english/2018-02/22/c_136991987.htm.

Conclusion

It is well-known that a source text can resist and even defy translation. A full-frontal approach may not work and can render translation dysfunctional. Not surprisingly, alternative approaches are often required and thus designed to avoid a sub-par result. However, the final result of the effort may still border on the lack of adequacy. Even if – or because – the resultant translation is adequate, its acceptability for the target reader can be in question. To address this chronic disparity, the concept of spaces can illuminate the multi-dimensional complexity of translation by providing more resources for translation practitioners, who are reminded to be more mindful of finding better alternatives. A heightened awareness of the usefulness of the concept of spaces is required to energize and empower translation. This is utterly necessary because, among other things, it is not uncommon to find a grimly determined translator ending up in frustration and despair. Translation problems are manifold and, depending on the situation, each may require different strategies and approaches. At the same time, it has to be said that among many potential risk factors, translation is subject to abuse and other unsavory or undesirable consequences. The chance for translator and author to come to an agreement is relatively rare, and it is even rarer that the author happens to have sufficient knowledge of the target language to be aware of any possible problems. In most situations, the source text is at the mercy of the translator who can either give it an after-life or destroy it. It all comes down to making full use of resources or/and making more resources available. In wrestling with constraints of all kinds, the translator must learn to be more resourceful, and exploring translational spaces can help overcome these constraints.

The instability of meaning remains one of the most arduous challenges to translation and warrants the consideration to break out of spatial confinements not only to liberate translation from the strictures of the source text but also to expand the scope of the available resources for maximal correspondence between source and target texts. To this end, hypotheses generated by the translator regarding possible solutions to translation problems can be better evaluated and refined in various related spaces, historical, linguistic, and cultural. This can represent a significant shift of focus from process to space, thus allowing for more possibilities to be explored and considered. To maintain an optimal balance between accuracy and acceptability that has perpetually dichotomized translation, it is necessary and imperative to approach the issue in spatial terms, which can bring fresh insights to our understanding of how translation works and functions. The spatialization of translation makes it possible to investigate exactly what happens to translation, which is viewed as movement from one language across space into another. It is not a linear movement as usually perceived. Instead, displacement, exile, and diaspora overlay the spatial dimensions of translation, all of which need to be mapped carefully to sort out different complexities resulting from a multitude of interrelated variables and relationships. Lack of accessibility and acceptability as envisaged necessitates the need to develop spatially integrated translation strategies. Since there is no direct access to the original, anything can happen in relation to the indirectness occasioned by translation. There is rarely a chance for direct, unmediated access to what is articulated in the original. This also entails that space is not only objectively given but is also produced through cultural and social forces.

It can be observed that a wider perspective has become increasingly important for Chinese translation scholars, for whom cosmopolitan spaces are deemed to be indispensable. Most importantly, the function of translation is for cross-cultural communication. In the instance of translating world literature as the ultimate testing of translatability and universal accessibility, the chronicle issue of untranslatability is brought to the fore and raises questions about the essential role of translation in introducing and promoting world literature. A greater challenge has emerged, almost imperceptibly, and as a result, a higher degree of both accuracy and adequacy is expected from translation. With this in mind, translatability should not be presupposed too easily, the lack of which, however, can easily undermine the validity and legitimacy of any form of cultural translation.

With growing cross-cultural and interdisciplinarity, the global academic landscape in the field of Translation Studies has changed significantly. An increasing number of Chinese translation scholars are publishing internationally, carving out an academic space unprecedented in Chinese cultural history to exchange scholarly opinions with international peers. Likewise, the international scholarly community now has the opportunity to learn more about Chinese translation practice, whose convoluted history provides a fertile testing ground for the investigation of various dimensions of cultural pluralism and variability. It is essential to find an effective way to balance or bridge the objective distance and artificial distance between the two different multifaceted cultural systems concerning Chinese-English translation. With the aim of opening new translational spaces for grappling with cross-cultural anxiety about difference and foreign otherness, more perspectives are needed because a single Chinese perspective has proved too narrow to be reflective of cross-cultural reality. Due to cultural alienation, there is bound to be a cognitive distance between the source reader and the target reader, especially in English Chinese translation and vice versa. The ontological instability of language is complicated enough, but if it is coupled with the ontological instability of another language, which is so different from the former, the situation becomes much more difficult regarding how to circumvent or overcome situational constraints imposed by all kinds of translation tasks.

Through the heterogeneity of different spatial dimensions, cross-cultural interpretations and considerations of national values are underscored to create different reading experiences. How to enable Chinese culture to travel globally has been a central priority in recent years and is fostering the need for more spatial coverage and resources. In view of the growing demand for high-quality translation, viable and varied forms of mediating cultures in multifarious manifestations must be developed to render energy and vitality to the translated text by way of enhancing readability and acceptability. More importantly, the question of cultural value is closely entangled with and defined by how a text is translated. Transcultural spaces are keenly needed for empowered and effective translation to be produced, on the strength of which a Chinese-Western convergence can be achieved through genuine cross-cultural dialogue and understanding. Translation is related to exploring and unraveling the complexity of transnational, transcultural, transdisciplinary transformative spaces, and the appropriations of these spaces and others represent an effort to integrate understanding the nature of translation with what is required in practical operation. Thus, the spatial practice is critical to developing a framework to focus on enabling and facilitating optimal cross-cultural communication that can contribute greatly to achieving Chinese-Western convergence.

Index

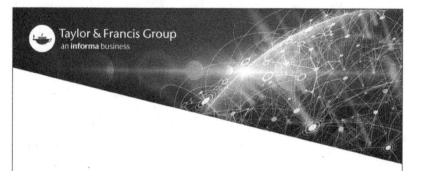